BUSINESS CPR

SOLVING THE PROFIT BUT NO CASH PROBLEM

Increase *your* **C**ash flow from **P**rofits
through **R**eporting in five easy steps

LORIN YOUNG

NEWMAN SPRINGS PUBLISHING
320 Broad Street
Red Bank, NJ 07701

First originally published by Newman Springs Publishing 2020

ISBN 978-1-64801-174-0 (Paperback)
ISBN 978-1-64801-175-7 (Digital)

Printed in the United States of America

CONTENTS

BUSINESS CPR
Solving the Profit but No Cash Problem

INTRODUCTION

In 2016, *Owning a GREAT Business* was published. Its purpose was to introduce the "7-P Framework," a decision-shaping model that leads those who own a good business to develop the insights and actions necessary to own a GREAT business.

The core truth laid out in *Owning a GREAT Business* is that business ownership is not for the faint of heart. Before owning my own business, I held many different job titles and enjoyed a wide array of experiences with two "Fortune 100" businesses. Yet nothing I had done previously had fully prepared me for operating my own million-dollar business without a financial safety net.

As the owner of Design Dynamics, I confirmed what works and what gets in the way. I wrote my first book for small business owners who work hard with passion and purpose, yet are unsatisfied with their results. I intentionally targeted those who wanted to own a great business and knew they weren't quite there yet. My goal was simply to help others enjoy greater success in owning their own businesses.

Not long after publishing *Owning a GREAT Business*, I faced a difficult decision: The factors that had made Design Dynamics a great business to own were rapidly changing. This was due to a combination of market forces beyond my direct control and the actions I wanted to pursue in the balance of my professional life. These realities, combined, led me to sell my business so that I could focus on what I *truly* wanted to do: help other business owners excel.

I sold my graphics and signage business to RR Donnelly (RRD), the world's largest commercial printer. They merged the assets of my large-format printing business, including key employees, into their Orange County operations. Upon completing my obligations to ensure a smooth ownership transition, I stepped out from being a small business owner to being a full-time business scientist.

BUSINESS SCIENCE VERSUS BUSINESS CONSULTING

Over the years, I have enjoyed the study of business frameworks and mental models that I have accumulated into a large library of the best that I draw from as the situation warrants. What I continue to find interesting to date is how I have yet to consistently apply any particular framework, even my own, to my client work.

I have found that locking in on one particular consulting framework with every client is too much like trying to force a square peg into a round hole. In medical terms, what I have come to appreciate is if it isn't good for the patient, it isn't good for the practitioner. From years of experience, I have come to know that the applying of business laws and principles to the unique needs and dynamics of each particular business rather than force-fit a particular framework is the best approach.

Because of the data-driven way I approach my work with each client, I function more like a business scientist than a consultant. Scientists set aside opinions, perspectives, and assumptions until they have concrete evidence to back them up. As such, a business scientist will never rely on opinions or assumptions to make educated decisions, whereas business consultants I've seen and worked with do this all the time.

By applying the scientific method to my client work, I better help clients identify what they need to do differently to produce better results. Just like the most effective scientists of any scientific discipline who apply the scientific method to problem-solving, I apply a similar approach to critical thinking, data collection, interpretation, and communication of the results.

As a business scientist, my initial hypothesis entering into each business can be simplified to a single question: "Is this a great business to own?" From the start of my working in the client's business, I actively work to prove whether this hypothesis is true or not, using the following approach:

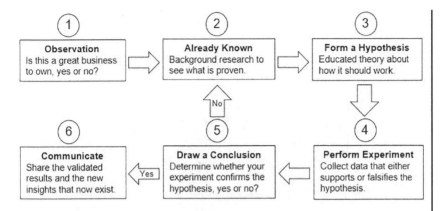

After working through the company's data and interviewing key employees, I move quickly and with a high degree of confidence to answer the question of whether this is a great business to own or not. Over the past few years, the answer to this core question has consistently been "no." This isn't surprising to me; I'm there to take a close look in the first place: The business isn't performing as the owner wants, and they are looking for help.

Answering this primary question with data positions me to explore the answer to the second question simultaneously: *Could this business produce better results? Yes or no?*

DON'T MAKE IMPORTANT BUSINESS DECISIONS IN THE DARK

In studying numerous businesses across this great country of ours, I have come to appreciate how nine out of ten small business owners fail to organize in a way that will ever lead to owning a GREAT business. In presenting the "7-P Framework," I offered the following figure to reinforce this fact. It sets the stage for how a data organizing framework can help you discover the truth about your business for those wanting to produce better results:

Since developing this visual, I have come to better see exactly why the majority of business owners don't know why they can have profits but no cash in the bank. It's because they don't have a good sense of when their business is operating at a cash profit or at a loss. This is because…

1. They don't have clear profit targets;
2. They aren't making decisions based on their potential cash impact;
3. They aren't consistently tracking their accounts receivable collections.

As I study struggling businesses, I see snowballing stress levels as cash flow tightens, making it impossible for the owners to identify by themselves what they need to do differently. At its core, those owners I find struggling are failing to grasp the relationship between cash, profits, and reporting on their ability to build and maintain a viable and successful business.

In those businesses I have studied that had cash reserves in the bank, I have found them to have eroding profits with ownership, not knowing why. In these cases, what I have found is a business owner with steady cash flow who isn't comfortable with using reports to track and manage needed improvements in their businesses and as a result are producing less profit.

What's even more amazing to me is how none of my clients to date recognize the true definition of lost income—the difference between the money actually being made and the potential money that should have been made but wasn't.

DON'T ALLOW YOUR BUSINESS TO BE ONE OF THE MILLIONS THAT WILL FLATLINE THIS YEAR

As an experienced small business owner, I appreciate firsthand why people achieve less-than-desired results, even with very hard work. The breadth of experiences I've enjoyed over my career has helped me to identify strategies for avoiding costly and time-consuming mistakes. I truly believe the answers to achieving better business results can be found in the insightful application of guiding principles that help produce a winning business formula. In other words, I believe in the "science" of business more than the "art" of business.

It's my honor to share some of the latest wisdom I've gleaned in life. You'll find this new principle-driven five-step model to solving the profit but no cash problem to be an easy-to-follow formula aimed at saving businesses in distress as well as helping those who want to excel and grow.

As a business owner, you work hard and deserve to have your energy result in owning an increasingly profitable business, one with predictable cash flowing through it. If you're not satisfied with the results you're getting in your business, here is my promise to you: If you put into practice the foundational principals offered in the following pages, you and those you work with will experience better results, personally and professionally. If not, I will personally study your business at no charge to discover what's holding you back.

To Your Continued Success,
Lorin Young
Business Scientist
Founder, Keystone to Profits
Author, *Owning a GREAT Business*
Architect, *Owning a GREAT Business Roadmap*
Practitioner, *Business CPR*

1

WHAT CAUSES BUSINESSES TO HAVE PROFITS BUT NO CASH?

The answer to the question, "Why does my P&L Statement show a profit that is higher than my bank balance?" is not solved by accounting. Solving the profit but no cash problem is more than using cash for things that don't show up on the income statement. It's also more than the timing difference of when revenues and expenses are recognized in relation to their collection and payment.

The reason your financials show you earning a profit that is greater than what you show in your bank account is caused by not understanding the relationship of your cash flow, profits, and reporting. It's aggravated by not understanding the timing of your cash inflows and cash outflows represented by your sales and expenses as reflected in the following example:

Financial Transaction	P&L Statement	Bank Transaction	Bank Statement
Net Sales for Month	$100,000	Balance Brought Forward	$10,000
Less Direct Costs	60,000	Customer Payment Deposits	50,000
Gross Profit	40,000	Total Withdrawals	58,000
Less Overhead Costs	30,000	Bank Fees	50
Operating Income	10,000	Balance Carried Forward	1,950

Your ability to have profits but no cash happens every time you spend more cash than you brought in during any time period ahead of actually collecting on sales made. Whenever expenses increase faster than sales, the sustainability of that business is put at greater risk immediately. This is even true when revenues minus the expenses associated with earning that income are positive.

By allowing expenses to grow faster than sales, the gap between what your P&L reports as profits and your bank statement reports as your ending cash balance is compromised. Part of this is a function of using the accrual accounting method versus cash accounting. Accrual accounting matches accomplishment (delivery of product or service) and effort (expenses incurred to generate accomplishments), regardless of cash flow timing. Cash accounting records income when cash is received and expenses when cash is paid out.

Claiming that the difference between profits reported and cash in the bank is solved by accounting is the easy answer. Yes, cash basis accounting can be used to track the movement of cash through a business, such that net income more accurately reflects a business's cash in the bank. The problem is reported cash balances are ultimately a measure of how profitable a business operation is over time. By matching expenses with their associated revenues in a reporting period, it gives you the truer profit. As a result, it is an excellent measure of the ongoing sustainability of your company.

Unfortunately, the accrual method of accounting doesn't give you a good measure of your ability to pay your bills week-to-week. While cash accounting shows you the cash received minus the cash paid out during the time period that tells you when you spent more cash in a period than you brought in. It doesn't solve the profit but no cash problem either. You solve the profit but no cash problem through weekly management of your cash. It is when you manage your cash inflows and outflows independent of your financial statements is how you stop being surprised by how much cash you have in the bank. Do this to avoid being surprised at the end of each month at the amount being reported on your P&L and bank statements.

Cash management is more than looking at your Statement of Changes in Cash Flow that shows you cash flows from operations, investment activities, and financing decisions. Cash management is how you manage the relationship of your opening cash balance and your ending cash balance week-to-week. It is how you know the amount of your cash inflows and their sources. It is how you manage your cash outflows and their uses. It is how you know week-to-week whether you are building cash reserves or burning through them?

To best appreciate what causes businesses to have profits but no cash, you need to understand what causes businesses to burn through their cash faster than they bring it in.

WHAT CAUSES BUSINESSES TO FLATLINE?

In appreciating what causes businesses to flatline, it helps to consider how every human being, regardless of race or gender, will flatline anytime their heart ceases to function. If this happens to you, not only will your heart stop, but all of your other organs will begin to deteriorate, one after another. If your heart fails to begin pumping blood through your body again quickly, your oxygen-deprived brain will begin to die, and as your brain fails to function, there will no longer be any life to sustain.

 A "flatline" refers to a flatlined electrocardiogram, in which the heart shows no electrical activity. It is represented by a flatline, the most severe form of cardiac arrest.

A *cardiac* flatline is the total absence of electrical activity from the heart. This means no tissue contraction from the heart muscle and, as a result, no blood flowing to the rest of the body. Whereas a flatline *electroencephalogram* will show when there is no electrical *brain* activity indicating brain death. If this happens while you are under medical care, and you have not specified that you do not wish to be resuscitated, every attempt will be made to bring your heart back to function again. If your heart can't be restarted within a medically reasonable time, a decision will be made to stop further resuscitation attempts, and a time of death is announced.

Yes, this is a morbid way to open a business book that solves the profit but no cash problem, yet one I believe you will come to appreciate given the strikingly similar correlation between a life you care about flatlining for real compared to a business you care about flatlining from running out of cash because there are insufficient profits.

CARDIAC ARREST CAN STRIKE WITHOUT WARNING

Business owners who are surprised when they have no cash in the bank are like a person who wakes up in the ER, learning they are lucky to be alive because they had just suffered a heart attack. The American Heart Association (AHA) defines cardiac arrest as "the abrupt loss of heart function in a person who may or may not have been diagnosed with heart disease. It can come on suddenly, or in the wake of other symptoms. Cardiac arrest is often fatal, if appropriate steps aren't taken immediately."

The AHA tells us what signs to look for if we suspect someone is experiencing cardiac arrest:

1. **Sudden loss of responsiveness.** To confirm if the person is in cardiac arrest, tap him or her hard on the shoulders or ask loudly if he or she is okay. If the person doesn't move, speak, blink, or otherwise react, they are considered to be unresponsive.
2. **Normal breathing has stopped.** If the person isn't breathing or is gasping for air, then they may be in respiratory or cardiac arrest. If a person remains in respiratory arrest for very long, they will proceed into cardiac arrest.

Every time your business is tight on cash, your business experiences a sudden loss of responsiveness. Your ability to manage your employees, serve your customers is compromised, because all of your attention is focused on finding cash. When this happens, normal operations come to a slow stop as it becomes increasingly difficult to meet payroll and source needed materials.

WHAT THE AMERICAN HEART ASSOCIATION RECOMMENDS

Consider what to do if you have tried and failed to get someone you love to respond, and you think they may be suffering cardiac arrest. Here are the actions the AHA professionals recommend:

1. **Yell for help.** Tell someone nearby to call 911 or your local emergency response number. Ask that person or another bystander to bring you an AED (automated external defibrillator), if there is one on hand. Tell them to hurry—time is of the essence. If you're alone with an adult who exhibits signs of cardiac arrest, call 911 and get an AED if one is available.

2. **Check for breathing.** Administer CPR if the person isn't breathing or is gasping for air ineffectively.

3. **Give CPR.** Push hard on the sternum, causing the chest to deflate at least two inches, and perform rapid compressions at a rate of 100–120 a minute. Keep your hands in the center of the chest, allowing the chest to return to its normal expanded position after each push.

4. **Use an AED** (automated external defibrillator) as soon as it arrives. Turn it on and follow the verbal prompts.

5. **Keep performing chest compressions.** Continue administering CPR until the person starts to breathe and move or until someone with more advanced training, such as a paramedic, takes over.

A visit to www.heart.org/en/health-topics/cardiac-arrest/causes-of-cardiac-arrest reveals that "most cardiac arrests occur when a diseased heart's electrical system malfunctions. This malfunction causes an abnormal heart rhythm such as ventricular tachycardia or ventricular fibrillation. Some cardiac arrests are also caused by the extreme slowing of the heart's rhythm," a condition known as bradycardia.

SUDDEN CARDIAC ARREST IS NOT THE SAME AS A HEART ATTACK

A heart attack occurs when the blood supply to part of the heart muscle is blocked. A heart attack may cause cardiac arrest. When the electrical impulses in the heart become rapid or chaotic, the heart is likely to stop beating, suddenly putting the person in cardiac arrest.

Failure to act quickly and decisively in a cardiac emergency leads to unnecessary deaths. The www.heart.org web page managed by the American Heart Association (AHA) shares the following causes of cardiac arrest:

- **Scarring of heart tissue** from a prior heart attack or another cause. A heart that is scarred or enlarged from any cause is prone to develop life-threatening ventricular arrhythmias. The first six months after a heart attack represents a particularly high-risk period for sudden cardiac arrest in patients with atherosclerotic heart disease.
- **A thickened heart muscle (cardiomyopathy)** causes damage to the heart muscle as a result of high blood pressure, heart valve disease, or other causes. A diseased heart muscle can make a person more prone to sudden cardiac arrest, especially if they also suffer from heart failure.
- **Heart medications,** under certain conditions, can set the stage for arrhythmias that can cause sudden cardiac arrest. Significant changes in blood levels of potassium and magnesium from using diuretics, for example, can also cause life-threatening arrhythmias and cardiac arrest.
- **Electrical abnormalities** such as Wolff-Parkinson-White syndrome and Long QT syndrome may cause sudden cardiac arrest in children and young people.
- **Congenital blood vessel abnormalities**, particularly in the coronary arteries and aorta, may cause cardiac arrest. Adrenaline released during intense physical activity often acts as a trigger for sudden cardiac arrest when these abnormalities are present.

- **Recreational drug use** can cause sudden cardiac arrest, even in otherwise healthy people.

The bottom line for the American Heart Association (AHA) is that "irregular heartbeats such as these that can cause cardiac arrest, and should be considered life-threatening."

The *same* bottom line can be seen in businesses whenever cash outflows exceed cash inflows. Prolonged exposure to poor cash flow puts business owners at increased risk of going *out of* business or, to stick with the analogy, flatline.

Should someone's life be threatened by cardiac arrest, then hands-only CPR—**C**ardio (Heart) **P**ulmonary (Lungs) **R**esuscitation (Revival) is the lifesaving emergency procedure performed when the heart has stopped beating completely. Some key facts can help us to appreciate the critical importance of CPR:

- Every minute without CPR, a person's survival rate decreases by 10 percent.
- Without CPR, 92 percent of those with cardiac arrest die before making it to the hospital. Put another way, only 8 percent of people who suffer cardiac arrest outside the hospital survive.
- Many victims appear healthy, with no obvious or previously known heart disease or other risk factors.
- The life you save with CPR is most likely to be a loved one, given the fact that four out of five cardiac arrests occur at home.
- Hands-Only CPR, solely with chest compressions, has proven to be as effective as CPR with breaths in treating adult cardiac arrest victims. Since 2008, the American Heart Association (AHA) has recommended Hands-Only CPR for adults.

Just as you would hope to have a CPR-certified person nearby if your heart should stop beating, it's critical that your business has a skilled, ready-to-practice *Business CPR* specialist any time your business **C**ash, **P**rofits, or **R**eporting practices need reviving.

The value of learning *Business CPR* is that the skills needed to revive your business are the *same* skills you should be using to *protect* it from ever needing to be financially resuscitated. This is how you solve the profits but no cash problem.

CPR: THE DIFFERENCE BETWEEN LIFE AND DEATH

While cardiopulmonary resuscitation may feel like it has been around forever, it wasn't until 1956 that Peter Safar and James Elam invented mouth-to-mouth resuscitation. In 1957, the United States military adopted the mouth-to-mouth resuscitation method to revive unresponsive victims. This led to the formal development of CPR in 1960.

Thankfully, the lives of many cardiac arrest victims around the world are saved daily because someone close by was able to get their heart started again using CPR. The power of CPR lies in getting the heart to resume functioning, blood to begin flowing again through the body, and the lungs to begin breathing again. Making the heart pump again is the difference between life and death for a person in cardiac arrest.

Now consider how many business owners struggle every day with a low sales or flatlined business caused by drowning in mistakes, overdosing on debt, or choking on costly errors. Far too often, these business owners close their businesses because they fail to grasp the relationship between cash, profits, and reporting. Their ability to build and maintain a viable and successful business is absolutely dependent on understanding and balancing this relationship.

WHAT IS BUSINESS CPR?

Business CPR or *B-CPR* involves managing the relationship between cash flow, profits, and reporting. Without all three working together, you are at risk of cardiac arrest in your business, just as you would be if your heart stopped pumping blood and oxygen to your tissues because of blood loss, clogged arteries, or failure in your nervous system.

Becoming competent in *B-CPR* doesn't require special certification, a college degree, or years of accounting experience. To practice *B-CPR*, you only need to know the relationships between your cash flow, profits, and financial reporting. Understanding these relationships thoroughly is the best way to protect your business from ever needing to be revived. By consistently applying the principles of *B-CPR*, you will have a profitable business with predictable cash flow to keep it healthy.

WHY SHOULD I CARE ABOUT *B-CPR*?

B-CPR involves managing the relationship between cash flow, profits, and business reporting. Without all three of these business fundamentals working together, your business is at risk of flatlining, just as you would be if your heart stopped pumping blood and oxygen throughout your body.

From a business perspective, *cash* equates to the blood flowing through our bodies; *profits* equate to the heart pumping blood to vital organs and tissues; and *reporting* effectively on all parts of our business equates to the way our nervous system sends and receives important and timely messages. Just as *cash* funds all of the important actions across your business, the blood in each of us performs many important functions from supplying the oxygen carried in red blood cells to our tissues to the supply of nutrients such as glucose, amino acids, and fatty acids processed by the digestive system and transported throughout our body. Blood also carries hormones released by the endocrine glands, distributing them to the body parts that need them, *when* they need them.

Blood is the fluid substance that primarily serves to carry oxygen and nutrients to tissues while shuttling away metabolic waste. Similarly, cash flowing from business operations is how employees, suppliers, lenders, and the government get paid. Any cash left over forms profits, which can be given to investors as dividends or returned to the company to reinvest.

In the human body, bleeding from a severed major artery can result in death in only ten to fifteen minutes. As a result of major blood loss, the heart begins to fail, leaving the surviving arteries and veins to starve for blood until the heart has nothing left to pump. This type of death is referred to as exsanguination or bleeding out. It occurs when the body loses 30 to 40 percent of the total blood volume. For an average-sized person, this is half a gallon or around three to four pints of blood.

FEW BUSINESSES FLATLINE DUE TO THE EQUIVALENT OF PHYSICAL TRAUMA

Few businesses flatline because they bleed out cash at such a rate that they are viable one day and bankrupt the next. The cause of *most* business deaths is far less dramatic but just as lethal: the equivalent of a blocked artery. In humans, clogged arteries most often do not cause detectable symptoms until a major event, such as a heart attack or stroke, occurs. At other times, especially when the arterial blockage is 70 percent or greater, the buildup of arterial plaque may cause symptoms that include chest pain or angina, shortness of breath, or other coronary artery disease signs and symptoms that can be treated, if they're diagnosed in time.

Healthy arteries have smooth interior walls that allow blood to flow through easily. Clogged arteries result from a buildup of a substance called plaque on the inner walls of the arteries. The buildup of arterial plaque will reduce blood flow or in some instances, block it entirely.

Healthy
Coronary Artery

Clogged arteries greatly increase the likelihood of heart attack, stroke, and even death. Because of these dangers, it's important to understand that when plaque builds up, it narrows your coronary arteries and decreases blood flow to your heart. Eventually, a complete blockage will lead to a heart attack.

Coronary Artery
with Plaque Buildup

Should your heart stop pumping blood, you will suffer sudden cardiac arrest (SCA), also called sudden cardiac death. SCA is always fatal unless treated right away. This is because brain cells begin to die after four minutes of no blood flow. After six minutes, those cells will cease functioning, and you will be effectively dead.

Even if you made a profit last year, you run out of cash this year from operations you are in business cardiac arrest. If you are unable to quickly raise cash through operations from the selling of assets, securing additional paid-in-capital, or raising cash through debt, your business will cease to function. If this happens, you will be out of business.

THE POWER OF ANY FUNCTION LIES IN THE CENTRAL NERVOUS SYSTEM

Our physical bodies are 100 percent reliant on our central nervous system, which consists of the brain, spinal cord, sensory organs, and all of the nerves that connect these organs with the rest of the body. Messages are communicated among the parts of the body through specialized cells called neurons. Without this unconscious and steady flow of back-and-forth messages from and to our brain, we would effectively cease to exist.

The business equivalent of the central nervous system is the business reporting system, particularly the financial reports built from the data collected from each transaction. Every financial report represents different roll-ups of each transaction, which we can think of as neurons. In business, these neurons are too often underdeveloped through poor transaction recording. As a result, the information they represent are never fully accurate nor utilized in most businesses.

While our physical nervous system is a complex collection of nerves and neurons that transmit signals between different parts of the body, the business reporting system is much less complex. It involves the timely recording of each of a business's financial transactions. Failing to report each financial transaction accurately contributes significantly to business cardiac arrest. Over time, failure to convert the financial data produced through each transaction a business conducts every day of every week, throughout the financial year, into useful information, robs business managers of key insights. And it blinds them to effective actions that could be taken to improve the results of their business.

WHY SHOULD I CARE ABOUT THE ACCURACY AND TIMELINESS OF MY FINANCIAL REPORTING?

Accurate financial reporting provides actionable information for critical decision-making. Your financial statements create business-specific information about the results of your operations, your financial position, and the cash flowing through your operations. This information will help you to make financial-statement-informed decisions regarding the best allocation of resources within your business operations.

Too many small business owners remain small because they have no interest in understanding the purpose and importance of the information reported in their financial statements. This lack of interest greatly increases their risk of going out of business. What's difficult to comprehend is that there are only *three* core financial statements to understand when operating any business:

	P&L Statement	Balance Sheet	Statement of Cash Flows
Formula	Sales - Expenses = Net Income	Assets = Liabilities + Owners Equity	Operating + Investing + Financing Cash
Definition	A summary of management's performance as reflected in the profitability (or lack of it) of the business over a certain period, irrespective of cash flow.	States (1) what assets the company owns, (2) what it owes (its liabilities), and (3) what is the amount left to the owners after satisfying the liabilities.	A summary of the actual incomings and outgoings of cash over an accounting period (month, quarter, year). It answers the questions: Where the money came from? Where it went?

	P&L Statement	**Balance Sheet**	**Statement of Cash Flows**
Key Fact	Net income is the owners' return from operations and represents an increase in the value of their investment in the business.	Owners' equity is not the owner's piggy bank; it represents the owners' claim on the company assets AFTER the liabilities have all been paid off.	Operating cash flow can be used to make new investments in the business, repay financial debt, or to return capital to the owners.

Failing to consistently use readily available financial reports on a timely basis will result in a flatlined business. You protect your business from flatlining by using the financial data that's produced through each transaction your business conducts every day of every week throughout the year. Your business transactions entered into your accounting system will show you how your business is performing. Use this foundational information to identify *where* corrective action is needed to improve your profit results.

Every business has to manage both cash and profits effectively. To WIN in business, you need both positive operating cash flows and sustainable profits. By consistently using financial reports, business owners and management teams know what is working well and what isn't. Disciplined use of your internal reporting system is how you intelligently decide *what* actions to *start, stop,* or *change* in your business.

IS YOUR BUSINESS A GOOD BUSINESS TO BUY?

Businesses with predictable cash flow, strong profits, and accurate reports never face the question, "Is this a good business to buy?" They don't face this question because they understand that cash, profits, and reporting all depend on their clear understanding of the "four key" numbers in any business:

1. Net Sales
2. Gross Profit
3. Operating Income
4. Working Capital

Business CPR can be used to effectively balance the combination of money, time, and risk that are the base inputs to any business. If you are in a high-risk business that consumes all of your time and money, you had better know whether you are earning a profit. If not, you run the risk of waking up in two, five, ten, or twenty years with nothing to show for your hard work, stress, and sacrifice.

YOUR BUSINESS'S GROSS AND OPERATING PROFITS ARE THE KEYS TO OWNING A HEALTHY BUSINESS

Every business starts with cash, which is invested in various ways to generate revenue. Ideally, any revenue is turned back into cash, and the cycle begins anew. The health of this business cycle is measured through gross and operating profits.

Your business is like a hollow muscular organ that pumps your cash investment through the circulatory system of your business operations by rhythmic contraction and dilation of cash inflow and outflow. Your heart lies at the center of your circulatory system, which consists of a network of blood vessels, such as arteries, veins, and capillaries that carry blood to and from all areas of your body. Similarly, the cash your business generates funds the activities occurring every day across all aspects of your business.

In its most basic form, profit is calculated by subtracting the sum of all expenses from total net sales. The profits a business produces indicate the health and potential wealth of a business. Cash flow, on the other hand, refers to the inflows and outflows of cash that may be occurring, whether or not the business is operating at a profit. No matter its size or length of operation, it's essential for any business to find that magical balance of cash flow and profit.

The hard reality is that every business is required to spend cash, but no business can spend its profits until those profits are converted into cash. Just because a business is profitable on paper doesn't mean it will have sufficient cash flow to sustain itself over time. This is especially the case whenever a business's money is tied up in assets, accounts receivable, or inventory, such that it can't pay its current expenses.

Unfortunately, most business leaders fail to see the cash or profit implications as quickly as they should. This is because they are not effectively utilizing the financial data created from their revenue-generation activities that report on the health of their business operations. As a result, they fail to understand the true picture of their business operations over a period of time as well as the current financial position of the company.

UNDERSTANDING VARIABLE AND FIXED COSTS IS THE START OF *B-CPR* SUCCESS

Ensuring that you have a profitable business begins with understanding the two principal *costs* of running any business: variable and fixed costs.

Variable Costs will vary according to how much a business produces and sells. The costs for resources used to produce and deliver what you sell are called the cost of goods sold (COGS.) Some common examples of variable costs include:

1. Direct labor required to deliver a service or produce a product;
2. Materials required to produce the product or support a service;
3. Shipping and service delivery costs required to get the product or service to the buyer.

Fixed Costs stay steady, regardless of how much a business produces and sells. If a cost doesn't change regardless of a sale being made, it is considered a fixed cost. These costs are considered "overhead" and are accounted for in selling, general, and administrative (SG&A) expenses. Some common examples of fixed costs include:

1. Advertising;
2. Owner and office salaries;

3. Insurance;
4. Rent and utilities.

Successful business owners must be thoughtful and cautious in taking on new fixed costs, because these costs don't go away when sales slow, whereas the cost of goods sold, if truly variable, are only incurred whenever a sale is made.

Other costs to be aware of are taxes and interest paid. These "costs of doing business" are imposed by the government or other agencies. As a business owner, you need to be aware of your tax and interest obligations and account for them when considering the pricing of your products and services. Failure to account for a variable cost, fixed cost, interest, or tax expenses in your pricing will negatively impact the profitability of your business every time, and your cash flow from operations will suffer as a result.

UNDERSTANDING GROSS PROFIT AND OPERATING INCOME

Gross is the money a business keeps after direct costs are subtracted from net sales. The first profit calculation is as follows:

Net Sales - COGS = Gross Profit

Gross profit margin is the percentage of money the business keeps after the variable costs are subtracted from the sales revenue. Below is the mathematical formula for calculating your gross profit margin expressed as a percent:

Gross Profit / Net Sales = Gross Profit Margin

The gross profit margin confirms how efficiently your business converts a sale into a profit, and it's the number one determiner of whether you will have any operating income. Put another way, decreases in gross profit without corresponding decreases in overhead expenses will guarantee that you're on track to losing money, not making a profit.

Operating Income is any money the business keeps after both the variable costs, *and* the fixed costs are subtracted from net sales revenue. This second profit calculation is as follows:

Net Sales - COGS = Gross Profit - SG&A = Operating Income

SG&A is referred to as Selling, General, and Administrative expense. These expenses are reflective of your fixed costs; those costs that don't vary with sales. Subtracting overhead or fixed costs from Gross Profit results in the second level of profitability in your business, often referred to as Operating Income.

Another common reference to Operating Income is EBITDA, which stands for *earnings before interest, taxes, depreciation,* and *amortization.* Knowing your EBITDA earnings is important, because this figure tells you how efficiently your business operations are converting sales to profits.

Net Income is considered the "bottom line," whereas Gross Revenue is the "top line." Net Income is the money left over after accounting for every business transaction that occurred during the accounting period. Put another way, your Net Income is the profit made by the business that is available to be reinvested in the business or returned to you as the business owner. Below is the mathematical formula for calculating net profit and net profit margin percent:

Operating Income - Interest - Taxes - Depreciation - Amortization = Net Profit

Net Income / Net Sales = Net Profit Margin

Most successful businesses have gross profit margins that are 45 percent or greater, EBIDTA earnings that are 15 to 20 percent, and net profit margins that are at least 10 percent or greater. Businesses achieving these types of margins are most commonly operating in a market where there is high customer demand and the possibility for their businesses to grow.

CONCLUDING WHAT CAUSES BUSINESSES TO HAVE PROFITS BUT NO CASH

Knowing when and how expenses and revenues are recognized on your P&L Statement is important, yet it doesn't solve the profits but no cash problem. Proactively managing your cash inflows and outflows is how you know whether you are building cash reserves or burning through them. You determine where to intervene to help your business improve profits to protect cash flow through reporting. This is how you protect yourself from "having more month left than you have cash" to pay that month's operating expenses.

If you are constantly stressing over how you are going to meet payroll or pay your bills or you are failing to earn at least 45 percent in gross profit, 20 percent in operating income, and at least 10 percent net income, the following chapters will introduce a proven five-step system for avoiding business cardiac arrest.

AUTHOR'S SIDE NOTE—APPRECIATING THE SIGNIFICANCE OF LUCA PACIOLI TO YOUR BUSINESS

Modern-day business failures occurring all around us each day are even more amazing when you consider a little bit of history: In 1494, Luca Pacioli published a twenty-seven-page treatise on bookkeeping. In effect, Pacioli explained double-entry bookkeeping to Italian merchants. His body of work, written over 500 years ago, led to his being recognized as the father of professional accounting and bookkeeping.

The purpose of double-entry accounting, he explained, is to provide a business owner with the opportunity to apply two equal and corresponding sides, known as debits and credits, to the financial transactions occurring in his or her business. *Debit* in Latin means "he owes;" *credit* means "he trusts."

Pacioli's book also gave instructions for recording transactions in a variety of currencies, thus establishing the "C" in *B-CPR* by enabling merchants to report their transactions and, ultimately, manage their cash. The ability to calculate the "P" for profits was established by learning how to record each business transaction accurately. This, in turn, established the "R" for reporting in Business CPR. By accurately reporting debits and credits, everything necessary for a business to succeed became available to the inquiring business owner in 1494.

Today, just as the merchants influenced by Pacioli, we can know whether revenues (R) are greater than expenses (E.) When R > E, the result is profits. And when R < E, the business has suffered a loss.

It was also referenced by Pacioli that merchants who failed to maintain their records were at greater risk of business failure. It was pointed out that the merchants who used double-entry bookkeeping had access to important information about their business so that they could take effective action to both stop losses and increase profits.

Over 525 years later, business owners around the world will still end a day, a week, a month, and even a year without accurately reporting on transactions, just like the struggling merchants Pacioli tried to help in 1494. Their failure to practice the "R" for "reporting" in *B-CPR* prevents them from knowing if they are "P," profitable or not. When a business is *not* profitable, it leads to immediate issues involving a lack of "C" for cash.

While this is obvious on the surface, my work with modern-day businesses each going through their own highly stressful and never-ending cycle of tight cash resulted in an epiphany that led to the development of *B-CPR*. Just as CPR can save your life, a highly committed business owner through the principles of *B-CPR* can protect their cash, even as they work on new ways to generate the profits needed to fund both ongoing and future business operations through the disciplined use of the right reports.

2

OVERVIEW TO *B-CPR*: YOUR FIVE-STEP SYSTEM FOR IMPROVING CASH FLOW FROM PROFITS

The true success of any business is not measured by the money actually made but by the difference between the money made and the money that should have been made but wasn't.

Even if your business made a profit last year, it doesn't mean you won't become one of the many businesses approaching flatline this year. Anytime you find yourself drowning in never-ending problems, overdosing on debt, or choking on costly mistakes, your business is at increased risk of failure.

You don't have to close your business should you be struggling to make the relationship between cash, profits, and reporting work for your business. *B-CPR* has been developed to help you learn how to improve your cash flow from profits.

WHY SUFFER THE EFFECTS OF BUSINESS CARDIAC ARREST WHEN YOU CAN AVOID THEM?

Avoiding the effects of business cardiac arrest is done through *B-CPR*, a proven easy-to-apply five-step business management system with the power to revive a flatlined business and help you achieve greater levels of financial success.

Owning a business that performs the way you want it to versus controlling your time and your life requires discipline and effort. Developing a clear understanding of the relationship between cash flow, profits, and financial reporting is the *only* way to effectively manage your business and achieve your desired result.

For several years, I've been engaged by multiple business owners to improve the results of their businesses. I have established over these years that the key to uncovering what needs to be changed to improve business results is in understanding how they use their business's financial reporting system. I have also confirmed that consistently applying the principles of *B-CPR* is the best way to hold onto cash from profits that protect any business from flatlining.

The first key is to use your business's financial statements to confirm how sustainable your profits are cross-checked against your bank statements to verify how predictable your cash flow is or not. If your profits aren't sustainable, and your cash flow isn't predictable, you need to identify what you must change to produce higher profits and predictable cash flow.

If you don't like feeling out of control, or worse, battling the pitfalls of running out of cash—the two leading causes of a flatlined business—then take the necessary action today to begin doing things differently. The best method I have found to identify what needs to be done differently to produce better results is to consistently act on the five business-saving steps in *B-CPR*.

MANAGEMENT EQUALS CONTROL, AND CONTROL EQUALS INCOME

To put it simply, effective management means that you have control over your business and, as a result, over the income your business produces. Control also means that you're able to start, change, or stop whatever you and your employees are doing whenever you need to do so. When you can't easily start, change, or stop what you are doing in order to generate better results, it is likely because you aren't sure what, why, or when to make these changes. You correct for this lack of control by following these fundamental and critical steps:

1. Never expose your business to cash outflows that exceed cash inflows, by
2. Knowing what you are trying to accomplish, and in what time period, through
3. Continuous confirmation of the quality of your profits, with
4. Unrelenting and decisive action to stop profit losses which keep your business at risk by

5. Always being accountable for your results.

Business CPR not only protects your business from failing; it is the surest way to realize your sales, profit, and wealth creation goals! Below is the visual representation of the *B-CPR* model that will help you *gain and maintain control over your business in five "must-do" steps:*

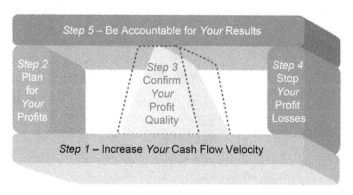

What holds this five-step model together from the top is Step 5—Be Accountable for *Your* Results. Without deliberate action on the critical few things needing to be accomplished each day, you'll never produce your desired results. I reference the fifth step first because, ultimately, you'll need to have the discipline to follow through on the actions your customers are paying you to take and the decisions your employees need you to make so that they can do what you need them to do.

Those who try to operate their businesses without a firm commitment to being accountable for their actions operate under the "hope" method. This usually means they are more likely to be hoping they'll have money in the bank than actually executing a plan that defines how they'll generate profits. Knowing what specific areas to focus on to achieve planned results is identified through each of the first four steps of the *B-CPR* model listed in order of importance.

Step 1—Increase the velocity of your operating cash flow today is how you fund your way into next week.

Step 2—Build your twenty-four-month profit plan that sets your direction and guides your decisions.

Step 3—Confirm the quality of your profits earned each month to identify what you need to start, change, or stop.

Step 4—Stop the losses that keep your business at risk beginning with quantifying your losses so you prioritize which issues to fix first.

Below is a high-level introduction to each of these easy-to-apply steps in the B-CPR model. Each step and their order came from extensive research grounded in how best to help business owners achieve their business goals while protecting their business from flatlining. As you read the overviews begin to consider where your business is most in need of you being more attentive as an owner in managing your business assets.

STEP 1—INCREASE THE VELOCITY OF *YOUR* OPERATING CASH FLOW TODAY

Nothing in your business happens without **cash.** To prevent *cash outflows* from exceeding *cash inflows,* maintain a four-week rolling cash forecast to confirm how much money from operations you are holding onto. Protect the health of your business by projecting your **cash flow** for at least the next four weeks. I recommend doing these projections every Monday to help you prioritize *where* you need to exert more effort each week. Your goal is to make sure your projected cash outflows *never* exceed your available cash. Chapter 3 shows you how to easily calculate these projections.

STEP 2—BUILD *YOUR* TWENTY-FOUR-MONTH PROFIT PLAN TO GUIDE *YOUR* DECISION-MAKING

Without knowing your sales and profit *targets* to be realized each month, it's impossible to know whether you'll make a profit, let alone accomplish your goals. Ideally, your Profit Plan is finalized in month eleven of each year, so you'll know your goals for month one of the following year. Chapter 4 guides you through the core steps to follow in building an achievable profit plan.

STEP 3—CONFIRM THE QUALITY OF *YOUR* PROFITS THROUGH LEADING AND LAGGING METRICS

To confirm how your business is doing while identifying where you are performing better or worse than your desired plan, utilize the following two tools:

KPI Scorecard: This tool comprises your leading metrics or key performance indicators (KPIs), which should be captured and discussed in your weekly management team meetings. Using a KPI Scorecard helps you confirm that your daily actions are on track to produce your planned weekly, monthly, and annual results.

Variance Reports: These lagging metrics are pulled from your monthly P&L statement and balance sheet. They should be used during the second management meeting of each month to confirm whether or not you realized your planned results for that month.

The information for both of these reports comes from data being generated and recorded through every transaction. If you capture this information accurately and on a timely basis you will be able to identify the needed actions you must take to position your business to benefit from Step 4. Chapter 5 lays out how to begin, now, to confirm the quality of your profits in greater detail.

STEP 4—STOP THE LOSSES THAT KEEP *YOUR* BUSINESS AT RISK

All wasted or lost cash costs you both cash reserves and profits. Every profit failure drains your cash reserves and puts your business at risk every time you fail to make money on a sale. **Profit Losses** are best identified through the leading and lagging metric "misses" monitored in Step 3. It's imperative to your business's survival to stop *any* loss that has a significant impact on your cash quality and velocity. Chapter 6 introduces a business "change" methodology, which you can use to stop cash from draining the life out of your business.

STEP 5—BE ACCOUNTABLE FOR *YOUR* RESULTS

You control *your* business through disciplined **actions.** In every business, there are always more smart actions one *could* take than time available to do so. The hard reality is that not every action you complete will produce the results you lay out in your Profit Plan. Know that without action, there is no profit. The key to long-term success lies in having a high bias for action and a passion for results. If your disciplined actions *aren't* creating the intended results, then change your actions to ensure that you realize your desired results. Chapter 7 guides you through the process of working smarter, not harder, by consistently following the principles of *B-CPR.*

Steps 1 through 4 of the *B-CPR* management system will better ensure that your hard work produces the desired results. By mastering the ins and outs of your profit plan, you'll be able to determine the *critical few things to do* among the noise of the *relevant many you could do.* This is how you will consistently produce the desired results that you are holding yourself and others accountable for generating.

THE "C" IN *B-CPR* REFLECTS HOW YOU MANAGE THE CASH FLOWING THROUGH YOUR BUSINESS

Your business may be profitable, but that doesn't mean you have adequate cash in the bank. There's a significant difference between profit and cash flow, one that most struggling business owners never fully comprehend. This is particularly true of those business owners who struggle with recording their financial transactions into their accounting software.

Successful business owners know that every time their business receives or makes a payment, it needs to be recorded within the week. Without recording these transactions, they'll never be able to generate an accurate P&L statement. Without an accurate and timely P&L statement, they'll never know if they are generating profits or suffering losses.

By having a timely and consistent business reporting system, smart business owners position themselves to create a P&L statement for any accounting period they can have confidence in using. The most effective use of your P&L statement is in isolating areas where you are at greatest risk of losing money by studying the areas of direct cost and overhead relative to net sales achieved by your business over a specific period.

In any language, profit is defined as the money left over for a business after subtracting expenses from revenues earned.

While net profit is the figure the government uses to assess tax liabilities, it's not the only number that demands your attention as a business owner. If you really want to know the pulse of your business, you must be vigilant in tracking week-to-week performance; *cash flow* from operations is a more important weekly metric than *profits.*

There is a reason why the windshield of our vehicles is bigger than our rearview mirrors. No one would ever drive their vehicle forward looking through glass the size of their rearview mirror with any speed.

The bottom-line profit or loss number in any P&L statement is a lagging number. It reflects what has already happened in your business. It's a very important number, just as your rearview mirror is an important part of safe vehicle operation, particularly when you want to see behind you.

Cash flow from operations is the lifeblood of every business, and it's particularly vital to any business that lacks large cash reserves.

When your business has cash available, you can pursue options for growth, make investments, and draw from cash reserves (savings) for any unexpected situation or emergency that arises. What gets misunderstood by many failed businesses is the hard reality that while your P&L Statement might show that your business is profitable, you can still go bankrupt whenever that business doesn't have enough cash to pay its current financial obligations. *Cash flow problems are the leading cause of business failure.*

THE NEED FOR *B-CPR* COMES DOWN TO YOUR "ACTUAL P" *(PROFIT RESULTS)* VERSUS YOUR "PLANNED P" *(PROFIT TARGETS)*

"Each year, as part of your profit planning for the coming year, you need to ask yourself a hard question: Do your planned gross profit and operating (EBITDA) earnings suggest that your business can be successful in the long-term?"

If not, what specifically needs to change during this profit planning cycle for your business to be successful?

The next question is, "How am I going to influence these factors so I'm making acceptable profits for the risk that I'm incurring?"

Never lose sight of the hard truth that business profitability in past years is no guarantee of profitability this year or next. Without a plan to direct and control your business, "How will you ever know if your business is profitable?" "How will you know if you're earning enough to be worthy of your valuable time and investment?"

Your annual profit plan confirms what you need to do to make money in the coming year. Or it may tell you that it's time to consider other opportunities. This is particularly true if, after creating your profit plan, you aren't *excited* about making it happen. If building your profit plan drains you of any desire to follow through, that's validation that you should consider making an alternative business and lifestyle decision.

Let's look at another important output from a profit plan: "Is my business structured and staffed to allow it to operate without me?" If your answer is, "No, there is *no way* I will hit my profit plan numbers if I'm not 100 percent involved in the day-to-day operations of my business," it's a sure sign that you have multiple problems to address.

Step back and ask yourself if you have it in you to press forward. Are you committed to resolving the daily issues and problems your business faces? If the answer is "yes," then this book will help you to move forward. If the answer is "no," you have a problem that is not addressed in this book, and you'll have to seek answers elsewhere.

B-CPR IS ULTIMATELY ABOUT MANAGING PROFITABILITY, USING THE RIGHT REPORTS

Successful business owners value the importance of keeping well-organized financial records. They understand that having a financial record system is the only way they can effectively and efficiently keep track of all financial transactions. Without an accurate recording of financial transactions, they would have no way of knowing whether they are making or losing money or whether their business is succeeding or failing.

They refuse to fly (operate) their businesses blindly in the dark without instrument controls. They've learned to avoid financial disaster by making accurate and timely business reporting information a key part of their weekly routine. They know that without good records that they can access at any time, they'll never know if their business is profitable. These business owners use accounting software like QuickBooks or Sage to know if they have been paid by all of their customers. They also use accounting software to track expenses, monies owed, and payment deadlines.

In contrast, running a small business out of your checkbook is not an acceptable alternative to managing your cash. It means constantly worrying about the money coming in and going out of the business solely through your bank account balance. Most business owners doing this have little interest in recording the transactions occurring through their business in their accounting software. As a result, they are limited in how they manage their business to what their bank account reports as it relates to money coming in and out each time they check their bank balance.

Yes, small business owners who run their businesses out of their checkbooks do have a rough sense of whether they have enough money in the bank to pay any bill that is due. The problem is they have no good way to know what money their business receives from selling services or products to customers and who still owes them.

I worked with a large towing and diesel repair business that had an owner who instinctively used his bank account to manage his $2.5 million business. The problem he didn't recognize was how he had no line of sight to those who had not paid, and as a result, he had a highly difficult time managing expenses. As a result, he never knew with any surety if he was making a profit or not. From my experience in working with this type of business owner, they're most often losing money, a great deal more money than they may realize.

B-CPR IS ANCHORED BY ACCURATE + TIMELY RECORD-KEEPING

Successful business owners keep daily-to-weekly sales, operations, and financial records; whereas, struggling business owners have often found record-keeping to be a difficult habit to establish. Therefore, they never practice this key routine to making a profit and controlling cash flow.

Effective record-keeping begins with recognizing two key factors: *First*, no game is fun to play over time when no one is keeping score. Part of the fun is knowing whether you are winning or losing (particularly when you know you are winning!) *Second*, if your goal is to enjoy the long-term financial benefits of operating a well-managed business, one that runs without you, you'll first need to learn to keep consistent and accurate financial records.

Many successful businesses started with a notebook and folders to record daily receipts. Revenue and expenses were entered into a spreadsheet every night or each weekend while those who failed to complete these tasks often went out of business. As their businesses grew, successful business owners progressed to accounting software packages. Over time, they might hire an outside accountant to help them manage their finances. Ultimately, the most successful of them would hire an office manager, then a controller, and finally, a chief financial officer to help them manage their financial business records and investments.

As a business owner, you will need to decide *which* tool or resources will best help you record your revenue and expenses this week. Although any accounting software, bookkeeper, or accountant can help with much of the record-keeping, you need to *understand* the financial records of your business and review them monthly. As your business grows, you will want to deepen your understanding of financial matters so that your money will work harder than you do.

The "P" for profit in *B-CPR* comes **after** you have converted your sales into "C" for cash inflow and paid your expense transactions representing cash outflow and **before** the "R" for whether you did this at a profit or loss through your reporting.

Creating an income statement or profit and loss (P&L) statement is easy. It starts with recording your revenue and expense transactions into your accounting software every week. It's amazing how many business owners fail to record both sales and expenses incurred in a timely and consistent manner. Too often, they'll try to do this at the end of a month or a quarter or never at all. All because they failed to develop the habit of timely and consistent record keeping.

As a result, they fail to record every transaction that occurs, every transaction that has one of two outcomes. The end result of each sales transaction is either more money coming into a business or more going out. Business management is ultimately this simple: you're realizing a profit as a result of cash remaining after total costs are deducted from a sale or you aren't.

Only after all of the revenue and expense transactions have been recorded for the accounting period can you create an accurate profit and loss statement. This is why it's a grave mistake to run your business out of your checking account. Calculating a realistic profit picture from your bank statement alone is impossible.

Your accounting system will easily create your P&L Statement for you by adding up the entries from the revenue and expense records entered for a specific period, such as a week, month, quarter, or year. Your P&L Statement will summarize sources of revenue and expenses and do the math for you. It will communicate whether your business is profitable or not during any chosen period by showing you:

Gross Sales

- Less discounts, returns, and sales write-off's

= Net Sales

- Cost of Goods Sold (variable costs)

= Gross Profit

- Selling General & Administrative Expenses (fixed costs)

= Operating Income (EBITDA)

+ Other (non-operating) Income
- Other (extraordinary) Expenses
- Interest
- Taxes
- Depreciation and Amortization

= Net Profit (or loss)

By aggregating revenue and expense transactions into their appropriate categories as reflected above, you get to confirm where you are making or losing money.

You may have dozens, hundreds, or even thousands of entries from your various transactions over any given accounting period. The recording of each transaction into your accounting software automatically records the data into its appropriate chart of account in your general ledger. All of these recorded transactions are ultimately reflected on your P&L, Balance Sheet, and Cash Flow statements.

Knowing how a P&L Statement is organized is the best way to analyze and understand your core financial data. It will provide you the most insights you can draw from to improve your business.

You will never know if your business is profitable unless you create and utilize a P&L or Income Statement. Remember, the "R" for reporting in CPR is foundational to your making a profit with cash reserves in the bank.

THE BOOKENDS OF *B-CPR:* WEEKLY CASH FLOW PROJECTIONS AND MONTHLY ANALYSIS OF YOUR FINANCIAL STATEMENTS

Cash flow refers to the *timing* and *amount* of the cash flowing in and out of your business. It's important to differentiate the two types of cash flow:

1. Positive cash flow occurs when the total amount of cash coming into your business during a specific period is greater than the total amount of cash leaving your business during that same period. For your business to be viable, you must have a positive cash flow cycle.

2. Negative cash flow occurs when the total amount of cash leaving your business during a specific period is greater than the amount of cash coming into your business during that same time. Negative cash flow is always a risky and undesirable situation. Anytime you're projecting negative cash flow, you need to immediately address what actions need to be taken to generate and protect cash before you begin to run a greater deficit. Often, difficult decisions must be made.

While the flow of money out of most businesses can be seen in a predictable pattern, rarely can the same be said for money coming into a business. As a result, it's far too common for business owners to have some combination of the following cash flow challenges:

1. The newness of the business or recent late payments makes it difficult to receive and pay on credit.
2. Growth opportunities can reduce the amount of available cash.
3. Unused or underutilized purchased inventory ties up cash.

4. Customers paying on credit delays the amount of incoming cash.
5. Selling to other businesses at less than full price and on credit delays both the amount of incoming cash and the quality of that cash inflow.
6. Uneven sales due to seasonality or other factors create peaks and valleys in the amount of cash available.
7. Nonpayment by customers robs you of cash that then becomes bad debt.
8. Unexpected expenses that force you to spend unplanned cash.

THE BOTTOM-LINE OF *B-CPR*

As you can see from the above list, you can't just assume that positive cash flow and profitability will automatically happen for any business. Cash reserves are achieved through thoughtful profit planning and follow-through on key actions supported by accurate and timely reporting. Failure to utilize accurate reporting and make informed key decisions will result in your business flatlining. If this happens, your business will need to be financially resuscitated, because you didn't apply the principles of

Unfortunately, business resuscitation *won't* always work. Sometimes the required action is taken too late, and the business can't be saved. The power of *B-CPR* lies foremost in the *prevention* of business cardiac arrest than in the saving of a business that's already in full-blown cardiac arrest.

CONCLUDING THE OVERVIEW OF THE *B-CPR* MANAGEMENT SYSTEM

Through daily, weekly, and monthly disciplined actions on the critical few versus the relevant many things needing to be done, you'll be able to realize your sales and profit goals with cash reserves in the bank. Protecting the flow of cash through your business allows you to generate surplus cash flow from operations and continuously improve profitability while also protecting your business from ever flatlining.

The principles of *B-CPR* will help you to more easily apply corrective action to fix what's not working in your business and allow you to simultaneously improve your business results and your quality of life. This is how you position yourself to stop worrying about the difference in your reported profits and bank account balance.

AUTHOR'S SIDE NOTE—APPRECIATING THE EASE OF REALIZING THE BENEFITS FROM APPLYING *B-CPR*

As stated in the opening of this chapter, the true lost income of any business is not the actual money lost but the difference between the money actually made and the money that should have been made but wasn't. No business ever performs to its potential year over year. There are always external and internal forces that impede a business's ability to make as much money they should.

What amazes me is the difficulty that business owners and senior executives have in identifying the actions they need to start, change, or stop in order to produce higher profits and protect cash flow. Their consistent inability to identify the necessary actions to take prevents them from ever having full control over their businesses.

What further amazes me is their willingness to live with the feeling of being out of control. Even worse, they're often in denial that they're running out of cash. As a result, they rarely take action on readily available, easy-to-access data. If the data is organized into a useful form and integrated with other key factors, they now have actionable information they can use to identify what practices they need to start, change, or stop with confidence.

Below is some foundational information that illustrates how your business can benefit from *B-CPR* in five easy steps. As you review your *B-CPR* data needs step by step, consider how this information is readily available in almost every business. The problem is the information is rarely used together in an organized way to help business managers get the results they're looking for:

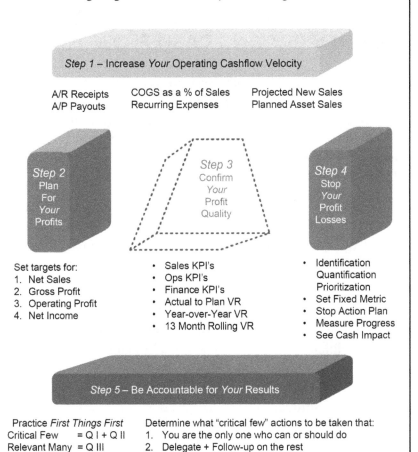

The balance of this book will show you how to develop the insights you need to act confidently if you are to significantly improve your cash flow and, ultimately, the profits generated in your business.

3

STEP 1—INCREASE THE VELOCITY OF *YOUR* OPERATING CASH FLOW TODAY

Cash is the "lifeblood" of every business, no matter its size. Everything any business does over its existence depends on an available and predictable cash flow. Making cash available to the business is the most important concern for management. And every time a business loses *control over* its cash, it will quickly find itself in financial trouble.

Two important phrases used with cash that need to be fully appreciated. The first is *cash velocity*—the speed of cash flowing in and out of any business. The second is *cash quality*—the degree of business excellence as reflected through gross, operating, and net profits.

Increasing the velocity of your operating cash flow is Step 1 in Business CPR (*B-CPR*). This follows from the hard reality that without cash, you are out of business. This is a law, not a principle (the key difference between a law and a principle is that laws have no exceptions). Every day, businesses close because they run out of cash, and this is why gaining and maintaining control over your cash velocity through your operations is Step 1.

THE NUMBER ONE PROBLEM ASSOCIATED WITH CASH VELOCITY

Most people think that the number one problem with cash velocity is collecting the money owed to you; this is actually the number *two* issue. The number *one* issue with cash velocity is cash quality. You'll do everyone associated with your business a serious disservice if your business is bringing in dollars to pay your employees, suppliers, and everyone else but not *you*. When you only leave yourself pennies after you pay everyone else, you will owe more than you collect, and then you will have a real cash velocity problem.

Consider the health of the following three businesses by looking at their cost structure through a dollar, then pick the one you would like to own:

	Business A	Business B	Business C
Sales of...	**$1.00**	**$1.00**	**$1.00**
Direct Labor	.20	.10	.35
Materials	.25	.20	.15
Equipment	.05	.10	.15
Gross Profit	**.50**	**.60**	**.35**
Marketing	.10	.10	.05
Office Payroll	.20	.15	.12
Outside Fees	.04	.07	.10
Insurance	.01	.03	.02
Rent	.08	.10	.05
Utilities	.03	.03	.02
Operating Profit	**.04**	**.12**	**-.01**

It doesn't take a complex financial analysis to determine which of these three businesses would be best to own. You only need to follow what happens to a dollar by converting all of the expenses flowing through the business into a percent of Net Sales and then apply that same percentage to a dollar.

You likely picked Business B, because it's generating twelve cents of operating profit on every dollar, not losing one cent like Business C. This is "cash quality." Business B clearly has better cash quality then Business A, whereas Business C has negative cash quality.

Cash quality only matters if you are collecting the cash owed to you. This is why Steps 2 through 5 are about cash quality, and Step 1 is about managing the cash you have collected. The velocity of cash flowing through your business is the most *urgent* business need, but not the most *important*.

No matter how profitable your business may be, if the money that should be in the business is still sitting in the bank accounts of your customers and not in your own bank account, you're in trouble. This is a contributing cause of the profits, but no cash problem. Your accrual based P&L statement has recorded the sale, but your bank statement doesn't reflect the same sale until you receive payment for that sale.

Step 1 of *B-CPR* starts with collecting the monies owed to you in a timely fashion. Step 2 is the bridge between improving *cash velocity* from Step 1 and confirming *cash quality* in Step 3.

Every business I have studied has cash velocity issues, because they fail to stay on top of their accounts receivable. Most of the time, it is because they don't like asking people for money, even when it's money owed to them. Too many business owners find collection calls to be distasteful, so they don't make them, even when they need to.

What's interesting is how those who dislike calling about invoices due are the same ones dodging calls from their own suppliers who aren't hesitating about getting paid. These owners are not connecting the dots. What they need to appreciate is that anytime they're making calls, asking to be paid, they need to address the calls asking them to pay. It's the only fair way to do business.

Businesses overcome their Step 1 cash velocity issues when they commit to managing their accounts receivable (A/R) collections process with great discipline. Failure to collect monies owed to you is the leading cause of unnecessary business cardiac arrest.

FULLY APPRECIATING THE SIGNIFICANCE OF CASH IN YOUR BUSINESS

The American Heart Association defines cardiac arrest as "the abrupt loss of heart function in a person who may or may not have been diagnosed with heart disease." See the illustration below to appreciate precisely how *B-CPR* starts with cash.

C = Cash

Cash flow from operations is like the blood that flows through our bodies. Just as our blood supplies oxygen to our tissues carried in red cells and nutrients through our blood lipids, we need cash flowing through our businesses to function properly.

Consider the following effects of low oxygen in blood called Hypoxemia:

- Confusion
- Restlessness
- Headache
- Shortness of breath
- Rapid breathing
- Dizziness
- Lightheadedness
- Fainting
- Lack of coordination

These same symptoms of hypoxemia are observed in business owners struggling to find cash to pay their bills.

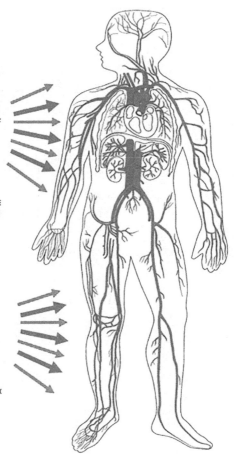

Just as your blood vessels carry blood to and from all areas of your body to sustain your life, the cash your business generates flows through your operations to sustain your business. Cash flow from operations funds the everyday activities needed to generate sales and deliver your products and services. Without cash flowing in from sales, you will never have the opportunity to earn the "P" for profits in *B-CPR*.

For the last several years, every business I've studied, with the exception of two, has suffered the same effects as a person with hypoxemia: low oxygen in the blood or, in *B-CPR* terms, low cash supplies flowing throughout their business. This "condition" creates restlessness in the owner and a lack of coordination across the business. These effects are due to confusion about what consumers will and won't buy. Its effects are particularly noticeable around payroll. When I see a client sweating his or her payroll, I know their business is suffering and approaching business flatline. At the very least, they can't achieve progress or advance their goals because they aren't generating enough cash to sustain their business.

I also find that a business's demise is close when the most exciting time of the day is mail delivery. All I have to do is watch their reaction as they thumb through their mail and notice whether it's elation or despair. Their elation quickly turns to relief when they see the business logo for a customer, indicating they've received monies to deposit. And when there are only bills—no payments—despair is plainly apparent.

Recently, I worked with a business owner who's employees rushed to the bank each payday to cash their paycheck. Experience had shown them that the last person to cash their paycheck was likely to see it bounce. This happened often enough that I heard this story retold multiple times as I interviewed both management and employees.

What's interesting is that this business's Office Manager maintained a daily "cash sheet," which tracked their check float. Based on monies deposited and checks cleared, the owner would either release checks that had already been written or continue to hold onto them. One obvious problem with this practice was that it only factored in each day. It was not an effective way to control cash throughout a week or a month, let alone a year. And that's playing it way too close!

THERE IS A DIFFERENCE BETWEEN CASH FLOW AND CASH MANAGEMENT

No matter what the amount of cash flowing through your business is, you'll face both internal and external obstacles that hinder timely cash flow. These obstacles can result in serious financial problems. Particularly when a business owner fails to understand the differences between these two important cash terms.

Cash Flow represents how the business receives cash, processes it through its accounting system, and disperses the cash to those owed money.

Cash Management represents the proactive control over cash receipts processed through their accounting system and dispersed through disciplined control over cash outflows based on accurate cash inflow projections.

MANAGING CASH STARTS WITH BEING CLEAR ON CASH SOURCES AND ENDS WITH ITS USES

At its core, successful management comes down to being more *proactive* and less *reactive* in managing the cash flowing through your business. The following table recaps the most common sources and uses of money in every business of any size:

Cash Inflows = Sources of Money	Cash Outflows = Uses of Money
Cash inflows represent any source of funds that come into the business:	Cash outflows are uses of funds by the business:
• Cash Sales • Sales Deposits • Customer Account Sales (A/R) • Line of Credit Advances • Loans from Lenders • Outside Investment Money • Personal Savings • Interest Earned on Savings • Repayment of Employee Loans • Other Money Receipts	• Payroll + Payroll Taxes • Sales + Other Taxes • Sales + Other Taxes • Recurring Expenses • Vendor/Supplier Payments • Rent or Mortgage Payments • Lease Payments • Interest Expenses • Credit Line Repayment • Long-term Notes Payable • Miscellaneous Charges

Knowing your sources of cash is key to projecting *when* that cash is coming in. Following the flow of your money through your business tells you *when* and *where* cash will be needed to fund operations. This is the only effective way to disburse your money wisely.

BUSINESS CONTROL BEGINS WITH ACTIVELY MANAGING CASH FLOWS

"Control" over cash implies critical thinking and decision-making by management in how to best use every dollar of cash. This process starts with understanding how cash is collected and paid out so that you have more cash remaining in your business than you are paying out.

Managers gain control over cash flow by following the money through week-to-week cash forecasting. This practice projects the timing of cash flowing into and out of the business. Knowing *when* cash is coming in and *when* cash will be needed to fund operations is the only effective way to disburse your money prudently.

The hardest part of this step is determining the amount of funds available for disbursement each week. I have found that a four-week rolling cash management forecast does this job best or you can choose a forecast period of any length from daily to fifty-two weeks.

For practical purposes, daily is too often and will rob you of quality time that could be used to improve the quality of your cash. Cash quality equals profits. This is the cash that matters, because it's the cash that you get to keep, not the cash that flows through your business.

Businesses with poor cash quality are typically businesses with high sales and low profitability. Any business trading the equivalent of a dollar for four quarters is a business that's break even at best. Business owners in this position are either continuously anxious about cash or clueless. Sometimes, these business owners are too proud of how much they are generating in sales while ignoring what they're making on each sale. They love to talk about their top-line number, yet when you direct their attention to their bottom-line number (the most important number on their Profit and Loss Statement), their confidence fades. It's vital to long-term business survival that everyone in a business appreciate that business is about the money held onto, not how much product it is able to sell. I've found that business owners who don't understand this concept to be the most difficult to help.

In contrast, the owner who *is* anxious about their cash (and its flow, management, and quality) is an owner I *can* help. To put this difference in attitude in medical terms, these forward-looking owners are like those who, after learning they're at increased risk of a heart attack, change their diet and lifestyle after learning. They follow their doctor's instructions to eat less, cut out alcohol and cigarettes, start exercising, and begin monitoring their blood pressure. We all know what happens when people with high risk for cardiovascular disease *don't* make these recommended healthy changes!

Projecting your weekly ending cash position is like monitoring your blood pressure. Just as you gain control over your blood pressure by following your doctor's orders, you gain control over your cash velocity and, ultimately, your cash quality by managing your cash week-to-week.

An effective *cash management tool* begins with calculating how much weekly cash is on hand. Next, forecast any cash funds that you can anticipate receiving. These monies represent your cash inflows. The law of cash management is that cash *inflow* must be greater than cash *outflow*.

THE MECHANICS OF CASH MANAGEMENT ARE EASIER TO ACCOMPLISH THAN LOSING WEIGHT

Cash management is the projection of the company's cash position over a predetermined number of weeks. If your goal is to have enough cash to run your business, you must proactively manage your cash flow from operations. Below are the key terms you need to understand to realize this important goal:

1. **Beginning Balance** is the cash available at the beginning of the week. For most businesses, this is what exists in your business checking and savings accounts.

2. **Cash Inflow** is *any* cash that is "expected" to come into the company within a given week. Cash inflows can include cash sales, A/R collections, cash from the sale of equipment, a loan, or you selling an ownership position in your company. It does not matter where the cash comes from; all that matter is when that cash is available.

3. **Cash Outflow** is *any* cash that is going to go out of the company within a given week. It does not matter who the cash goes to; all that matters is when and how much of your cash each week will be flowing out of the company.

4. **Ending Balance** is the balance projected at the end of a given week after "receiving" all of the Cash Inflows and "paying" out all of the designated Cash Outflows.

The projected ending balance after accounting for all known cash inflows and cash outflows for a given week will be either positive, negative, or zero (zero is essentially the same as negative). When cash is tight the key is to decisively hone in on the limited number of actions you must take, based on which of the following ending cash balance is being projected:

If Positive: Invest the excess cash, take a dividend, pay bills in advance to take advantage of a discount, or save the money for a slow period that is coming;

If Negative: Delay payments, offer discounts to clients for early payment, require cash deposits on new orders, take a loan from a bank or employees, or take on an investor.

Your problems multiply when you fail to manage your cash. In contrast, disciplined weekly cash management will position you to anticipate upcoming obstacles to cash flow so that you can make informed decisions. By knowing *when* cash will be tight, you can make better decisions on *when* and *how* to distribute the cash you have available to fund your core business operations.

THE GOAL OF *WEEKLY* CASH MANAGEMENT

The projected cash position for each week is driven by when your customers decide to pay you. Their decision to direct their cash to you sets the timing of your Accounts Receivable (A/R) collections.

Your goal is to project each week's collections by customer invoice, plus any cash sales you expect to make, to establish your projected cash inflow amount for each week. This amount (inflow) must be greater than that week's financial cash *outflow* requirements, as outlined below, or your business will have a negative cash position.

Projected negative cash positions call for an immediate adjustment to cash outflows, both through delaying payments and by increasing A/R collection efforts. These are the best available options for most businesses. The pursuit of an outside cash injection into the business—through a line of credit, loan, or investor funding—is another option but a difficult step to take for most small business owners.

The goal of weekly cash management is to determine, in advance, probable shortages or excesses in cash that may occur in the business. This allows you to adjust inflows and outflows as needed. Ideally, you determine these needs weekly so that you can maintain the appropriate amount of cash on hand at all times. This requires a clear understanding of the following types of routine business expenses drawn from your accounting system data to establish your weekly cash outflows:

1. **Payroll expenses**: Payroll is the primary expense that must be accounted for in its entirety. The most important asset of the company resides within its labor. If labor is not paid, the risk that the business will lose its best labor is great.
2. **Taxes**: If taxes are not paid, the IRS may move to freeze all of the business assets and eventually shut the business down. In addition, the IRS will demand payment for all interest charges and penalties on the money owed.
3. **Fixed expenses**: These include rent, insurance premiums, owner's salary, and other items that don't tend to vary with

sales and production volumes. These fixed expenses are difficult to adjust in the near-term.

4. **Vendor payables and other operational expenses**: Here, management has some near-term flexibility on when to disburse payments. These payments can be strategically delayed or dispersed over a period. This tactic will preserve cash when inflows are tight with minimal disruption to business activities.

If you project a highly positive cash position, you must analyze your cash data to determine *what* is driving your good fortune *before* you spend the excess cash. Here are some questions that Robert P. Magnus identified in *Cash, It's Always About Cash*:

1. Is your company at the top of a collections cycle? I.e., in the busy season, or, did you receive a large payment from a customer?
2. Are you current on all of your debts?
3. Have you paid your taxes, including estimated taxes?
4. Do you have any "lump sum" payments coming due?

If you have confirmed that excess cash *does* exist, verify that those additional funds are providing a reasonable rate of return, i.e., the interest that you will earn and report as "Other Income."

Whenever cash shortages are revealed, the business must immediately alter its cash outflows until a suitable cash inflow-to-outflow balance is attained. See below for some alternative management options to consider for overcoming a temporary negative cash position.

KEY COMPONENTS OF AN EFFECTIVE CASH MANAGEMENT TOOL

It is *never* enough to manage your business out of your bank account nor by your monthly P&L Statement or your cash position at the end of each month's bank reconciliation to determine how your business is doing. Too much time elapses between each of these activities. The purpose of a structured cash management system is to *identify* and *project all* cash movement in and out of the company by *week*, over a four, eight, twelve, or fifty-two-week period.

Any cash management tool you choose to utilize will have columns represent each week, over the identified cash management period. You will also likely have rows for Accounts Receivable, Accounts Payable, Payroll, Recurring Expenses, and Debt Payments in a single unified table. Below is a commonly used approach for populating a cash management tool:

1. **Beginning Bank Balance:** Start the system by recording your current bank balance. This is the first cell of your cash management table representing the beginning cash balance you have to build from.

2. **Accounts Receivable**: Report your Accounts Receivable records, captured by exporting the "Open Accounts Receivable" report from your accounting software into Excel, categorized for import into the cash management system by Name, Invoice Number, Invoice Date, Type, Terms, and Amount.

3. **Future Sales Projections:** Now that all monies owed for past sales made is reflected in A/R, you need to make projections for likely Sales Invoices to be issued. These are your future week cash inflow projections for work that is highly likely to take place but for which you do not yet know the actual amounts. This is best done by estimating a "normal" or "expected" weekly total for A/R receipts based on historical and expected future levels of production. Be sure not to duplicate your future sales with your actual A/R. If any projected sales subsequently become part of your actual A/R, you need to delete these future sales projections. It's important since you want the A/R reflected to be actual cash obligations to your business.

4. **Accounts Payable**: In your Accounts Payable section, capture your exported "Open Accounts Payable" reports from your accounting system and enter them into your cash management system. Make sure the A/P report includes Name,

P.O. Number, Date, Terms, Type and Open Balance, in that order.

5. **Future Expense Projections:** Once your current payable obligations is captured, you'll need to make projections for likely Vendor Bills to be received. These future weeks payable projections must also be made to account for any expenses, tied to work that will take place but for which you do not yet know the actual amounts. To account for future payables you will have to honor it is best to estimate a "normal" or expected weekly total for projected A/P Payments based upon a balance of history and expected future levels of production. Be sure not to duplicate your future payables with your actual A/P. If you have values projected in the future that have become part of A/P, you will need to delete these future projections, since the goal for your A/P is to be a reflection of actual cash obligations from your business.

6. **Payroll**: Enter the Gross Payroll amount in the Payroll Section of your cash management system. Note the frequency and date on which the next payroll will be processed. Should you have any hourly employees whose hours vary week-to-week, use the average for the last twelve weeks.

7. **Recurring Expenses**: Use this section to capture regularly recurring expenses that don't appear as a vendor payable on your Accounts Payable listing. Include the normal amount paid, frequency, and day of the month on which the next payment is required. One-time expense items or items with irregular timing or amounts should not be entered in this section. Enter these amounts directly in your summary section of the cash management tool since these amounts and their timing will vary month to month.

8. **Calculated Ending Cash Balance**: First, add your beginning cash balance to your cash inflow balance. Then, subtract all of your cash outflows to calculate you're projected ending cash balance for each week. Your ending cash bal-

ance then becomes the beginning cash balance at the top of your next column for the following week.

Your ending cash position will be calculated as follows by week for the next four to twelve weeks:

Beginning Balance	Cash Inflow	Cash Outflow	Ending Balance
Current bank balance less any check float	Projected by week: • A/R collections • Future sales • Other cash receipts	Planned by week: • A/P payouts • Future COGS • Payroll • Recurring payments • Other cash payouts	Projected ending cash position by week

WHAT IS THE BEST WAY TO COMPLETE A BUSINESS CASH FLOW ANALYSIS?

Once you have calculated your ending cash position by week it is time to analyze your forecasted cash results. Your goal during your cash management analysis is to identify which weeks you are projecting to have low or negative ending cash balances. Wherever your ending cash balances are negative, more cash has been forecasted to be paid out than cash received in that week.

Your business cash flow analysis is how you apply your cash projections to better "control your cash" today by either making more cash sales, accelerating A/R collections, eliminating expenses, or slowing down A/P payments this week vs. waiting for your business to run out of cash because you failed to take immediate action to improve the velocity and quality of your cash flowing through your business.

The output of your business cash flow analysis needs to result in clear actions you will take to better manage your business according to your projected cash position for the next four to eight weeks. The most important actions you must take will be triggered when your ending cash balance in a given week is negative because you planned your cash outflows to exceed your beginning cash balance, plus cash inflows.

WHAT TO DO IF YOUR BUSINESS CASH FLOW PROJECTIONS ARE NEGATIVE?

To correct for negative cash flow balance in any of the next four weeks you must first decide how best to solve your negative cash flow position? Will you resolve your negative cash position by accelerating cash inflows or by slowing down your cash outflows?

Negative Cash Flow Decision

Path A   Path B

Increase my   *Slow down my*
cash inflows *cash outflows*

If you choose Path A your first step is to review your A/R forecast data to identify any customer receivables that can be accelerated. Next, adjust the forecast date to adjust your cash inflow projections.

If you choose Path B your first step is to revisit your A/P forecast data to identify any payable items that can be strategically delayed without negative impact on operations. This is the best way to protect your cash outflows from exceeding your cash inflows.

Below are more strategies to consider when managing a temporary negative cash position. The challenge with these strategies is their degree of difficulty implementing them in the next few weeks:

a. Increase sales.
b. Decrease overhead expenses.

c. Develop weekly payment plans with those to whom you owe money, in order to control outflows in a wise manner.
d. Obtain loans from friends, family, or financial institutions.
e. Provide cash to the business from personal resources.
f. Secure a line of credit to help you manage cash through the lows.

A LEADING INDICATOR OF BUSINESS COMPETENCY IS CASH INFLOW PROJECTION ACCURACY

The forecasting accuracy of your customer payment deposits is the number one driver of business success. Your business lives and dies by your ability to project your cash inflows accurately. You improve this skill by making your customer payment deposits the same day they are received. Same day payment deposits do two things for you. The first is it ensures that cash is available when you need it. The second is in how it helps you develop a better sense of payment timing practices of your customers as you process their payment to you each day.

HOW BEST TO HANDLE MY PAYMENT DISBURSEMENTS

Electronic or check disbursements are your cash outflows. Until you master your cash management process you should turn off all auto payments and restrict your payment disbursements to no more than once per week.

The best days to write checks to those you owe is Thursday, for release on Friday, so that the deposits can be stored in interest-bearing accounts or as payment against any outstanding lines of credit. Should you have a line of credit, and until that line is paid down to zero, all monies should be paid against the line of credit, and not deposited into your checking account. On Thursday, a sufficient amount is transferred from the line of credit to the checking account to cover all checks mailed on Friday and any additional expenses that must be paid during the week, such as payroll. Committing to this process will effectively cut your outstanding LOC in half.

HOW DO I KNOW IF I'M GETTING ANY GOOD AT MY BUSINESS CASH FLOW MANAGEMENT?

The benefit to your business of your cash flow projections is proportionate to the accuracy of your cash flow projections. The best way to gauge your business cash flow management skills is to track your actual cash inflows and outflows for a week against that week's forecasted cash in and cash out.

Every time you compare any estimated information with the actual data, you further develop your ability to understand how you thought something would happen actually does. When your cash management projections mirror your actual cash flows, you'll be in a position to use your cash flow projections to set new goals and better plan your operations for higher quality profits and less week-to-week worries about how you will meet payroll.

NEVER FORGET...

The key to effective cash management is in knowing who owes you how much and when you will collect that money. Ultimately, the cash you collect from your customers is the definitive measure of the value that your customers place on your goods and services. The flip side of this fact is that the failure to collect the monies owed you when their due is the best reflection of how much your customers value your business. If they never pay you, they never valued what you provided them.

CASH FAILURE IS MORE OFTEN CAUSED BY FAILURE TO COLLECT THAN BY OVEREXPANSION

Many popular business books point out that a common problem many startup entrepreneurs face is their highly reactive propensity to invest in new opportunities in an effort to expand their businesses. All too often, it is stated, in their fast drive for sales success they forget to consider the cash needed to fund their expansion which, of course, leads to business failure.

In my experience, failing to collect monies owed for work delivered is a far greater problem than overexpansion. While "growing too fast" is an attractive idea to write about, the reality is that getting people to pay up is the more serious problem, and it needs to be addressed.

Another cash problem business owners face is the occasional "cash bonanza" that occurs in a "boom time." This situation often results in the business investing heavily in fixed assets, such as equipment, vehicles, and buildings. Or it may result in taking on additional staff overhead or frivolous spending while the cash is flowing. Anytime an owner feels the false sense of security that "the cash will always be there when it's needed," it's an indication that his or her business is at increased risk of suffering a business cardiac arrest.

When the cash bubble bursts, as it almost always does, the business owner comes to the hard realization that those must have assets they took on debt to finance aren't being used as expected. Next they find themselves working harder to find the cash to pay for those "borrowed" assets but with less cash coming into the business. What's really disheartening is that at the same time the struggles to make the loan payments increases the pressure to cover routine payroll expenses and unavoidable taxes becomes unbearable.

Business owners operating under the "hope method," which presumes that the amount of cash received by the business is going to be greater than the amount it will need to disperse, is at increased risk of business cardiac arrest. They can avoid suffering this pain by recognizing that "hope" is not a method of conducting business. Implementing the principles of Business CPR is a proven method that works in any type of business.

TEN FUNDAMENTAL WAYS OF IMPROVING YOUR CASH POSITION

You can position your business for success while suffering much less stress by taking decisive action on any combination of the following ten most fundamental ways to improve your cash position. They are listed here in order of cash velocity importance:

1. Collect on past-due A/R (Accounts Receivable) from all of customers who owe you money.
    a. Send out your invoices at the same time you ship product, make a delivery, or perform a service. There is no need to wait until the end of the week or month.
    b. When you send out an invoice, call the client to make sure it's been received and that it's correct; also take this opportunity to identify any potential payment delay issues.
    c. Three days before the due date, CALL the customer to remind them of the invoice, and get confirmation that they will mail payment insufficient time for you to receive it by the due date.
    d. When customers miss due dates, freeze their accounts. Don't let them train you by repeat performance to accept late payments; instead, retrain them to pay on time and keep their promises.
2. Speed up payments through cash deposits and reduced terms on future sales.
    a. Require deposits on new or large sales.
    b. Change the "terms" under which you do business. Don't assume that you have to give thirty, sixty, or ninety days for a customer to pay. This step works particularly well when you have a good reputation for quality and timely delivery.
3. Sell underutilized assets to free up cash.
    a. Assets exist to generate sales at a profit. If you have assets that are not realizing this objective, sell them to free up cash.
    b. An asset sold for cash today is always more valuable than an asset that's depreciating faster than it can produce profits.
    c. An asset that is fully depreciated and is not being used to make money is not actually an asset; it

should be converted into cash now, no matter how much money you already have in the bank.

4. Delay or reduce recurring expenses.

    a. Move payroll from every week to every two weeks. This will make your administrative life much easier and allow your bookkeeper to take a vacation on the off weeks.

    b. Hold back pay one week. If your work week ends on Friday, don't drive your staff crazy by paying the following Monday. Pay the following calendar week.

    c. Don't treat 1099 employees as employees but as subcontractors. They are NOT employees, and you need to treat them as you would any other vendor. Pay them once per MONTH, based on the invoice they submit to you. Failure to treat them as regular vendors could mean that you become liable for both the company's and their personal share of taxes. Along with incurring possible fines, you may have to pay interest on the amount you would have paid for an employee.

    d. Renegotiate loans, particularly banknotes, seeking longer terms and lower interest rates.

    e. Refinance equipment loans to lower rates (interest) and terms than your original loan agreement to free up cash in the near-term.

5. Delay or reduce payments to existing suppliers and vendors.

    a. Keep your word; don't start delaying things. But DO call those you owe in advance and discuss a change in terms before instituting a unilateral delay. It's the professional and respectful way to do business.

    b. If there is a particular key vendor with whom you have a large balance, negotiate with them to make some or all of the balance into a "TERM NOTE" with specified interest paid over twelve, twenty-four, or even thirty-six months.

    c.   Delay payments. As with credit cards, although you're required to pay in thirty days, you aren't considered late and won't get reported to the bureaus until you are another thirty days late. So as long as you pay on/before fifty-nine days late, you are not likely to get "dinged" in a credit report. Just remember to make sure to pay the vendor on or before the sixtieth day! And don't mail it on the sixtieth day and expect it to arrive at the vendor on the same sixtieth day.

6. Reduce COGS on future work.

    a.   Seek price reductions on future work coming in. Many times, on big projects or long-running engagements, it's advantageous to seek multiple vendors' bids for your work.

    b.   Push hard for labor efficiency improvements as the anticipated savings in your weekly cash payroll projections. You will know these efficiencies are holding when you see that your lowered payroll expenses begin to match your projections.

7. Change supplier terms to delay paying COGS on future work.

    a.   When negotiating future purchases, open discussions with competing vendors and reach agreements in advance to have different terms for that new project versus what you have had for existing or past work.

    b.   Request to delay Vendor Payments until the week after you yourself are paid. Sometimes key vendors may request that you agree to a joint check, i.e., your client issues you a check made out to both you and your vendor for the vendor's share of supplies. When agreeing to receive a joint check, quite often, a joint "release" will be required.

8. Delay, pay down lesser amounts, or borrow greater amounts against capital expenses.

a. While it is generally better to pay cash for a needed item to avoid having long-running debt, maintaining CASH reserves is also critical, thus making a partial payment on loans a more prudent move when cash is tight.

b. Differentiate between Want versus Need by identifying the ROI (Return on Investment) before you ever take on debt financing to fund capital investment.

Know what sales need to occur on a daily, weekly, and monthly basis to justify or prove the validity of the investment in hard numbers.

9. Increase future sales.
   a. Become proactive in searching for new customers.
   b. Develop a new product or service to expand what you are selling to customers.
   c. Develop a new market to reach beyond your existing customers.
   d. Expand geographically into a new market area.
   e. Go back to past customers and ask what can be done to get them to buy from you again.
   f. Ask all of your past and existing customers if they can refer you to a friend or someone who could refer you on to a friend.

10. Increase capital or the money invested in the business.
   a. Lend personal money to the company through "additional paid-in capital."
   b. Borrow money from a friend, a bank, or a private investor as a "long-term liability."
   c. Take on a partner to invest in the company as a shareholder.

STRATEGIES FOR IMPROVING THE VELOCITY OF YOUR CASH FLOW FROM OPERATIONS

The goal of this chapter is to establish that your cash flow from operations is a direct function of the quality and velocity of the cash coming into your business. Again, the quality of cash is a function of your gross profit and operating income. Cash quality represents the amount you have left in the bank from your sales after your COGS, SG&A, and other expenses are paid. In the long-term, your business needs to be about continuously improving your cash quality.

Businesses with high profits are like athletes with healthy hearts. Both perform exceptionally well with the athlete having little to no need for someone to administer CPR. Similarly, the profitable business is unlikely to require resuscitation through *B-CPR*.

Where *B-CPR* is urgent and important is in managing *cash velocity* or how fast your business is paid for its products and services. Those who require prepayment before work can begin have the highest cash velocity, whereas those who allow their customers to pay even one day past their "agreed to" payment terms will have slower cash velocity.

And in the worst-case scenario, those who *never* collect payment for their products and services have ZERO cash quality and NO cash velocity. They *only* have cash outflows draining the life out of their business.

Sustaining a positive cash flow cycle begins with having a plan for managing cash. This includes the weekly discipline of projecting cash inflows and outflows. Through a multiweek rolling cash forecast, you'll have the ability to protect your business from possible cash outflow surprises that often arise from cash inflow setbacks.

Maintaining a positive cash flow cycle for any business is a never-ending battle that begins with the following critical success factors:

1. Issue sales invoices promptly, ideally at the time of delivery.
2. Understand the payment terms for your industry so you don't exceed them.
3. Manage your accounts receivable (A/R) collections consistently.

4. Set up favorable payment terms with your suppliers and vendors.

Once you have set up smart collection and payment strategies, you can help keep your repayment commitments by adopting one of the following cash flow improvement strategies. Unfortunately, each of these strategies for improving the cash flow of your business has pros and cons: The pros typically come down to protecting cash, while the cons lead to negative impacts on profitability. As you consider the following list, don't forget to consider the profit implications, should you decide to act on any of these cash flow improvement strategies:

1. Require deposits or insist on cash payment at the time of service or product delivery.
2. Offer discounts to customers who pay early.
3. Cease offering payment on credit or establish strict terms of payment on credit.
4. Implement a late-payment charge that is communicated upfront and strictly enforced.
5. Accept credit card payments.
6. Offer automatic bill payments to customers.

An even better cash flow strategy is to conserve cash whenever sales slow. This strategy is particularly useful in the near-term for businesses with few fixed costs. For most businesses of significant size, conserving cash in the near-term comes down to using one of the following cash conserving strategies:

1. Cut unnecessary expenses.
2. Reduce inventory.
3. Delay paying invoices until a few days before they're due.
4. Negotiate delayed payment terms with suppliers, if necessary.

In the long-term, conserving cash for larger businesses comes down to managing expenses downward as a percent of revenue. This is most effectively done through P&L statement variance reporting for both actual-to plan and year-over-year results for the same accounting period.

The best cash flow strategy is proactively managing the flow of cash through a cash management tool. Accurately planning for cash inflows and cash outflows is necessary in order for you to maintain a cash reserve as reflected in your statement of cash flows.

CONCLUDING THE IMPORTANCE OF STEP 1— INCREASE THE VELOCITY OF *YOUR* OPERATING CASH FLOW TODAY

The key to business survival lies in the recognition that you must always have cash on the hand because *cash is not profit,* and *profit is not cash.* You need *both* to sustain and grow a business (though not in equal measures) throughout its lifecycle.

Never lose sight of this hard truth: Lenders only *want* to lend money to companies that don't *need* their money. They're not interested in putting their money at risk with those who need a loan, because they don't practice effective cash management. And any lender willing to lend to those tight on cash will charge higher interest rates to those who marginally qualify.

Accurate cash flow forecasting is the key to predicting *when* money will be needed. Gaining a handle on your cash flow will help lower your stress in the near-term. It will enhance your ability to obtain a loan at the lowest possible interest rate, when, and if, you choose to expand your business. It will also end you asking yourself why your reported profits are so different than your reported bank balance.

AUTHOR'S SIDE NOTE—IT DOESN'T MATTER WHAT *YOUR* VISION, MISSION, AND STRATEGY IS IF YOU DON'T HAVE CASH

Initially, when I began applying the *B-CPR* model to the businesses I worked with, I had made cash management one of the later steps. I'd been influenced by the standard idea of helping a business first through *vision, mission,* and *strategy.*

Originally, I had "Step 2—Build *Your* Twenty-Four-Month Profit Plan"—as Step 1. I'd had some experience working with several businesses that had enough cash to survive, yet they had no plans to expand into a more profitable business. I saw expansion as the number one element in B-CPR, because I was locked into the common view that a healthy business comes down to having a plan to achieve greater and greater profits.

My initial business improvement approach led with building a profit plan drawn from the business's income statement in order to appreciate past profit performance as part of projected profits. I chose this approach in order to determine whether the business could be profitable before I considered cash flow. My reasoning was that according to a long-held law of business, "without profits, a business will never survive" in the long-term.

But I'd lost sight of another higher law of business: "When you're out of cash, you're out of business." In following up with business owners who had well-developed twenty-four-month profit plans, I came to appreciate that while they had profit plans demonstrating how much profit they should make each month, in the near-term, I had failed to help them master the skill of projecting cash into the future.

What I clearly recognize now with 100 percent certainty is that *B-CPR* truly is ordered, as lettered, by **C**ash, **P**rofits, and **R**eporting. Yes, a profit plan will show you what kind of money you should be expected to make, but it doesn't tell you precisely *when* cash is coming in. And this is why having a weekly cash management plan is so critical to your business success.

"Business CPR" is the key to avoiding business flatline. It starts with knowing when and where the money is coming in and going out of your business. It's more than projecting how much money you will have flowing out your business before your profitable sales start. It's about holding onto more of the cash coming in. It's about collecting ten, fifteen, or twenty cents or more on every dollar of sales. Remember, these are profits, but profits don't happen until you master Step 1—Increase the Velocity of *Your* Operating Cash Flow Today.

If your favorite part of the day is checking the mail, followed by running to the bank to deposit any checks you've received, stop reading NOW. Go to www.mybpitsite.com for a ready-to-use cash management tool that will make it easier for you to meet payroll. Then you can stop paying COD with your vendors, because they'll be happy to put you back on credit terms.

If you have good control over your cash velocity, and you know when your cash is flowing in and out of your business, read on to learn how you can improve your cash quality through *B-CPR* Steps 2 through 5.

4

STEP 2—PLAN FOR *YOUR* PROFITS TO SHAPE *YOUR* DECISION-MAKING

Every business owner I have ever met wants their company's performance to be stronger than the previous day, week, month, quarter, and year's results. The smart ones want to achieve this by growing their cash reserves from higher profits. These business owners know that the success and future of their company ultimately depends on their ability to be profitable both today and in the future.

Any company's ability to remain profitable depends on many factors impacted by varying degrees of an owners ability to control. Political, economic, societal, and technological developments can rock their business, just as their own strengths, weaknesses, opportunities, and threats can have significant impacts. The constant among the factors that are in or out of a business owner's control is *the thoroughness of their planning for profits* and their effective execution of this plan. These are the two key ingredients to owning a great business, one that will be worth more tomorrow than it was yesterday.

The critical thinking employed in planning for profits in each of the next twenty-four-months cannot be overlooked. It is the *best* way to ensure you and your management team embrace your vision for your current and future business position. Your close attention through *B-CPR* Step 2 will set your roadmap to success, one that will take your organization from where it is today to where you want it to be tomorrow. The output of Step 2 defines what actions you must take to get there through creating and executing your "Profit Plan."

THE SIGNIFICANCE OF PLANNING FOR PROFITS

Successful business leaders are masters at knowing how to use their employee talent, company assets, and resources to their greatest advantage. Profit planning is the core management tool or process for achieving this advantage.

Your profit plan identifies the targets you plan to achieve by month for sales, gross, operating, and net profit. As your profit targets become clear, the actions needed to realize those targets also become clear. Use this information to define your goals, objectives, strategies, and tactics you'll act on to realize your plans for profitability. Your twenty-four-month profit plan helps you to direct the work of your employees in a controlled and coordinated way toward the accomplishment of your documented goals and objectives. As you work your profit plan, you will achieve your profit targets.

The goals and objectives set forth in your profit plan establish the course of action your company will follow to reach its desired destination. Nevertheless, you must first define the intended *means* by which you will reach those objectives. Effective leaders use the *means* to identify what *value* they desire to create for their customers. Then they use their management skills to direct their employees to accomplish their stated profit plan's goals and objectives. They make strategic decisions and changes, as required, to keep the business progressing toward the planned destination.

Step 2—Build *Your* Twenty-Four-Month Profit Plan is not about planning for *all* contingencies or possibilities. It is about creating *structure* and *priority guidelines* for your team to follow. This framework is necessary to help your business stay on course and realize its monthly profit goals. In studying businesses of all sizes, I've come to realize that a company that has *planned* to make a profit is 100 percent more likely to achieve its goal than a company that does not.

THE UNFORTUNATE CONSEQUENCES OF *NOT* HAVING A PROFIT PLAN

Failure to set clear targets that will direct your company through each month of your plan is a giant mistake. The likely and ill-advised result is running your business by one crisis to the next by the pressing problem of the day. Or equally as shortsighted, running your business "the way you have always done things." This results in misaligned employees working in different directions, all due to a lack of shared vision derived from documented profit objectives and goals. Lack of a clear profit plan also creates confusion, inefficiency, and higher costs through waste and inefficiency. The result? Smaller profits with decreasing levels of cash in the bank.

Without a profit plan, any sales growth occurs "by chance" rather than by planned actions. Any efforts you and your employees make are hampered by day-by-day problems, which you are forced to face, without any direction from your plan. Profit plan direction—on a daily basis—better ensures that your actions will lead to company growth and profit. Without a plan, you and your employees are "flying blind," hoping that your profits and cash flow results will mirror the intensity of your efforts. Unfortunately, all too often, this is not the case.

Every viable business will earn revenue and incur associated expenses in fulfilling its purpose. Whether this purpose fulfillment is by strategic intention or accidental, every business will produce "results." The ultimate question is whether the results of revenue minus expenses are favorable or unfavorable? The size of your profits is the ultimate measure of how your business is performing and on which side of the equation your "results" fall.

Every profit dollar earned is a reflection of the quality of your past management decisions. Profits are a "lagging indicator," whereas customer loyalty, employee engagement, operating cycle times, and cash in the bank are the core "leading indicators" of your profit quality and velocity. Effective managers use monthly profit planning to facilitate communication so the people on their teams know what to do and what role they are expected to play. Effective managers will also visibly communicate *how* they will know whether they are winning or losing through each month of the profit plan.

HOW THE QUALITY OF YOUR PROFITS
MIRROR THE STRENGTH OF YOUR HEART

As stated in Chapter 1, the American Heart Association defines cardiac arrest as "the abrupt loss of heart function in a person who may or may not have been diagnosed with heart disease." In this chapter, we likened "cash" to the blood flowing through your body. As long as the heart is pumping, the blood is flowing. Keep both working as intended and you significantly reduce your risk of cardiac arrest, "the abrupt loss of heart function."

Abrupt loss of heart function occurs through heart failure more often than through blood loss. Bleeding to death from a major severed or partially severed artery takes ten to fifteen minutes. As large volumes of blood are lost, the heart begins to fail until the heart has nothing left to pump. While this is a morbid thing to think about, it is not a very common cause of heart failure.

The *more common* cause of heart failure is a combination of lifestyle choices and hereditary conditions. In any case, your heart's job is to pump blood to and from all areas of your body. When your heart is healthy and strong, this process goes unnoticed, because it happens naturally, efficiently, and effectively. Nevertheless, when this vital muscle fails to perform, you have serious problems immediately.

Your best chance to avoid an emergency application of *B-CPR* is to practice Step 1—Increase *Your* Operating Cash Velocity Today. As your business receives planned cash flow from operations, you decide how these funds are paid out for the completion of activities occurring every day across your business.

Just as poor lifestyle choices eventually create heart health issues, bad business decisions and ineffective actions have the same negative effects on business profitability. Consider the same visual used in Chapter 3, but this time viewed through the lens of business profitability:

P = Profits

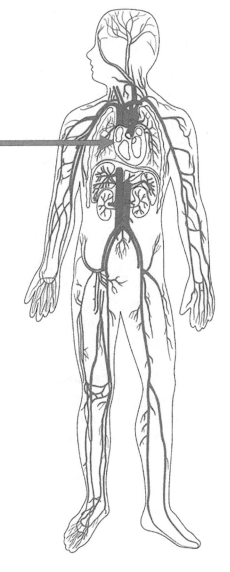

At this minute, your heart is pumping your blood and oxygen throughout your body without any voluntary thought or action. If this process were to stop, you would immediately go into cardiac arrest.

Your heart is the center of your circulatory system that consists of a network of blood vessels, such as arteries, veins, and capillaries.

Your business's profits are pumping cash through your business operations by rhythmic contraction and dilation associated with cash flowing in and out of your business each day.

Your business slips into cardiac arrest when it *stops* pumping cash as a result of repeated profit losses tied to the inability to generate profitable sales.

At this minute, your heart is pumping your blood and oxygen throughout your body without any voluntary thought or action. If this process were to stop, you would immediately go into cardiac arrest.

Your heart is the center of your circulatory system that consists of a network of blood vessels, such as arteries, veins, and capillaries.

Your business's profits are pumping cash through your business operations by rhythmic contraction and dilation associated with cash flowing in and out of your business each day.

Your business slips into cardiac arrest when it *stops* pumping cash as a result of repeated profit losses tied to the inability to generate profitable sales.

In reflecting on the previous illustration, consider how your brain's cells will begin to die after only four minutes without blood flow. After six minutes, these cells will cease functioning completely. You will be brain dead. No one *wants* to be brain dead, nor does any business owner *want* to own or run an unprofitable business. These situations are not anything that any of us plan for.

Step 1 of *B-CPR* taught you how to improve your cash velocity. *Now* it's time to lay the foundation for improving your *cash quality*. When you understand both your cash velocity and cash quality, you never question why your reported profit is different than your bank balance.

WHAT DOES PLANNING FOR PROFITS LOOK LIKE?

Profit planning is more than projecting numbers you would like to see on your P&L statement. It is the *set of actions* you commit to taking in order to achieve a targeted profit level. These actions involve the development of an interlocking set of short-term budgets that roll up into a master plan. In most cases, the intended goal of your profit plan is to put more cash in the bank through each month in the coming year.

An effective Profit Plan tracks and communicates your progress by the variance of actual results to planned results for each month. Each variance report you utilize in Step 3—Confirm the Quality of *Your* Profits will either confirm that you are moving closer to or farther away from having a profitable business. It is up to you to establish your parameters for success. Is your business one that will be worth buying? Another common measure of success is how much surplus cash is available to invest or to distribute as dividends to you and your investors as a result of your profit plan?

Your profit plan also confirms whether the anticipated sales, gross profit, and EBITDA earnings (earnings before interest, taxes, depreciation, and amortization) suggest that your business is likely to be successful in the twenty-four months ahead based on planned production and sales.

Moving forward, it doesn't really matter what profit margins your business produced in the past or whether you had a profit plan. What *does* matter is the hard reality that every business must face: There is no guarantee that your business will be profitable *this* year.

Ensuring that you *will* have a profitable business in the year ahead starts with building a profit plan. And most notably that you use this plan to manage your business throughout the coming year. Without a profit plan, you will never know if you are tracking above or below your profit goals through the year. On a personal level, you will not have an accurate sense of whether your business is capable of providing enough profit to be worth your time and investment risk if you don't have a plan.

Your annual profit plan will either confirm that your actions, and those of your team, are working or not. It is important to remember that your Profit Plan is dynamic and alive, not some theoretical document to sit on a shelf or in a file cabinet. Your profit plan represents *your best thinking* on what you need to *start, stop,* or *continue doing* to make money in the coming year. As the months roll by, your profit plan will confirm that you were right in your thinking or your results will tell you that now is the time to begin considering other approaches or opportunities. This second course of action is particularly important if, after creating the profit plan, it drains you of any desire to continue working toward your business goals. If this is the case, you should consider doing something different.

One of the underappreciated benefits of creating a profit plan is its timeliness, its ability to provide you with a near-term performance outlook. Each month's results, compared to your profit plan, tell you whether your profit plan is on track or unrealistic. If you *aren't* hitting your profit plan numbers in months one and two, and you are below the previous year's profit performance, then you have the necessary data to immediately identify what area(s) you specifically need to change in order for your business to be successful.

In playing any game, when it isn't going as you would like, you think of strategies to make real-time changes. You more thoughtfully consider your next moves. You do this because you aren't playing the game to lose. The same is true in business. When you have a well thought-out profit plan with goals that aren't supported by your most recent P&L report, you have reliable data on which to act. The question is, "What are you going to do differently to influence those factors performing below planned?" Answering this question through action is how you end the profit plan period with acceptable profits for the risk you incurred. There's another important output from an effective profit plan. It's the answer to the question, "Is my business structured and staffed to allow it to operate without me?" If your answer is *no*, "there is no way I will hit my profit plan numbers if I'm not 100 percent involved in the day-to-day operations of my business," then you have a serious problem. Learn how to address this problem by following Step 5— Be Accountable for *Your* Results in Chapter 7.

DON'T UNDERESTIMATE THE IMPORTANCE OF ACCURATE FINANCIAL RECORDS

Your confidence in developing an achievable twenty-four-month profit plan starts with the quality of your historical data. Successful business owners understand the importance of keeping accurate and organized financial records. They know that having an accurate system of transaction recording is the only way to effectively and efficiently keep track of financial details.

Without the financial details that accurately confirm whether they are making or losing money, they would never know if they own a succeeding or failing business. Business owners who work with their financial statements on a regular basis, not just at tax time, are refusing to operate their businesses blindly. Rather, they know it's essential to their business to have in place day-to-day routines that enable them to have accurate financial records.

These business owners use accounting software like QuickBooks to know if their customers have paid them, to track their expenses, and to keep track of who the business owes money to. They use the reports generated from their financial information management system (FIMS) to build their profit plan. And then they use these same reports to track their actual-to-planned performance.

Before you begin to design and build a profit plan, it's important that you have an appreciation of the following key financial tools beginning with your Chart of Accounts (COA).

YOUR FINANCIAL CHART OF ACCOUNTS IS THE CORE OF YOUR FINANCIAL INFORMATION SYSTEM

The backbone of all accounting programs is the Chart of Accounts or COA. It forms the underlying foundation that allows you to record and track your company's financial progress. Smart business owners maintain an accurate COA as part of their habit of timely record-keeping.

These financial statements give them direct insight into where their business is doing well and where it is underperforming or failing. They know a poorly designed COA results in misleading information leading to poor decisions and, in turn, undesirable results. What I see most commonly in misaligned COAs is the understating of the cost of goods sold (COGS) by overstating their selling, general, and administrative expenses (SG&A). This situation occurs anytime a COGS item is listed with SG&A items in the chart of accounts.

Why is this a problem? When you understate your COGS, you incorrectly inflate Gross Profit. This leads to an inaccurate belief that you are pricing your products and services correctly, because, "look at all that gross profit being produced." This is the most common reason why people get confused about the difference in profits being reported through their P&L Statement and what's shown on their bank statement.

The reality is you *aren't* making the money you *think* you are on each sale, particularly when you aren't factoring in an accurate overhead absorption. This results in less cash being generated to cover your nonoperating expenses, which leads to less cash in the bank. The solution for this is to always place your variable and fixed expenses in their proper chart of accounts categories.

Your COA is the equivalent to using a seven-drawer filing cabinet to store all of your different business transactions. Each drawer represents a different account type created within the COA as virtual "folders" that will fit into one of the following seven drawers.

1. **Assets**—These are the items that your business has in its possession: monies that you have in your bank accounts, inventory that you have on-hand, or equipment used in your operations.
2. **Liabilities**—These include monies that your business owes to others: an auto loan on a car you use for business, a mortgage that you carry on your warehouse, or sales tax you've collected from your customers and that has not yet been paid to the state.
3. **Owner's Equity**—Equity is everything your business owns: any money that an owner invests in their business is considered equity.
4. **Income**—Income is the proceeds from the sale of products or services. For example, plumbing services sold or the sale of five lamps to a customer is considered income.
5. **Cost of Goods Sold**—These are items that require payment in order to complete the work, such as direct labor, materials, and equipment in order to produce goods or services that are then invoiced to your customers.
6. **Expenses**—These are items that you pay to run your day-to-day business operations. For example, advertising

expenses, office payroll, insurance, and office supplies are all categorized as expenses.

7. **Other Income and Expenses**—Transactions kept in this drawer involve all nonoperating income and expenses. Here you will find interest income, tax refunds, insurance settlements, extraordinary expenses, interest expense, taxes, depreciation, and amortization expenses.

UNDERSTANDING THE CORE PURPOSES OF THE PRIMARY FINANCIAL STATEMENTS USED IN SUCCESSFUL BUSINESSES

Every business starts with cash, which is invested in numerous ways to generate revenue. Ultimately, any revenue is turned back into cash, and the cycle begins anew.

This cash cycle produces financial data that, when recorded, can be used to report on the results of operations. If the data is accurately recorded, you will know with confidence the financial position of the company for any given period. The following table summarizes the logic behind the three primary financial statements used by nearly all successful business owners:

P&L (Income) Statement	Balance Sheet	Statement of Cash Flows
Sales - Expenses = Net Income	Assets = Liabilities + Owners Equity	Operating + Investing + Financing Cash
1. A summary of management's performance as reflected in the profitability (or lack of it) of the business over a certain period. P&L itemizes revenues and expenses of the past that led to the current profit or loss and can be used to identify what may be done to improve future profits. 2. Net income is the owners' return from operations and represents either an increase or decrease in the value of their investment in the business.	1. Listing at any point in time of a company's measurable assets (the capacity to produce revenue), liabilities (borrowings), and equity (owners' investment or the claim the owner has against the assets.) 2. States (1) what assets the company owns, (2) what it owes (its liabilities), and (3) what amount is left to the owners after satisfying the liabilities.	1. Provides a comprehensive picture of the company's cash flows beyond operations to see how cash changes from the beginning to the end of a period. 2. A summary of the actual or anticipated incomings and outgoings of cash over an accounting period (month, quarter, year). It answers the questions: Where the money came or will come from and where the money went or will go?

P&L (Income) Statement	Balance Sheet	Statement of Cash Flows
3. In contrast to a balance sheet, an income statement depicts what happened over a month, quarter, or year.	3. Owners' equity is not the owner's piggy bank; it represents the owners' claim on the company assets leftover AFTER the liabilities have all been paid off.	3. Operating cash flow can be used to justify making new investments in the business, repay financial debt, or to return capital to the owners.

To WIN in the game of business, you need both positive operating cash flows (Step 1) and healthy net profit (Step 2) to remain a viable business. This is because cash is allocated to employees as wages to suppliers as accounts payables, to lenders as interest, and to the government as taxes with whatever being leftover forming profits to give to investors as cash dividends or to reinvest back into the company.

Positive cash flow and profitability are achieved through thoughtful planning, disciplined work, and accurate plus timely reporting of the results. This is how you know if the results of your never-ending hard work and sacrifice are worth the effort.

WHAT IF I KNOW MY P&L STATEMENTS AREN'T ACCURATE?

If you have doubts about the accuracy of your historical P&L Statements, you should hold off building your profit plan until you have improved the accuracy of your chart of accounts. The good news is once you have a properly aligned P&L, a quality accounting software program will easily allow you to access both forward-looking and retroactive data that reflects the changes you make.

This means that not only will all future transaction recordings use the new account structure. Your financial system will also transfer historical data into the new COA format. In other words, you won't have to "restate" historical Balance Sheets or Income Statements to make them consistent with future reporting. This is a huge time-saver and also helps to ensure that your historical data will be reflected accurately, allowing comparisons to be made more easily.

Once you are confident that you have your variable and fixed cost transactions properly mapped to your COA expense categories, you can proceed with building your profit plan.

WHICH ACCOUNTING METHOD SHOULD I USE FOR PROFIT PLANNING?

Most experts believe the difference between positive profits and not so positive cash flow is essentially an accounting issue. Their argument is grounded in the fact that the reason profits don't equal cash is blamed on using cash for things that don't show up on the P&L statement. Or they argue it's a function of the timing difference of when revenues and expenses are recognized in relation to their collection and payment.

While there are fundamentally two accounting methods, the generally accepted accounting practice (GAAP) used by accountants to prepare financial statements is accrual basis accounting. With this method, expenses are reported only when goods or services are completely consumed, regardless of when the bill got paid. Likewise, revenues are reported only when the product or service has been delivered to the customer and the company has earned the right to receive a cash payment, regardless of when the business gets paid by the client. The two accounting methods are defined as follows:

> *Accrual accounting* matches accomplishment (delivery of product or service) and effort (expenses incurred to generate accomplishments) regardless of cash-flow timing. This is the preferred accounting method for profit planning, because it most closely correlates the timing of the revenue to the expense.

Cash accounting is the simpler of the two major accounting methods to perform. Put simply, this method records income when cash is received and expenses when cash is paid out. What's interesting is how many accountants advise small businesses to adopt cash accounting for tracking their *tax liability*, a method that is *not* considered a good management tool. This is because it leaves a time gap between the recording of the cause of an action (sale or purchase) and its result (payment or receipt of money).

Pulling down your historical financial statements on an accrual basis is the recommended view for profit planning. If you are unsure of the payout timing for any particular expenses, particularly your SG&A expenses, it is advisable to look at your P&L statement by month on a cash basis.

The balance of this chapter focuses on building your twenty-four-month profit plan. It will help you work through the thoughtful planning components that will best help ensure your business has a positive cash flow that results from healthy profits.

SHOULD I START MY PROFIT PLAN BY ESTABLISHING GOALS OR BY REVIEWING PAST PERFORMANCE?

Most strategy experts believe that past performance is *not* a good indicator of future results. This stems from the fact that the conditions that led to that past performance are likely to have changed in some way. This is particularly true if you are in a rapidly changing industry like high-technology where a new development can make what you sold *last* year obsolete *this* year.

For those businesses essentially supplying the same product or service this year, it won't have any such significant changes. If you expect to carry out similar business this year and don't believe there are any significant market changes to wrestle with, past performance is a good indicator of future results.

If you are in a rapidly changing industry where it is often hard to anticipate customer demand, then developing your strategic plan is a mandatory precursor to building your profit plan.

If you have been doing the same thing over and over and are getting worse and worse results, then developing a strategy is a "nice to do," not a "must do." Even if you have decided to make significant product changes, having a new and accurate profit plan that reflects those changes is the "must have" for the next year. This is because profit planning defines the set of guided actions you will need to take across sales, operations, and finance in order to achieve your profit targets.

Rather than set arbitrary targeted profit levels for sales, gross profit, and operating income, it is advised to review and appreciate your business's performance over the last four years by month.

START YOUR PROFIT PLAN WITH AT LEAST YOUR LAST THIRTY-SIX MONTHS OF P&L REPORTING

The most efficient way to build your Profit Plan is to start with a download of your previous thirty-six to forty-eight-months of P&L results. Only take this step *after* determining that your historical P&L statements are an accurate reflection of your management's performance. Make sure it is reflected in the profitability, or lack of, for the business over your most recent years. Note: this type of P&L statement confidence only occurs when your COA is properly aligned (it's always helpful to review your "drawers").

P&L Statement *accuracy* is the key to building a realistic Profit Plan derived from the previous year's results in setting *this* year's targets. This is because your past statement itemizes the revenues and expenses of the *past* that led to your *current* profit or loss. As you review the results for the previous years by month, you will get an idea of what needs to be done to improve your results.

If your financial system of record is QuickBooks, you can use the following guide to export a forty-eight-month view of your income statement from QuickBooks into a Microsoft Excel file:

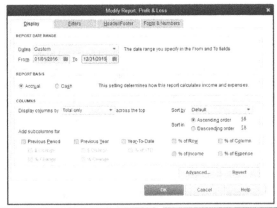

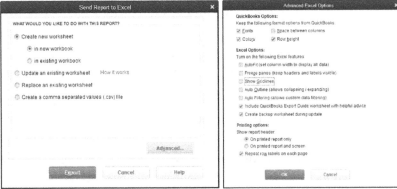

Following this data download, your goal is to begin your profit planning with your historical insights. It's essential to review them first to identify what needs to be done *differently* to produce higher profits. Once you are clear on what needs to be done differently, you will be in a position to set realistic profit plan targets by major product, cost of goods sold, and selling, general, and administrative expenses.

PROFIT PLANNING COMES DOWN TO THREE KEY FINANCIAL RESULT PROJECTIONS

The most effective and efficient approach to building a twenty-four-month profit plan starts with projecting the next twelve months for Sales, Gross Profit, and Operating Income. Start with these three core profit results from your P&L statement, because your profit is that matters most is the surplus amount remaining after total costs are deducted from revenue as determined by the following:

1. Sales must be greater than the cost of producing the goods and services you sell or else there will be no monies left over to pay for operating expenses.

2. Costs for resources used to produce and deliver what you sell are called the cost of goods sold (COGS). COGS are the variable costs of your business I.e., any costs that vary directly according to how much a business produces and sells. Some common examples of variable costs include:

    *   Direct labor required to sell or produce the service or product;
    *   Materials required to produce the product;
    *   Shipping and service delivery costs required to deliver the product or service to the buyer.

3. Gross Profit is the amount by which sales revenues exceed production costs (cost of goods sold). You can work toward improving this number by either raising selling prices or reducing COGS. Gross profit is calculated as follows:

    Net Sales - COGS = Gross Profit

4. The dollar contribution from gross profit represents the amount of money available to pay all other operating expenses, interest, and taxes. It's the difference between Net Sales and Cost of Goods Sold.

5. The amount of your gross profit contribution is the number one determiner if you will have any operating income. Put another way, decreases in gross profit without corresponding decreases in overhead expenses, will guarantee that you are not on track to being profitable. The occurrence of this problem is why most business owners struggle with the question of why their P&L shows a profit greater than what their bank balance reports.

6. Gross profit margin is the percentage of money the business keeps after the variable costs are subtracted from the

sales revenue. Your gross profit margin tells you how efficiently your operations are converting a sale into a profit as a percent of sales. Gross profit margin is calculated as follows:

Net Sales - COGS = Gross Profit / Net Sales

7. Any business expenses that occur, regardless of a sale being made, are considered overhead or "fixed costs" and are accounted for in selling, general, and administrative (SG&A) expenses. Some common examples of fixed costs include:

- Advertising;
- Office salaries;
- Insurance;
- Rent and utilities;
- Outside fees paid to a lawyer, an accountant, or your bank.

8. Operating Income is the profit resulting from your primary business operations, excluding extraordinary income and expenses. This figure is also called "earnings before interest, taxes, depreciation, and amortization" or (EBITDA). Operating Income is the money the business keeps after subtracting both variable costs and fixed costs from sales revenue. This profit number gives a more accurate picture of a company's operating profitability than gross profit, and is the primary measure used to determine how profitable a company is in managing its operations. Operating income is calculated as follows:

Gross Profit - SG&A Expense = Operating Income

9. Knowing how much you expect to sell, what you expect those sales to cost, and how much overhead you will need to cover through your gross profit are the core building blocks of your profit plan. Ultimately, your profit plan will look like your P&L Statement in that it will tell you what

you are projecting to do by month for the following "big three" financial results.

Net Sales
- COGS (variable costs)
= Gross Profit
- SG&A Expenses (fixed costs)
= EBITDA (Operating Income)

10. Should your business have a lot of Other Income (non-operating), Other Expenses (extraordinary), Interest, Taxes, Depreciation, and Amortization expenses, then you should consider planning for these targets to establish a more accurate view of your Net Profit in your profit plan. Taking this tenth step is not encouraged, unless the above is true. This is because it adds a distracting level of complexity to your deliberate and thoughtful focus on the "big 3" numbers laid out in steps one through nine.

It is these "big 3"—net sales, gross profit, and operating income—that ultimately anchor your profit plan as you lead your business through the year to your planned results.

THE *MOST* IMPORTANT NUMBER YOU PROFIT PLAN FOR IS *SALES* BY MONTH FOR THE NEXT TWELVE MONTHS

The key to understanding this most significant profit planning number comes from Thomas Watson Sr., the president of International Business Machines (IBM) from 1914 to 1956. Mr. Watson, one of the greatest capitalists to ever live, coined the phrase "Nothing happens until a sale is made." This business truism is the cornerstone of *your* profit plan too.

Your profit plan should *not* include any expense or profit targets until you are 100 percent clear on what you will sell by month. It is impossible to set your profit plan target until you identify your sales goals by core product and service. Knowing how much you plan to sell and how much you expect to make on those sales. This is how you protect yourself from incurring a lot of expenses before a sale is even made.

Here are some examples. You don't need to line up and pay for tech support unless you are selling something that requires it. The semitrucks and trailers you see on our interstate highways have nothing to deliver unless someone sells something. The roads themselves won't be paved until someone sells the asphalt. The auto mechanic has no automobile to work on unless someone sells an automobile that, eventually, will need work.

At a minimum, projecting income involves knowing the following numbers for your business:

1. Gross sales by product.
2. Number of orders by product.
3. Average transaction dollar value by product.

Ideally, you will have access to these three fundamental sales projection numbers by month for the last forty-eight months. At a minimum, you need these numbers for the past twelve months if you are to have any expectation of accuracy in projecting your gross profit.

It is necessary to have the results for gross sales and the number of orders so that you can calculate the average transaction value by product for the last four years. These average numbers will help you to know what you're generating on gross sales on every transaction in real terms. If you are generating *less* on each sale year-over-year that puts greater and greater pressure on your operations. If you are generating *more* gross sales per transaction, than congratulations are in order: You are on track.

If you only have gross sales numbers, then you can back-calculate the number of orders. Then determine the average transaction value from the total gross sales by estimating your average per product transaction. You need to know the number of units and the average transaction value, because this information will shape your operating volume. Knowing these details will have a significant influence on how accurately you will be able to plan for your gross profit.

If your business doesn't often use sales discounting to generate sales nor has substantial write-offs for uncollectible accounts receivable, then your net sales will closely approximate gross sales. If so, you're good to go on to the next step.

If you *do* frequently discount sales, handle quite a few returned goods, and regularly write-off some sales, then you need to project these numbers as well in order to accurately establish your net sales.

Now you can confidently set your "most likely," *not* your "best case," net sales number into a twelve-month seasonalized view segregated by product and month. This is the starting point for your profit plan. Next, it's time to plan for your first measure of profitability.

WITH MONTHLY REVENUE PROJECTIONS IN PLACE, IT'S TIME TO PLAN *YOUR* COGS

In building a profit plan, *less* is *more*. You don't need to project out *every* COGS line item in your P&L statement. Rather, your goal in projecting your gross profit is to focus on the major COGS category totals. The most common areas to consider for COGS are the following:

1. Sales Commission
2. Direct Labor
3. Subcontractors
4. Materials
5. Equipment
6. Shipping
7. Other Direct Costs

Again, the goal is not to achieve decimal point accuracy by profit planning for every variable cost item. The goal is to plan for your *total COGS* so you can subtract that number from your planned revenue by month to calculate your monthly planned gross profit and your projected year-end gross profit.

Profit Planning around COGS is best determined by considering your *historical* percent of sales for each major expense category. For example, if your goal is a 40 percent gross profit margin, that means you can't have COGS totaling greater than 60 percent, no matter how many COGS categories you plan for.

Download your historical P&L data into a spreadsheet to easily calculate your major COGS areas as a percent of projected revenue. This allows you to establish the COGS profit plan budget by major area, by month. Remember, your cost of goods sold should always vary according to how much your business produces and sells. As a result, you always build the gross profit component of your profit plan as a percent of projected net revenue by month and year.

AFTER DETERMINING GROSS PROFIT, IT'S TIME TO PLAN FOR *YOUR* OPERATING INCOME

Your P&L Statement aggregates all revenue and expenses into categories that then allow you to determine *where* you are making and losing money. This is why you must profit plan at both the gross profit and operating income levels.

You also plan for your selling, general, and administrative or fixed expenses differently than you do for your variable expenses. The fixed costs flowing through your business will either be close to an average number by month or will occur in a regular, often predictable pattern for any given month of the year.

Knowing your fixed costs and how much you have paid out by the monthly average for the last forty-eight months is the best way to establish your SG&A expense targets within your twenty-four-month profit plan. Again, your goal is to stay focused on totals *by major expense categories* versus wading through hundreds or thousands of transactions over the last several years. Your P&L statement will summarize these expenses into the assigned category based on your chart of account logic for revenues and expenses. The most common SG&A expense categories are as follows:

1. Marketing and Sales
2. Travel and Entertainment
3. Office Expenses
4. Office Payroll

5. Insurance
6. Outside Fees
7. Property Expenses
8. Utilities

Most of the above SG&A expense projections will be a fixed number, by month, resulting in an easier number to project. Some overhead expenses will more closely mirror sales and will be projected similar to COGS. Either way, it's good to look at each SG&A expense category as a percent of revenue for the *total profit plan year*. You should do this to make sure that you don't have an over or understated expense number in any one month.

Remember, your SG&A expenses are supposed to be fixed costs that are easily identified. So this should be the easiest aspect of building your profit plan. Once your total indirect operating expenses for the profit plan period are established, you can now project your operating income by month and by year.

Remember the following example from Chapter 3? It involved looking at the cost structure of three different businesses, through a dollar, then choosing the one *you* would like to own:

	Business A	Business B	Business C
Sales of...	**$1.00**	**$1.00**	**$1.00**
Direct Labor	.20	.10	.35
Materials	.25	.20	.15
Equipment	.05	.10	.15
Gross Profit	**.50**	**.60**	**.35**
Marketing	.10	.10	.05
Office Payroll	.20	.15	.12
Outside Fees	.04	.07	.10
Insurance	.01	.03	.02
Rent	.08	.10	.05
Utilities	.03	.03	.02
Operating Profit	**.04**	**.12**	**-.01**

Let's look at planned COGS and SG&A expenses in terms of cents lost out of every dollar. Doing so will help you appreciate how much you're risking cash quality with every dollar of sales. This is particularly true if your P&L history shows you have had months like Business C in the table above.

If you have even *one* month of negative cash quality projected over the next twelve months, stop reading here and jump to Chapter 6 on page 132. Here is where you will learn Step 4—*Stop Your Profit Losses that Keep Your Business at Risk*. As a small business, planning for *losses* without lots of angel investors patiently backing you until you turn a profit is like preparing to suffer business death by business cardiac arrest: It's going to happen. It's much better, easier, and less stressful to plan for profits each month!

USE *YOUR* TWENTY-FOUR-MONTH PROFIT PLAN TO BETTER MANAGE *YOUR* BUSINESS

Every P&L statement produced reports *lagging results;* in other words, for transactions already completed. When you add the perspective of a P&L aligned profit plan by month to your *actual* P&L statements, you create both *leading* and *lagging* financial data. This is how you see a side by side comparison of what you *expected* your business to perform in a given month versus how it *actually* performed.

The most effective way to improve your business performance is to view your business data like a scientist. Compare your actual results by planned area to your planned results. Do they significantly differ? If yes, you now see areas where definite action is needed. Then it's time to commit. In contrast, without a monthly profit plan, you will never know whether your business is as profitable as you had planned it to be. It's one of the most significant reasons that businesses with predictable cash flow, strong profits, and accurate reports rarely face the question, "Is *this* a good business to buy?" The answer is in the numbers, which they consistently have right in front of them.

Most successful businesses have gross profit margins of 45 percent or greater, EBIDTA earnings that are 15 to 20 percent and net profit margins that are 10 percent or greater. Businesses achieving these types of margins most commonly have highly-efficient operations in a market with high customer demand and weak competitors.

If your business *isn't* producing these types of profit results, then tracking your actual performance against your monthly profit plan is how you determine where you can best make up the difference. By monitoring your actual-to-planned profit performance by month, you will never lose sight of a very important fact: Profit is the money a business *keeps* after subtracting all of the associated costs and expenses from the sales revenue that is collected.

CONCLUDING THE IMPORTANCE OF STEP 2—BUILD *YOUR* TWENTY-FOUR-MONTH PROFIT PLAN

Positive cash flow and profitability do not "just happen" for *any* business. They are achieved through thoughtful planning, committed work, and accurate plus timely reporting. They are the reward for your never-ending hard work and sacrifice.

Failure to *plan for profits* will result in your business needing to be financially resuscitated, because you didn't learn to apply the five steps of:

Achieving balance by utilizing the *B-CPR* five-step system to avoiding business cardiac arrest is the best way to ensure you have the cash to fund your business operations at a continuously increasing profit to you.

AUTHOR'S SIDE NOTE—FOCUS ON PROFIT, *NOT* ON STRATEGIC PLANNING IN STEP 2

Most academics, business consultants, and recent MBA graduates are likely to find issues with Step 2. Why? Because this step is really about budget, not strategy. They'll say that strategic planning involves clearly "determining your path to success" in the planned period ahead. They will also say that business strategy is built through the process of defining the strategies and tactics you will use to attain the short and long-term objectives for your company.

Then, these experts will remind you that a well thought-out business strategy forces you to think about the future and the challenges you will face. It forces you to consider your marketing and management plans, your competition, your overall strategy and, yes, your financial goals. They will explain that a viable business strategy can and will help you confirm your vision and define your goals as you lay out a clear plan to realize them.

I am in 100 percent agreement with these common statements about strategy. I'm not saying you should *skip* defining your strategy. Not at all. If you have an interest in building a strategy for your business, it is a very worthwhile exercise. Navigating through the steps of any strategic planning process will help you to think about your business and determine how you want to proceed into the next three-to-five years.

I highly recommend completing an annual strategic planning exercise if you are in a rapidly changing industry or if you're in an industry that is in decline. Your strategy will help you identify what you will and won't do. I also advise you to develop a formal strategy if you're unsatisfied with the results you have been getting by conducting business as usual. Your goal through the strategic planning process is to *rethink everything* about your business, yet all of these things are *not* as important as building a plan to realize your profit targets.

Ultimately, every "strategy" ends with the same goal, which is to make a profit over the next three-to-five years. During my career at Nationwide, I was part of the Corporate Strategy Council with the responsibility for bringing forward the Human Capital strategy. We had a team of talented people who worked hard to bring the respective business and functional strategies forward. We created large binders full of strategic plans, which the C-Suite executives reviewed with the Board of Directors each December.

The issue was how these well thought out strategic plans would never be used again through the next year. At best, they would go into an executive's bookshelf. They'd almost never be open on a desk. And more often, these carefully prepared binders would be hid away in a closet or used as a doorstop.

During these same four years, I was also part of the Finance Council, which was comprised of the business unit and staff function controllers. Within this group, I was the only one who overlapped as I also sat on the Corporate Strategy Council. I was in a unique position to see what was important to both groups and what wasn't.

The Finance Council had no interest in the Strategy Council's work outside of what the staff function strategic initiatives were going to cost them. And this was where the real profit planning work occurred. This consisted of getting the controllers to allocate funding to one of the strategic initiatives identified in the strategy. Their support of taking on any new expense was proportionate to the savings or other cost reduction moves that the strategic initiative was intended to make.

In the end, all that mattered was whether we hit our profit goals or not at the end of the year. That's the measure that funded the incentive pool. You could fail to deliver a strategic initiative and still get some bonus money as long as the company hit its profit goal. Miss the profit goal, and nobody got any bonus, no matter how well they did on a strategic initiative.

Here's the challenge to consider: It takes *time* to see the results of the goals you set out in your strategy. To keep yourself and your management team from operating blindly while you wait to see the results of your strategy, you need to lead with a *profit plan*. Then confirm the *quality* of your profits through utilizing Step 3 before moving on to stopping any profit losses, Step 4 of *B-CPR*.

Most small business owners don't need to spend a lot of time seeking to answer strategic questions. They then need to know how much they think they can sell, how much they intend to make on each sale in gross profit. They then need to manage their sales function to hit their sales target and manage their operations function to produce at their targeted gross profit. It's all in the *Profit Plan*.

Consider *your* business. If you want these same numbers to be much larger in months thirteen through twenty-four of your twenty-four-month profit plan, there's a help. Go to www.business-cpr.com\startegytool to find a strategic planning tool. Download this tool for free, and it will guide you through building a successful business strategy, just like the publicly traded corporations and large, pricey consulting firms do.

If you *aren't* hitting your Profit Plan sales and gross profit targets, it may be because you don't have a well thought-out strategy. It's more likely, though, that you are failing to follow through on your planned actions (*B-CPR* Step 5.) If this is true, you are likely to be *spending* more than you planned (Steps 2 and 3) or you aren't proactively stopping your profit losses (Step 4).

The number one benefit of the *B-CPR* management systems is that it is built on five proven steps that you don't need an MBA to follow. Individually, each of the five steps is already being followed, to a greater or lesser degree, the world over. What's been missed is the widespread understanding that failing to follow all five steps consistently is the most common cause of business failure. It is the solution to the profit but no cash problem.

Go to www.businessfitnesscheck.com to assess the health of *your* business to compete. Then read on to learn the remaining three steps to owning a profitable business with predictable cash flow.

5

STEP 3—CONFIRM THE QUALITY OF *YOUR* PROFITS

The third step to avoiding business cardiac arrest is grounded in a popular truism: *You can't control what you can't manage, and you can't manage what you can't measure.* Anything you want to improve starts by *first* accurately measuring to confirm your baseline. What are you currently doing? And how is it working for you? Then, once you have your targets set in place, you can measure to determine if you are better or worse than where you had planned to be.

Consistent action on *B-CPR* Step 3—Confirm the Quality of *Your* Profits is critical to your business success. Every profit dollar you earn is the result of *past* actions that produced a profitable result. So the sooner you identify *where* corrective action is needed the sooner you will see improvements in your current and future results.

MEASURES, INDICATORS, AND METRICS IS HOW YOU CONFIRM THE QUALITY OF *YOUR* PROFITS

Measures record a *directly* observable value or performance. All measures have a unit attached to them, such as an inch, a centimeter, a dollar, or a liter.

Indicators, in contrast, *indirectly* measure a value or predict an outcome, such as customer satisfaction and leading indicators of performance listed in the table below.

Metrics are standards of measurement by which efficiency, performance, progress, or quality of a plan, process, or product are assessed. Effective managers use the following two types of metrics to measure the performance of their employees, operations, and ultimately, the profits of their business:

Leading Metrics	Lagging Metrics
Leading Indicators are *inputs*—they measure the activities that are necessary to achieve your goals.	Lagging Indicators are the *outputs*—they measure the *actual results* that confirm whether you hit or missed your goal.
These come *first*. They describe how to achieve your goals, serving as indicators of the likely results of your actions. These metrics are *outcome predictors* that are harder to measure, but are easier to influence and improve upon directly.	They show the final score of your strategy execution. These metrics summarize the *outcome* of an event and as a result, are easy to measure, but impossible to improve upon directly, or influence, in the near-to-short-term.
• Measures ACTION • Key Performance Indicator (KPI) or Key Behavior Indicator (KBI) • Activity-based • Shorter—measures hours, days, and weeks • Shapes BEHAVIOR	• Measures RESULTS • Key Results Indicator (KRI) that confirms what happened • Financial-based • Longer—measures months and years • Shapes GOALS

LEADING AND LAGGING METRICS NEED TO WORK IN TANDEM

You need to utilize both types of metrics to manage your business. *Leading* metrics are the best way to ensure that behaviors and actions are managed as they need to be. *Lagging* metrics confirm how your business is performing relative to your goals. They consider your financial results for revenue, costs, and profit measuring, and they indicate the effectiveness of these past activities throughout your company during any given time period.

When you combine your profit plan targets with your financial statements, you create a reoccurring indicator, one that is likely to predict your year-end financial results. And as you approach the end of the year, the more accurate your updated predictions are likely to be.

It's amazing how many business owners fail to consistently view their financial statements to gauge the health of their businesses. It's even more amazing when these business owners operate their businesses without clear targets in place to gauge their month-to-month progress. They are operating in the dark! Those who do this are also the same people who don't understand why their bank statement balance and P&L statement have numbers that are so different from each other.

A MONTHLY REVIEW OF *YOUR* P&L STATEMENT IS NOT ENOUGH

As I have worked across the United States with some very well-intentioned business owners, I continue to be stunned at how few review their P&L Statements each month. They're often so caught up in dealing with the problems of the day that they don't take time to monitor, at a minimum, their monthly financial reports.

In reality, a quick monthly P&L Statement review will help them identify precisely where they need to begin taking new actions if they want to shape better results in the following month. Unfortunately, every P&L statement is a *lagging,* not a *leading,* indicator of results. Fortunately, each accurate P&L statement *does* readily inform on the quality of the *decisions* you have already made and the *actions* you have already taken.

It is better to have leading and lagging metrics working in tandem to help you track the progress of your activities, start to finish, through to the final results. Think of it as a simple equation where "actions = results." To make the equation work, start with the results you *want* represented by your key *lagging* indicators. Then work backward to identify the necessary actions, the *leading* indicators you will need to act on in order to *realize* your planned results.

Use of Step 2 in the *B-CPR* system establishes your revenue and profitability targets by month. Your efforts here define what success will look like for the year ahead and each individual month. Step 3 focuses on confirming the *quality* of your results. It allows you to check, in real-time, whether you need to make adjustments to the quantity, quality, efficiency, and effectiveness of your actions. And it's the best way to assist you in your goal of achieving the planned profit results established in Step 2.

Failure to carry out Step 3—Confirm the Quality of *Your* Profits through leading and lagging metrics is the surest way to develop serious problems with cash; not just cash *quality*, but cash *velocity* too. Put simply, the negative consequence of bypassing Step 3 is likely to include trading a dollar for four quarters at best. Not an effective way to operate your business!

Time is an important factor as well. Ideally, you want each dollar that passes through your business to be worth *more* than the dollar you spent to earn it. Until you reach this goal, you're at increased risk of suffering business death by cardiac arrest, because you won't have profits pumping cash flow from operations through your business.

A SIMPLE ILLUSTRATION MANY OF US CAN RELATE TO...

For many of us, our personal goals have, at least once throughout our lives, included weight loss. Let's say I weigh 220 pounds, which is my baseline. But I would *like* to weigh 190, my goal weight. The thirty pounds I want to lose is a *lagging* indicator that is easy to measure by comparing where I am week-to-week versus my starting point and my goal.

The power of a lagging metric is its ability to easily tell you *where you are* relative to *where you want to be*. If you have a set goal (your desired result) and a baseline (your starting point), you have the basis for accurately measuring the results of your actions. In this example, every time I step on a scale, I will know whether I'm progressing or not toward my goal.

Let's say at my end-of-month weigh-in, I register 212 pounds as I step on the scale. That's eight pounds closer to my goal. The message I get is, "Keep doing what you're doing, because you're getting favorable results." That seems pretty clear to me!

What if at that first-month milestone, I step on the scale weighing in at 224 pounds? While the result confirms that I'm not progressing toward my goal, it *does* show me that what I'm doing *isn't* working. And that's still an accurate measure, isn't it? The challenge is that now, I'm a month behind in reaching my goal, because the only measure I've thought to consider is my monthly weigh-in.

This is the problem with taking only a *single monthly look* at your financial statements, particularly your profit and loss statement. Keep in mind that you're looking at what has *already* happened. Seeing historical results always puts you at least a month behind if you are off-track and need to make adjustments in order to realize your annual profit plan goals.

Let's say my goal to lose thirty pounds is time-bound at six months because I want to slim down before my daughter's wedding. By relying *only* on the scale through that first month, I've put myself behind with a *new* need to now lose thirty-four pounds in only five months. If this were really the case, I think I couldn't help but be discouraged!

The *better* approach to realizing my weight-loss goal is the adoption of *leading* metrics that will help me *consistently* measure the actions I'm taking to realize my six-month weight-loss goal. Now, you don't need to reinvent the wheel when setting up leading metrics. A little research will tell you what most people in a similar position are already doing to realize their desired results. In my weight-loss example, the two best "leading" metrics in the opinion of many professionals are calories taken in and calories burned.

The challenge is that both of these metrics are easy to influence but hard to measure. When you order lunch in a restaurant, the number of calories isn't always listed on the menu. And if you are without a smartwatch or Fitbit to help you track your physical activity, you would also have no clue how many daily calories you burned.

If you're serious about your desired result, you'll need to be creative in finding a way to measure the *key actions* you must take to reach it. In the weight-loss example, the desired result is to enjoy my daughter's wedding at 190 pounds, not 220-plus, in six months.

In order for that to happen, the *key actions* I'll need to take will be to 1) significantly reduce my calorie intake by watching what I eat; and 2) be consistently more physically active.

Keeping track of both calorie intake and physical activity on a daily basis will give me a strong predictor of whether I will have lost weight or gained weight the next time I step on the scale. This is the power of *leading* metrics.

ANOTHER EXAMPLE...

Now, let's imagine you own an IT outsourcing company, and your goal is to be 100 percent compliant with the SLAs (service level agreements) you've reached with your new customer. For example, one SLA you've agreed on is that the maximum allowed time for resolving high priority incidents is forty-eight hours.

You obtained this new client because their previous IT service provider failed to hit this target, and it cost the client, on average, $25,000 per month. Because you knew you were up against some strong competition and you wanted their business, you offered to refund the customer 10 percent of their monthly invoice if you were ever to fall below 90 percent on priority incident resolution within forty-eight hours.

Similar to stepping on the scale, this output is easy to measure: You'll either solve your customer's priority incidents within forty-eight hours or you won't, and you're betting you'll succeed 90 percent of the time. The question is, how can you best influence the outcome of this clear lagging result measure?

The answer is, by identifying the activities your people must undertake in order to achieve the desired outcome of resolving priority incidents in forty-eight hours. Specifically, 1) you'll need to ensure that your staff starts working on "high-priority incidents" as soon as they occur; 2) you'll need to make sure that priority incidents are assigned to the right people with the right skillset; and 3) you'll need to confirm that the assigned person isn't already overloaded with other work. These activity options could translate into the following "leading" indicators for managing your performance for high-priority incidents:

1. Percent of priority incidents not handled successfully for two hours.
2. Number of open priority incidents older than one day.
3. Percent of priority incidents dispatched more than three times in the last month.
4. Average backlog of priority incidents handled per technical expert.

If your goal is to score perfectly on your high-priority SLA incident metric, then you would begin by measuring the above listed KPIs daily. As the results are reported to you each day, you would focus management attention on improving those KPIs most likely to lead to an improvement in high-priority incident SLA compliance. In other words, use your metrics results to prioritize your actions and those of your team.

Leading indicators are often related to activities undertaken by employees. Remember, the example of losing thirty pounds in six months is ultimately a measurable result, as is having a 90 percent or greater high priority incident resolution within forty-eight hours. The challenge is that without the activity of exercise and eating right, one's weight-loss goal will not be achieved. Nor will the high priority incident resolution goal be reached if you aren't monitoring the appropriate actions and activities daily.

THE RIGHT *METRICS* MATTER, BECAUSE THE RIGHT *ACTIONS* MATTER

Per author David Parmenter, in his book, *Key Performance Indicators*, a characteristic of a KPI is that it's "nonfinancial in nature [and] can be measured daily, yet can have a significant impact on operations."

Every profit dollar earned is the result of past decisions and the actions triggered by those decisions. Some of those profit contributing actions were planned and carried out deliberately. Others occurred by chance. Either way, "profits" equal "results" and "results" equal "action."

Many companies with high-energy owners operate their businesses by observing the value, "bias for action, and passion for results." This value reinforces the goal of using metrics to measure the results of the activities they are pursuing.

While the focus of the finance function will always be to track changes to the P&L and Balance Sheet statements, these items also represent an excellent source for metrics in every business, no matter its size. And yes, the use of these financial statement measures is *far* better than no measurement of performance results at all! The bottom line is that financial statements represent the scorecard for the results of your leading metrics (KPIs) whether or not you are intentionally tracking them.

DESIGNING *YOUR* METRICS MANAGEMENT SYSTEM STARTS WITH *YOUR* MONTHLY PROFIT PLAN

The ultimate purpose of any metrics measurement system is to confirm the quality of your results. Identify the results you *want* to confirm you are achieving using the profit plan you built in Step 2. Ideally, your chosen metrics will tell you whether you're achieving your desired sales and profits each month or not. Your profit plan also tells you what situation you are trying to *prevent*. And that is spending more in COGS, SG&A, and other expenses than you planned for or you need to offset the higher than planned expenses by lower spends in other areas. If this doesn't happen, you are guaranteed to have smaller profits.

As stated in Chapter 4, I've discovered that this line of thinking is best initiated through the development of your Profit Plan. This is because the Profit Plan directly sets the targets you want to achieve.

As you confirm the quality of your actions through weekly KPIs and the quality of your results through monthly variance reports, you'll establish *where* your business is on track. You'll also identify where you are *not* tracking to meet your profit plan goal. Note that profit plan goals can, and do, overlap with your strategic goals whether or not you have a strategic plan mapped out.

For example, let's say you have a strategic goal of $1,000,000 in new product sales revenue with an average per unit value of $10,000 and that your expected sales cycle for this new product is six months long. Rather than waiting the full six months to see if you've reached your goal of 100 planned new product sales, try tapping into some valuable *intermediate* metrics. Define your own shorter term key leading indicators, such as the number of sales calls your sales team needs to make each week in order to hit the $1,000,000-mark in new product sales in six months.

As you track weekly activity for both sales calls made and closed sales, you'll gain a sense of whether you're in reach of 100 deals sold and whether you're in shooting distance of achieving your lagging strategic goal of a $1,000,000. You don't *need* to wait out the six months to find out. Instead, you'll be able to operate with a solid sense of probable success during each week's KPI review.

Here's another example common among the strategic plans I experienced at Nationwide and PPG. Strategic initiatives often lead to the implementation of a new process or capability. As such, strategic initiatives are an excellent vehicle for changing how something is done, particularly when you track actual performance to your milestones throughout the initiative process.

Let's say you are implementing a new sales process to reduce the length of your sales cycle. One approach is to measure how compliant your sales reps are with the new process (i.e., are they using the required marketing materials and following the correct sales script). In this example, it would be most effective to measure the *exceptions* to the new process. These might include the numbers of required marketing materials being requested tied to the numbers of sales calls completed.

Another leading metric would be to compare the length of time required to complete each step. For example, the time it takes for a marketing qualified lead (MQL) to proceed to a sales qualified lead (SQL) and then to a sales accepted lead (SAL). You could also consider the amount of time it takes to get a proposal out the door. Here you would need to be sure of your baseline numbers, which establish what length of time *has* been, your *goal* for the sales cycle time reduction, and what your *actual* performance results reflect.

Once your activity measures are performing better than baseline, you'll know your strategic initiative is on track. And when these measures are *consistently better* than the goal, you'll know with certainty that you have accomplished your strategic initiative. Now it's time to set *new* goals!

DEVELOPING PRACTICAL KPIS

We've covered some common measures of performance that can be used as *leading* indicators of potential performance issues. Yet, before implementing these, we first need to understand some of the most common metrics used for measuring *lagging* indicators. In the table below, right column, I've listed some of the core *lagging* metrics used to confirm long-term trends. In the left column, I've listed some of the most commonly used *leading* indicators.

Leading Metrics	Lagging Metrics

SALES
• Sales Activity
  - Touches (calls, e-mails, apps)
  - Quotes, RFP, RFQ, or Bids
  - Closes or Sales
  - Conversion Rate
  - Avg. Transaction Size
• Customer Loyalty (customer retention)
  - Customer Satisfaction
  - Customer Value
	P&L
	• Sales Revenue
	• Net Revenue Growth
	• Cost of Sales
	• Gross Profit
	
	BALANCE SHEET
	• Accounts Receivable

Leading Metrics	Lagging Metrics
OPERATIONS	P&L
• Cycle Time—measure of lead times	• Cost of Goods Sold
- On-Time Delivery Percent	• Gross Profit
- Critical Path Measures	BALANCE SHEET
• Productivity—measure of output vs time	• Inventory
- Billable Hours Percentage	• Fixed Assets
- Labor Capacity Utilization Percent	• Total Assets
- Units per Labor Hour	• Accounts Payable
• Efficiency—measure of process throughput	• Current Liabilities
- Yield	• Long-term Liabilities
- Inventory Turns	
• Quality	
- Scrap	
- Rework	
• Capacity	
- Utilization Percent	
- Equipment Up-Time, Down-Time	
• Safety—to focus safe work behaviors	
- Days without Incidents	
- Days without Violations	
- Training Hours Percent	

Leading Metrics	Lagging Metrics

FINANCE
• Cash Flow
  - A/R Days
  - A/P Days
  - Cash On-hand
    Percent to Desired
  - Collections Funnel
    ▪ Orders shipped
      to invoices
    ▪ Orders shipped
      to deposits
    ▪ Orders shipped
      to CODs
    ▪ Number of cour-
      tesy calls
    ▪ Collections
      calls per day
• Investment
  - Return on Inventory
  - Return on Assets
• Coverage
  - Days of Liquidity
  - Working Capital Ratio
  - EBITDA to Fixed
    Cost Ratio
	P&L
	• SG&A Expense
	• EBITDA
	• Net Income
	
	BALANCE SHEET
	• Accounts Receivable
	• Current Assets
	• Fixed Assets
	• Total Assets
	• Accounts Payable
	• Current Liabilities
	• Long-term Liabilities
	• Owners' Equity
	• Retained Earnings

Another approach to establishing the most useful leading metrics is to identify *what problem you are trying to solve* by identifying each of its steps. Below are some examples of a "problem-based" approach:

Problem to Solve	Metric
Late deliveries	Cycle time-critical path measures
High rework	Quality—rework at control point
High scrap	Efficiency—yield
Low margin	Sales—average transaction size COGS—cost of labor, materials, outsourcing, etc.
Poor productivity	Productivity—units per labor hour; billable hours percent
Injured worker	Safety—days without violations
Capacity	Capacity—equipment up or down-time
Declining sales	Sales activity—leads, number of calls, conversion rate

Below are a few examples of metrics used by top companies in the world, to affirm that the use of leading metrics is not "rocket science."

Company	Leading Metric
3M	Number of new innovations Number of patents Customer service perception
Dell Computer	Customer satisfaction Days of supply in inventory
Coca-Cola	Number of cases shipped Sales growth in new markets

METRICS MANAGEMENT SYSTEMS MUST AVOID "GIGO"—GARBAGE IN, GARBAGE OUT

The challenge with Step 3—Confirming the Quality of *Your* Profits is the quality of data inputs used to measure metrics. If the data inputs are *accurate*, you'll have quality results to act on. On the other hand, *inaccurate* data will result in misleading information. This is particularly true when you have data coming at you from every corner of the business. It's tough to have confidence in your metrics tracking if you don't have confidence in the data feeding *into* those metrics.

An important goal of establishing optimal metrics for your business is to design your data-collection platform to feed you accurate metric calculations. For those management teams who are committed to managing their businesses through dashboards, there are many software providers available to help with this task. These valuable services will save you time chasing down the data to populate your leading metrics. You'll then have more free time to spend working with your metric *results* in order to identify any needed corrective actions.

Populating your lagging metrics is as simple as consistently entering your daily sales and expense transactions into your existing accounting software on a timely and accurate basis. Incorporate into this routine a monthly bank reconciliation, and you will have the quality financial records you need to track your progress accurately.

For those just starting out in business and who are using QuickBooks, know that you have a ready tool to begin developing your metrics management system as long as you're willing to make the following enhancements:

QuickBooks As a Quantitative Management System	
Sales & Marketing —*Get Work*	1. Use QuickBooks Customer Center as the system of record for your estimates submitted and customer database.
	2. Set up your Item list to track income vs. using outdated categories
	3. For each new customer and job for which an estimate is submitted, capture under New Customer & Job
	a. Name, job title, company name, key phone numbers, e-mail, and billing address.
	b. Under Additional Info capture the type of customer and indicate if they are a Key Account
	c. Under Payment Settings establish what their payment terms at the time of customer data entry.
	d. Use Job Info to capture Job Description, Job Type, Start, Projected End Dates.
	4. Use QuickBooks Estimates to Submit Bids and Invoices to Get Paid. This is how you will track your bid conversion rate by sales item.
	5. Update Job Status when awarded Job and enter the Start Date. Note "When Closed" in Job Status, and enter the "End Date" when completed. If confirmed that the job is not awarded, indicate "Not Awarded."
Operations —*Do Work*	1. Properly align QuickBooks expenses via your Chart of Accounts into Cost of Goods Sold and SG&A categories for more effective cost and expense monitoring and management.
	2. Set up staff by Department in QB COGS so you can track Revenue, COGS, and Gross Profit performance by Department. Use this data to monitor performance and share in wealth creation.

Financial —*Enable Work*	1. Use realigned QB expenses and expanded service line revenue (item list) reporting to manage P&L business performance according to
	   a. Actual vs. profit plan variance (monthly/quarterly)
	   b. Actual vs. same time period (monthly/quarterly)
	2. Use Cash Management tool to manage anticipated cash inflow timing against planned cash outflows.

THE KEY TO USING WEEKLY KPI METRICS IS *CONSISTENTLY MONITORING RESULTS*

All activity metrics need to be viewed in aggregate, and you should include some traditional financial ratio analysis. Remember that *leading* metrics are meant to predict or inform on what your *lagging* measures are likely to report eventually. When used together, these metrics can effectively communicate the quantity, quality, efficiency, and effectiveness of your day-to-day business operations.

An effective metrics measurement system provides the following benefits:

1. Linkage of sales, operational activities, and trends with financial performance.
2. Ability to anticipate changes in business conditions before they "bite" you without warning.
3. Better-informed decision making leading to continuously improving results.

If you choose *not* to implement a metrics management system, you are choosing to surrender any control over your business. You're choosing to operate your business blindly via the "hope method," hoping your daily activities of operation will produce the results you want to see. The problem is "hope" can never be counted on to deliver your planned results.

STEP 3 ALSO INCLUDES MONTHLY
VARIANCE REPORTING AND ANALYSIS

In completing Step 2, you will have invested considerable time and effort to confirm that your financial statements are accurate and "make sense" to you. These monthly statements, for the last forty-eight months, would have been analyzed and used as inputs into setting your twenty-four-month profit plan.

Step 3 comes down to confirming the quality of your profits-to-plan results through a disciplined review of your monthly financial statements. This review is anchored by your monthly P&L statement where you learn, monthly, whether you are making the intended profits or suffering losses. Each month, you *must* review your P&L to ensure that your business is on track to achieve its expected profits as well as its revenue targets and expense budgets.

Over my years of working with small business owners, I've observed something interesting: they're never sure exactly *what* they should be looking at when they walk me through their P&L. Below are some foundational lagging metrics by sales, operations, and finance that *should* be included in your metric measurement system:

SALES—Get Work

Monthly Metrics	Metric Formula
Monthly Net Sales	Monthly Gross Sales - Refunds - Bad Debt = Net Sales
Year-to-Date Net Sales	Year-to-date Gross Sales - Refunds - Bad Debt = Net Sales
Year-over-Year Monthly Sales Percent Change	Current Months Sales – Previous Year Month Sales / Previous Years Month Sales = Year-over-Year Month Percent Change

Year-over-Year Year-to-Date (YTD) Sales Percent Change	Current YTD Sales – Previous YTD Sales / Previous YTD Sales = Year-over-Year YTD Percent Change
Monthly Actual as a Percent of Monthly Sales Goal	Actual sales divided by planned sales for the month
YTD Actual as a Percent of Total Sales Goal	Actual sales divided by planned sales year-to-date

OPS—Do Work

Monthly Metrics	Metric Formula
Gross Profit Percent Month-to-Date	Net Sales - COGS for the month divided by Net Sales
Gross Profit Percent Year-to-Date	Year-to-date Net Sales - YTD COGS divided by YTD Net Sales
Revenue per Direct Payroll	Net Sales divided by Direct Payroll Costs for the month
Cycle Time	Customer Authorization Date divided by the Payment Receipt Date
Average Order Value	Order Gross Sales divided by the number of orders received for that period
Merchandise Cost as Percent of Sales	Material Cost divided by Net Sales
Direct Labor Billable Rate	Total number of billable hours divided by total number of direct labor hours paid for the week
Direct Labor Overtime Ratio	Total direct labor overtime paid divided by the total direct labor regular hours paid

Percent of jobs closed ahead of contracted completion date	Total number of jobs completed early divided by the total number of jobs completed in that period
Equipment Availability Rate	Total number of days equipment is unavailable divided by the total pieces of equipment times 30
Return on Asset Ratio	Net Income for the month divided by Total Assets

FINANCE—Enable Work

Monthly Metrics	Metric Formula
EBITDA for Month	Gross Profit - SG&A Expense for the Month
EBITDA Year-to-Date	Year-to-date Gross Profit - YTD SG&A Expense
A/R Current	Total A/R that is Current (less than 30-days)
A/R 1 to 30 Days Past Due	Total A/R that is 1 to 30 days past due
A/R 31 to 60 Days Past Due	Total A/R that is 31 to 60 days past due
A/R 61 to 90 Days Past Due	Total A/R that is 61 to 90 days past due
A/R > 90 Days Past Due	Total A/R that is greater than 90-days past due
Average Days Payable	Accounts Payable divided by COGS times 365
Return on Capital Employed	Capital Employed = Total Assets - Current Liabilities; ROCE = Operating Income divided by Capital Employed

Change in Investment Fund	Current account balance less the previous months account balance
Gain on Asset Sales	Amount of Gain or Loss being reported in current month P&L Other Income

A monthly review of the measures of performance similar to the above confirms the quality of the monthly, quarterly, and annual results you're getting from your sales, operations, and finance functions. One of the easiest keys to success available to *every* business is the use of readily available *lagging* metrics reported in your financial statements. Your business will benefit greatly through your regular monitoring of these critical parts of your company. It's essential in order to ensure that the decisions you're making and the actions you're taking are producing the desired results month to month. The key to you having more cash in the bank is in how this information better positions you to eliminate unnecessary profit losses.

The primary benefit to your business from completing Step 3 each month is *confidence*. Because you will know through your reported numbers how well you are doing each month and through the year. If you are failing to reach any one of these *lagging* indicator goals for a given month, you have identified a specific area for considering corrective action.

As you identify *what* corrective action needs to be taken, think in terms of *who* is responsible for accomplishing it and *when* it needs to be completed. Being clear on the *who, what,* and *when* associated with each corrective action is essential to avoid falling short of your goal. Remember, over time, each repeat *lagging* metrics miss, if not corrected, will also cause you to miss your monthly, and ultimately, your annual profit goals.

UNDERSTANDING MONTHLY VARIANCE REPORTS

How often you should review your financial statements varies with the speed at which your financial statement data is changing. For most businesses, a monthly review works well. Your goal is to examine your financial statements in a disciplined way each month. Ideally, they're reviewed during the second management meeting of the month along with the monthly KPI dashboard.

Your first variance assessment should involve your monthly Profit & Loss statement comparison of current result versus the result for the same previous period. Make sure that the results reported for the current year are relatively consistent with the same period in the previous year. Or be very clear on the reason(s) they might differ. If the difference is significant and can't be readily explained, then you likely have a data entry error. Again, large variances by major sources of revenue and expense should be relatively easy to explain based on known changes in the business this year compared to last year.

If you *can't* explain the variance in results for this year versus the previous year, then you have discovered another area where corrective action needs to be taken. Again, any corrective action involves identification of *what* is to be done, *who* is responsible for accomplishing it, and *when* it needs to be completed. *Follow-through* on each assigned corrective action is essential in order to avoid falling short of your profit goals.

Your second variance report helps ensure that your business is on track to achieve your planned profits—the same goals you established during Step 2—Build *Your* Twenty-Four-Month Profit Plan. Here, you'll confirm your actual performance against your planned performance by month and year-to-date. A positive variance indicates that your actual performance is exceeding planned. A negative variance tells you *where* you are falling short relative to your profit plan targets.

Any *negative* actual-to-plan variance will cause you to miss that planned amount, unless a corresponding *positive* variance in another area can correct for the miss. You can avoid these misses by identifying *what* corrective action needs to be taken, *who* is responsible for accomplishing it, and *when* it needs to be completed. Timely follow-through on each assigned corrective action is the best way to avoid falling short of your profit plan goals.

GETTING THE MOST OUT OF *YOUR* MONTHLY VARIANCE REPORTS

Every month, plan to generate the following financial reports from your accounting software:

1. Monthly P&L Statement comparing the actual versus the previous same period.
2. Monthly "Variance to Budget" report comparing actual versus profit plan.
3. Month-end Balance Sheet.

At the "top" level, we need to verify that the following three numbers meet your expectations based on the targeted figure in your annual profit plan:

1. Revenue
2. Cost of Goods Sold (COGS)
3. SG&A Expense (Overhead)

The following is the key component to remember in the "actual versus previous same period" report:

> Did the actual COGS percent of revenue remain consistent? Or did the COGS percent of sales go higher or lower for the given review period compared to the same previous period time? If the percent changes aren't consistent with your changes in sales, then your COGS expenses aren't as variable as they need to be.

It's important to remember the following two key components in the "Variance to Plan" report: The "Percent of Budget" is a calculation that reflects the degree to which the actual result met the budgeted expectation. Any number greater than 100 percent indicates that the actual was higher than planned. When considering Revenue, this is a good variance to have; for Overhead, this is a bad variance. Consider the following core questions:

1. Did the budgeted **Gross Profit percent** come in as expected, regardless of the actual revenue dollars for the given review period?

2. Did the budgeted **Operating Income percent** come in as expected, regardless of the actual revenue dollars for the given review period?

Keep these basic tenets in mind during your monthly variance review process,

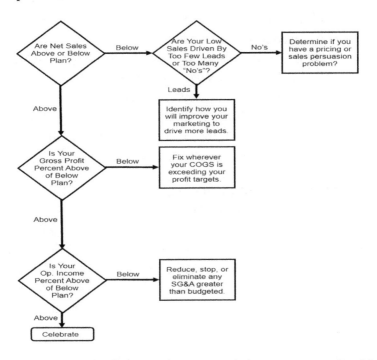

A minor variance-to-plan is to be expected; however, one should be mindful of trends. If trending below plan, you must boost sales revenue as needed, given how quickly money is lost anytime sales fail to cover expenses.

While minor variances in COGS are to be expected, significant differences as a percent of sales to plan indicate that your direct costs are not variable. This must be corrected or you will have insufficient Gross Profit contribution to cover your overhead and leave a profit for you.

Overhead should essentially be equal to budgeted if all items are categorized correctly. The only exception would be months with planned variances such as an extra pay period or when an insurance policy premium is paid over nine months to ensure a full year's coverage.

On the Balance Sheet, you'll want to check the following each month:

1. Accounts Receivable: This should be growing but not faster than the business in general. Many businesses get in trouble because they do not collect, on a timely basis, the monies owed to them.
2. Accounts Payable: This should not be growing at a rate faster than business growth in general. If it is, then you are borrowing from your vendors. This practice is not necessarily bad, but it is not sustainable over the long-term. Anytime A/P is growing faster than gross profit, you have a severe problem that needs to be fixed quickly.

CONCLUDING THE IMPORTANCE OF STEP 3— CONFIRM THE QUALITY OF *YOUR* PROFITS

You're most likely in business to make a profit. Never lose sight of the fact that the quality of your profits enables healthy cash to flow through your operations consistently. Profits are the day-to-day driver of your business, not just a number on your monthly P&L statement or an annual number you and your tax accountant discusses when he or she tells you how much money you owe in taxes.

Step 1 of *B-CPR* comes down to *sustaining* your healthy business through ensuring that *cash inflows* are always greater than *cash outflows*. Your business can survive, for a while, without profit; but it will *never* survive without cash. *Cash* is like air, *profit* is like water, and your personal *vision* is the nourishment that sustains your business.

As a result, every business must succeed in two critical areas; everything else is a means to this end:

1. Generate Cash to *Survive;*
2. Produce Profits to *Make Money,* so you earn a return on *your* Investment.

Your financial statements are your scorecard for tracking whether you are winning or losing:

- Balance Sheet is your company's health thermometer.
- P&L Statement tells you how you got that way and what you can do about it.

The critical success factors required for *avoiding* the negative consequences of business cardiac arrest include:

1. Knowing where you are in your profit plan, in order to know your next move with confidence;
2. Awareness of the "surprises" that can cost you unplanned expenses and drain your business of cash;
3. Having goals, objectives, and metrics to gauge how well you are performing;
4. Knowing what specific actions will cost you in carrying out your business operations;
5. Using your financial statements consistently to shed light on the quality of your results.

You earn profits by continuously pushing yourself to more effectively manage your business's assets as you control your expenses through sales, operations, finance, and admin functions. Step 3 helps you confirm whether these activities are being carried out effectively and as planned or not.

AUTHORS SIDE NOTE—APPRECIATING THE POWER OF ACTIONABLE INFORMATION

After the publication of my first book, *Owning a GREAT Business*, I received some feedback that the book lacked an easy-to-follow analogy or story that people could readily relate to. In reflecting on this feedback, I agreed.

My *Seven Organizing Principles for Owning a Great Business* does make it easier for business owners to make hard decisions relative to owning a great business. Very shortly, I will be updating the opening of this first book with the "Allegory of the Profit Tree" in order to set a better stage for the 7-P Framework I present throughout the book.

Why am I sharing this oversight from my first book with you now? Because I better appreciate the power of an analogy. They're easy for readers to relate to. In my work with a broad cross-section of small-business owners whom I helped, I've come to recognize with perfect clarity that every business owner was struggling with _cash_, _profits_, and _reporting_ in one way or another.

As I reflected on this recurring problem, I saw an immediate connection to the lifesaving process of CPR. I recognized it as an easy-to-understand analogy to the problems I was addressing with my clients. "Business CPR" provides a clear corollary to the power of cardiopulmonary resuscitation when someone suffers a heart attack. More importantly, I saw another correlation in cash, profits, and reporting in line with what medical science has taught us about avoiding cardiovascular disease.

In writing this chapter, I kept wanting to insert the analogy I have for the "R" reporting in _B-CPR_. In the end, I decided not to, because effective business reporting is not very complicated. It comes down to following through on the following key principles:

1. Effective business reporting must be timely and grounded in accuracy.
2. Informative business reporting involves a mix of leading and lagging metrics.
3. Use of variances to the previous year, to planned results, and to twelve-month rolling averages makes financial statements much easier to understand setting you up to take effective, corrective action.
4. If you want to see improved results, you must take corrective action.
5. If you want to make sure that planned actions are producing the planned results at the expected time you need a return and report "loop" best done through your weekly management meetings.

Confirming the quality of your profits doesn't get more complex than this. What makes Step 3 difficult is the _disciplined fol-_

low-through required to undertake the necessary corrective actions. Too often, this disciplined follow-through is lacking. When this is the case, misses continue to occur because there isn't a built-in "return and report" system. This is precisely the issue addressed by Step 5—Be Accountable for *Your* Results.

In writing the conclusion for this chapter, I *do* think the analogy for "R" is worth sharing. I will share it here, because it is such an effective correlation to what the ideal return and report system should resemble—our central nervous system as reflected below:

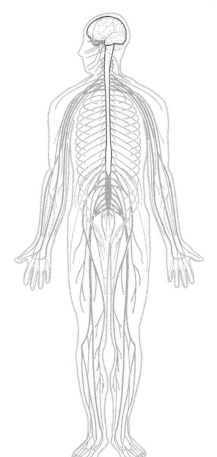

You and I are 100 percent reliant on our nervous system, which consist of the brain, spinal cord, sensory organs, and all of the nerves that connect these organs with the rest of the body. Without this vital system continuously sending messages to and from the brain and spinal cord, we would have no control over our bodies.

Communication throughout the body occurs through specialized cells called neurons. These cells transmit every communication signal. Without these signals constantly communicating, we would cease to exist.

The business equivalent of our "central nervous system" is our "business reporting system" which tracks the results from data produced through each transaction. You could say that all "transactions" are represented by "neurons," because they communicate information.

Failures in reporting that lead to business cardiac arrest stem from not using the financial data being produced through each transaction a business conducts every day of every week throughout the year.

The primary objective of financial reporting is to provide useful information to inform your decision-making. If your financial statements and dashboards fail to confirm the quality of the cash flowing through your operations and your financial position compared to plan, then your business is at risk. This information is key to making informed decisions regarding your best allocation of resources.

You and I are 100 percent reliant on our nervous system, which consist of the brain, spinal cord, sensory organs, and all of the nerves that connect these organs with the rest of the body. Without this vital system continuously sending messages to and from the brain and spinal cord, we would have no control over our bodies.

Communication throughout the body occurs through specialized cells called neurons. These cells transmit every communication signal. Without these signals constantly communicating, we would cease to exist.

The business equivalent of our "central nervous system" is our "business reporting system" which tracks the results from data produced through each transaction. You could say that all "transactions" are represented by "neurons," because they communicate information.

Failures in reporting that lead to business cardiac arrest stem from not using the financial data being produced through each transaction a business conducts every day of every week throughout the year.

The primary objective of financial reporting is to provide useful information to inform your decision-making. If your financial statements and dashboards fail to confirm the quality of the cash flowing through your operations and your financial position compared to plan, then your business is at risk. This information is key to making informed decisions regarding your best allocation of resources.

Our central nervous system is amazing in its complexity, efficiency, and effectiveness. The core intent of Step 3—Confirm *Your* Profit Quality is not about creating the equivalent of your central nervous system. This chapter comes down to appreciating the value of *actionable* information readily available in your monthly financial statements for those who take the time to study them in the context prescribed above.

Turn the page to learn exactly how Step 4—Stop *Your* Profit Losses that Keep *Your* Business at Risk has its origins in the human central nervous system analogy just described. Here, you will learn something that I only *wish* I had appreciated nearly thirty years ago when I began my corporate career fresh out of graduate school.

6

STEP 4—STOP *YOUR* PROFIT LOSSES THAT KEEP *YOUR* BUSINESS AT RISK

The Mayo Clinic states that "coronary artery disease is the most common form of heart disease and the most common cause of heart failure." They go on to say that "the disease results from the buildup of fatty deposits (plaque) in your arteries, which reduce blood flow and can lead to heart attack."

Arterial plaque arises from the buildup of calcium, fat, cholesterol, cellular waste, and fibrin. Over time, this buildup causes arteries to narrow and harden. Regrettably, the hardening of the arteries cannot be reversed once it has occurred. Lifestyle changes—including diet, exercise, prescription cholesterol-lowering medications, and quitting unhealthy habits like smoking—can prevent coronary artery disease or slow the process from becoming more serious. Unfortunately, failing to initiate these changes and commit to new lifestyle habits robs you of the opportunity to decrease your chances of having a heart attack or stroke as a result of coronary artery disease.

In business, the equivalent to coronary artery disease is the buildup of *profit losses* through mistakes, inefficient operations, and waste. Every wasted dollar reduces cash flow and leads to the complications caused by business cardiac arrest. As these waste dollars accumulate, it robs the business of accrued profits, and more significantly, it reduces cash in the bank by every wasted dollar.

You can correct for profit losses the same way you can reduce the chance of having a heart attack by making the necessary changes before it's too late. Start with reducing expenses, addressing inefficiencies, and ending unprofitable habits that lead to profit loss buildup and declining earnings.

THE KEY TO CONSISTENT PROFIT GROWTH IS ALWAYS TO BE FIXING YOUR #1 CONSTRAINT

While you *can't* reverse hardened arteries, you *can* stop profit losses. The key to consistently growing profits is to resolve the #1 constraint impacting business profitability. Step 4 of *B-CPR* details the process used to stop your business from "bleeding" out cash and, ultimately, profits.

Profit losses encompass business issues, waste, poor productivity, failed actions, and missed profit opportunities that cost you money. These losses typically manifest as lost sales or unnecessary expenses, which should have been avoided and that you now have to pay for. The key to this fourth step for avoiding business cardiac arrest is to identify and quantify the actual problem costs and opportunities lost in the business based on their calculated profit impact.

Just as your doctor can scientifically determine good and bad cholesterol to check whether you're sticking with his or her prescribed changes, you too can determine whether the processes in Step 4 are working optimally. You'll see these positive changes occurring in your gross profit, operating, and net incomes. On the flip side, fail to stop the profit losses, and you'll see continued declines in these same numbers.

The core steps in this process are much more than accounting exercises. They encompass behavior changes that result in your business performing differently through your continuous execution of Step 4—Stop *Your* Profit Losses that Keep *Your* Business at Risk.

Unwanted profit losses restrict the flow of cash through your business. So it makes sense that ending these losses is the most effective way to ensure that your business makes and holds onto more money. And it's easy to confirm your success in making and sustaining the changes that stop your profit losses. You'll see increases in weekly cash on hand levels and improving monthly profit results. This will end you're ever asking the question, "Why is my bank balance so different than my reported profits?"

WHAT'S THE BEST WAY TO IDENTIFY
WHERE PROFITS ARE BEING LOST?

The most efficient way to begin identifying and quantifying profit losses is by following Step 3—Confirm *Your* Profit Quality. Step 3 examines leading and lagging metric "misses" and unfavorable variance results. It isn't enough to identify *where* you are losing money; you need to quantify *each* profit loss, so you can prioritize *which* loss to stop *first,* based on its impact to your cash quality. This begins with a close look at the areas of your business managed in Step 1—Increase *Your* Operating Cash Velocity. And then, move on to the areas subsequently measured through Step 3—Confirm *Your* Profit Quality.

Once you have prioritized *what* to "fix" in your business, you are ready to establish your *who, what,* and *when.* The key is to focus first on the "who." No problem in your business can be effectively addressed until you establish *who* is accountable for fixing it. Assigning a specific person to own *what* needs to be done by *when* is required if any problem is ever to get effectively fixed.

Stopping your profit losses seldom needs to involve complex project plans with accompanying supporting documentation. It does require effective action by the person with the "A," the employee or manager accountable for fixing the problem and stopping the particular profit loss.

You will know that you have stopped a specific profit loss through your Step 3 variance reporting the next month *after* the loss is stopped. You confirm you have stopped the loss when you can see the value captured from stopping the loss reflected in your weekly cash management, the core component used in Step 1—Increase *Your* Operating Cash Flow Velocity.

BENEFITS *BEYOND* BETTER CASH FLOW AND
HIGHER PROFITS FROM STOPPING PROFIT LOSSES

The obvious benefits of Step 4 are higher business profits and greater cash flow from operations. The less noticeable benefit comes through the ability to identify, quantify, and resolve the most critical issues impacting profitability and cash flow. Through this

B-CPR step, you gain the kind of strong team awareness that is built through fixing a prioritized problem—one that has been creating stress for you and your team and costing your business real money.

Profit losses create unnecessary costs, and until they are fixed, they continue to waste cash and drain profits. Your employees likely know already *where* waste, inefficiency, and losses are occurring. They know, because these inefficiencies often make their jobs much more difficult than necessary.

Through the process of determining your "fix" priorities, you'll set quantifiable goals that will confirm *whether* and *when* the problem is fixed. Through the process of fixing the prioritized areas in your business, you measure progress on an hourly, daily, weekly, or monthly basis. Keep in mind that the sooner you measure things, the easier it is to fix the problem and confirm that it *stays* fixed.

There is another benefit to consistently following Step 4. Participation in the process creates urgency, buy-in, and focus on the *critical few issues* that must be corrected to stop profits from leaking out of the business. Throughout this process, issues that employees, including managers, want to see fixed are dealt with, resulting in less pressure and stress across your company in the long run.

Beyond seeing higher profits, more cash in the bank, and less-stressed employees, it's ultimately your customers who benefit. These customer benefits come in several ways: from engaged employees efficiently performing their jobs, to improved delivery of your products and services providing a better customer experience. Every time you eliminate waste, inefficiency, and delay, you ultimately provide a higher value-to-cost ratio for each and every customer.

Keep in mind that no customer wants to pay for your mistakes, nor should they. They are willing to pay you a profit markup, but they won't do so at their own expense because you fail to stop your business's profit losses.

WHEN YOU PLAN, QUANTIFY, IMPLEMENT, AND MEASURE—YOU ENSURE CORRECTIVE ACTIONS WILL TAKE EFFECT AND STAY IN PLACE

After a needed change has been identified, quantified, measured, and assigned, it must be started. By understanding the costs associated with a problem they are being asked to fix, those impacted will be much more engaged in making the necessary changes. As a result, their desire to be part of resolving the issues that are holding you back from improved profit and cash flow will result in new and improved efforts.

The following are the core objectives from acting on Step 4—Stop *Your* Profit Losses:

1. Focus efforts on quantifiable high-profit loss issues, not just annoyances.
2. Maintain a high sense of urgency for working through the difficult problems causing profit losses.
3. Obtain a high commitment from participants to make the required behavior changes to sustain the profit loss fixes.
4. Ensure a safe environment to discuss the next hard truth so that continuous improvement becomes the norm, not the exception.
5. Confirm greater value to the business is created through increased efficiencies, as reflected in higher profits and more cash in the bank.

Use this proven business improving process to focus both you and your management team. Through this process, you will change their priorities from "tasks" to "CASH" and subsequently to "PROFIT" by identifying what specific actions each of them needs to take to improve results. You can ensure that your team is doing what needs to be done by measuring their progress through your Step 3 scorecards during your Step 5 weekly management team meetings.

THE PROCESS STEPS FOR STOPPING *YOUR* PROFIT LOSSES IS LIKE ASCENDING A STAIRCASE ONE STEP AT A TIME

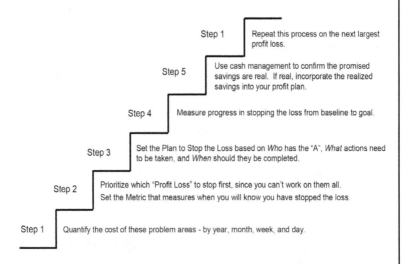

Identify where you and your people are most frustrated and having difficulty producing desired results.

Climbing any staircase begins with taking the first step. You can't take that first step to earning higher profits until you identify what is costing your money. The easiest place to start in identifying where you are losing money is with where you and your people are most frustrated and having difficulty producing desired results. Once you think you know what's holding you make, you can then use the following five steps of this proven business profit improvement process:

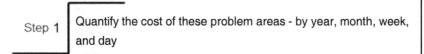

Step 1   Quantify the cost of these problem areas - by year, month, week, and day

You should hold off taking this first step until *after* you list out the "top five" most significant issues currently facing your business. Your goal in completing this first process step is *not* to quantify *all* of the issues facing the company; it is to quantify the *critical few issues first*, then move to other issues as those confirmed to be most critical are resolved.

Keep the math simple, estimate as necessary; focus on the profit dollar impact of the issue as it affects sales, cash flow, and profit. Working to achieve a precise cost of a specific profit loss is often a waste of time. Especially when simple math will allow you to establish a reasonable estimate of what the problem you need to solve is costing you. The calculation is necessary because you can never effectively stop a profit loss if you can't quantify what makes up the loss.

QUESTIONS TO ASK IF YOU CAN'T QUANTIFY WHAT A PROBLEM IS COSTING YOU.

If you are finding it difficult to quantify the cost of a "top five" issue, the following questioning sequence is useful in completing the math for any item perceived to be a profit loss:

1. Where does the cost show up?
2. How many employees are affected?
3. What is the number of hours lost each time?
4. What is the average hourly rate paid to those impacted?
5. What is the frequency of the impact—hourly, daily, weekly, monthly?

Below is the basic formula for calculating the cost of an employee influenced profit loss:

> nonpayroll costs + the number of impacted employees
> x hours lost x average hourly rate x the frequency
> of impact = cost of the identified profit loss

For example, your Gross Profit this year-to-date is 38 percent when you budgeted it to be 42 percent on sales of $1.5MM. You are on track to hit your sales goal, but you will be more than $60K short in gross profit contribution if you don't stop this profit loss immediately. You have determined that the source of this gross profit loss is that a key part of your product assembly has had to be special ordered twenty-nine times this year. While you wait for the part to come in, your eight product assemblers are kept busy with equipment cleaning and building maintenance while they wait for the missing part to come in. The math for this problem works out as follows:

Nonpayroll costs	$ 5,800.00	$200 rush fee per order
# of Impacted Employees	8	Product assemblers
Hours Lost per Occurrence	16	Two hours on average per shift
Average Hourly Rate	$ 14.62	Labor burden rate
Frequency of Impact	29	Number of special orders
Profit Loss Cost	$60,069.44	

In calculating the cost of this $60K loss in profit, you learn the reason for the twenty-nine special orders is no one has changed the reorder point for the part. It continues to be special ordered. Secondly, the reason you run out unexpectedly is due to excessive part breakage during assembly. As you research the cause for the part breakage, you learn that your three fastest assemblers, based on units assembled each day, are breaking the part when the holes don't line up exactly and then grab a new one. In researching why the part holes don't line up, you find that your supplier has allowed the tolerances in your sub-assembly part to slip so that a continuously growing number of parts being delivered from your out-of-state supplier are out-of-spec. The end result is you are losing both profits and cash.

It can be easy to identify the *source* of a problem, but until you quantify the *cost*, you won't fully appreciate what the specific issues are driving the profit loss or how to stop them.

Step 2	Prioritize which "Profit Loss" to stop first, since you can't work on them all
	Set the Metric that measures when you will know you have stopped the loss

After the "top five" issues are quantified and prioritized, set the metric that tells you when each particular profit loss is fixed. Remember, you can never know if you have truly solved a problem if you can't measure when the problem has been fixed.

In the example above, the measure isn't the change in gross profit. This is a lagging metric, one that you can only react to after the results are in. The leading metric for this example is the percent of rejected sub-assembly parts. As your baseline, you should be rejecting 6 percent, and you have actually been rejecting 0 percent. You want the sub-assembly rejection to be less than 2 percent on each order received, so you begin measuring your sub-assembly rejection rate. Once you are consistently below 2 percent, it's an indicator that you have likely solved this profit loss. But you won't know for sure until you see the improvement in Gross Profit margin in the months to follow.

Set the metric that measures when you will know you have stopped the profit loss. Next, force rank the "top 5" issues from the number one constraint to number 5. It's okay if you only have the resources to take on the number one constraint at this time. The key to continuously growing profitability is to resolve your number one constraint first, and when that's proven to be fixed, through a reliable metric, move on to the next most critical constraint.

If you are able to work on more than one issue at a time, then do so today. Just don't give the "A" (accountability) for more than one issue at a time to yourself or one of your managers. Giving multiple "As" to the same person who already has a day job to perform is a sure recipe for failure. The last thing you want is for no one to accomplish any one of their assigned "As" as planned.

| Step 3 | Set the Plan to Stop the Loss based on *Who* has the "A", *What* actions need to be taken, and *When* should they be done by |

For each quantified and prioritized issue with a known "fix" metric, identify who is the best person to be accountable. The specific employee who will see the required actions through to completion. In some cases, fixing the profit loss is already part of a direct accountability of the person assigned to fix the loss (the "A"). At other times, the "A" will go to the best person to lead the fix on top of the other work they are already accountable for performing. Either way, you don't have the luxury to assign people to work full-time on fixing your profit losses. Common sense is that these fixes must be worked into existing work routines, responsibilities, and accountabilities.

Once you have identified the *who*, and they've accepted the "A" for fixing the problem, it's time to get organized. List the major actions that the person accountable and others will need to complete to fix the profit loss. Ensure that each identified action lists the 3-W's: *Who, What,* and *When.* If anyone of these W's is missing, the task will not be completed efficiently nor in a timely manner.

In many cases, an action will need to be completed by the person with the "A," the accountable person. In other cases, a specific action needs to be completed by a responsible person *other* than the person with the "A." In this case, we call this responsible person "R." The "R" means that they are responsible for completing a specific action by an assigned date, but they are not the person accountable ("A") for stopping the specific profit loss. Being clear on *who* is responsible for completing each action and by when is the key to completing each step of the profit loss process as planned.

There can be only one person responsible for each action, just as there should be only one person accountable for each profit loss. An action with more than one responsible person usually results in a lot of finger-pointing, rather than working together to solve the problem. If a *team* is required to complete the action, assign the *leader* of the team. You can include the participants in the description of the action to be completed, but only one person can be the leader responsible.

After establishing who has the "A" for fixing the profit loss and who has the "R" for completing each action by a specified date, ask yourself if each action is an "easy" or "difficult" action to complete. If the action is *not* easily completed, it's not the right action. Complicated solutions involving difficult actions are unlikely to be successfully completed. While it may take longer to break down the actions involved into smaller, more discreet components of work, it's worth it to take this extra time. By doing so, you'll improve your likelihood of success in fixing the profit loss, which is your ultimate goal.

The person with the "A" is also accountable for establishing and maintaining the performance sheets tracking the issue to be fixed and reporting on the progress made in the weekly management meeting.

| Step 4 | Measure progress in Stopping the Loss from Baseline to Goal |

After you have established the "who, what, and when" involved in stopping the profit loss, you've committed to fixing. Now it's time to populate both the baseline and goal performance metrics established on the second step of this business improvement process.

The baseline number is the result of the metric formula established for the end of week one after work on fixing the profit loss is formally underway. In the example above, the baseline number on sub-assembly parts rejected was 6 percent.

The goal metric is the target established during the planning step that confirms *when* you will know that you have stopped the profit loss. In the example discussed earlier, we set the rejection rate target number at 2 percent.

Going forward, your goal is to maintain *clear* and *concise* tracking of your weekly results. Without tracking these specific numbers, the profit loss issue that you are attempting to fix will become lost in the flurry of everyday actions occurring across your company. You really need to maintain your focus and commit to accurate reporting.

During each weekly management team meeting, part of your agenda will be to review the progress made toward each assigned action item and the performance metric associated with each profit loss. Emphasize forward progress. If actions aren't being completed in a timely manner, apply corrective action to achieve your desired results.

Being proactive means you should never "miss" a metric for longer than three consecutive weeks without identifying and implementing corrective action. If you neglect to follow this advice, you'll surely see even worse performance results in the weeks to follow.

Each member of the management team assigned the "A" for a specific profit loss is responsible for reporting their numbers and for stating whether they are on track, or not, at the weekly management meeting. If off-track, they must also report how far off-target they are, and state their corrective action plan for how they are going to reach their target in the future.

| Step 5 | Use cash management to confirm the promised savings are real. If real, incorporate the realized savings into your profit plan. |

The purpose of action and results tracking is to move profit dollars from "planned" annual impact to "realized" annual impact. As the identified actions are completed, performance tracking improvements will become evident. As a result, you will begin "realizing" profit gains.

You complete Step 5 by confirming that promised savings are real as evidenced by your weekly cash management report. If you are spending less or taking in more cash in your specific area of focus, this confirms that you are capturing the expected benefits of changes made through the Step 4—Stop *Your* Profit Losses process.

After a few weeks of confirming positive results and improved cash management, it's time to apply these realized savings to your profit plan. You can choose to either increase a specific sales target or reduce a budgeted category so that your Step 3—Confirm *Your* Profit Quality further confirms that the fixed profit loss is holding.

If you begin seeing negative variances for the updated budget category, then your fix isn't holding. Or there may be another yet-to-be-discovered area that needs fixing in the same sales or expense category. If this is the case, go back to the beginning and repeat the business improvement actions of this process before taking on another profit loss to fix.

Step 1 | Repeat this process on the next largest Profit Loss

After you know each profit loss has successfully been stopped, it's time to start the process again for your most costly constraint. Revisit the remaining constraints identified to choose the next issue you want to put through this business cash flow and profit improvement process.

One trick used by many business owners is to maintain a running list of the "top five" constraints. Simply add a new item to the list each time you remove an item that's successfully fixed. By following this profit improvement process, you will quickly move through the issues you have identified and resolve the different constraints holding you back from making the profits you deserve to be making.

CONCLUDING THE IMPORTANCE OF STEP 4—STOP *YOUR* PROFITS LOSSES THAT KEEP *YOUR* BUSINESS AT RISK

As established in the Theory of Constraints (TOC), an overall management philosophy introduced by Eliyahu M. Goldratt in his 1984 book, *The Goal*, there will always be issues to resolve in any business.

It is important that the management team understands this when faced with the challenge of identifying, quantifying, and fixing problematic issues in the business. It is also helpful for employees to keep in mind that attacking these issues is the key to unlocking higher profits and, ultimately, seeing the rewards of higher compensation. As new issues are identified and typically uncovered in weekly management meetings, it will become a habit to go back to the first step and restart the process with each additional identified issue. Remembering Goldratt's philosophy that "there will always be issues to resolve" may help to prevent feelings of frustration. Reassure managers that you are indeed moving forward.

AUTHOR'S SIDE NOTE—DON'T JUMP IN WITH THE SOLUTION UNTIL YOU KNOW THE COST OF *YOUR* PROBLEM

If I could go back to 1992, two years out of graduate school, the way Marty McFly (Michael J. Fox) was thrown back into the 1950s in *Back to the Future*, I would introduce this Step 4 process to my younger self. Unfortunately, time travel isn't an option. As a result, I had to learn the power of quantifying the *cost* of a problem before jumping in with the solution much later in my career.

During my PPG Industries and Nationwide Insurance corporate days, many superiors valued my quickness with solutions to problems they wanted to be solved. This enabled me to climb the corporate ladder rapidly, but it came with a career cost.

While many of my managers valued my out-of-the-box solutions, I often jumped ahead of those who would be impacted by these solutions. I would move forward into implementation and, as a result, I would often encounter resistance to what I wanted to do. I was focused on immediate action when I *should* have used the power of quantifying the cost of the problem to set up the need for the solution. Like a salesman, I would emphasize the perceived benefits of the solution. In fact, I would get "constructive" feedback that I was "always selling," and I could never fully appreciate what my peers were trying to tell me, because I never felt that I was "selling" anything.

I genuinely felt that I was merely working to advance an idea to solve an accepted problem. What I appreciate now is that while I saw a specific problem, others either didn't see the *same* problem or they didn't appreciate the *significance* of the problem. Looking back now I see how my approach often alienated people, particularly when I would work *around* them. That was a career blunder, particularly when the senior executive sponsoring my innovative idea moved into a new role, and I suddenly found myself without the necessary support to complete the implementation.

What I failed to appreciate during my corporate years is the power of anchoring people to the *solution* by helping them see the *cost of the problem*. Before people can fully agree on a path forward, they first need to agree on what the problem costs and whether they want to continue living with that cost. Earlier in my career, I failed to appreciate this important step. Now, if I could go back to those years, I would more patiently sit on the proposed solution until I had reached an understanding on the cost of the problem and confirmation that this cost was unacceptable. In other words, I would provide enough information or education to achieve peer "buy-in" from those responsible and more importantly, those affected by my proposed solution.

In my experience, the cost of any solution is always greater than the cost of the problem until the people involved understand the cost of the problem. Now I spend the necessary time quantifying, in real numbers, the cost of a problem before jumping into the solution. As a result, I gain real commitment to making the necessary changes. This remains true, even when the required changes are slow to take hold. And that is what Step 5—Be Accountable for *Your* Results is all about.

7

STEP 5—BE ACCOUNTABLE FOR *YOUR* RESULTS

Lack of follow-through is the number one challenge holding small-business owners back from owning profitable businesses with more predictable cash flows. Consider some of Merriam Webster's synonyms for follow-through: accomplish, achieve, commit, execute, fulfill, and perform. The antonyms or opposites of follow-through are: fail, skimp, and slight.

When business owners fail to follow-through on an action, they fail to see a job, task, chore, duty, or obligation through to completion. Most of the time, these well-intentioned individuals will make a commitment to follow through when they initially begin, but then they become distracted by daily problems, and their best intentions fade into inaction. The "relevant many" things requiring their attention cause them to lose sight of the "critical few" things on which they *must* follow through. This is why Step 5—Be Accountable for *Your* Results is the step that holds the other four *B-CPR* steps together. Take another look at the *B-CPR* model for avoiding business cardiac arrest below.

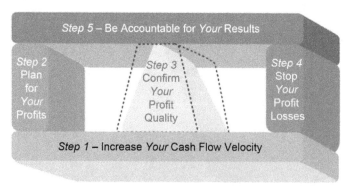

Consider the great lengths a doctor will go to in order to help a patient establish a commitment to life-saving lifestyle changes.

They are willing to put in this concerted effort, because they know these changes are *essential* to their patient who they know is at increased risk of a heart attack. Doctors who care will recommend specific changes such as losing weight, exercise, medications, and any other additional strategies unique to that patient with the goal of slowing the effects of cardiovascular disease. The caring physician will then *follow through* with their patient to see how they are doing with their healthy lifestyle changes.

HOW DO YOU KNOW WHEN YOU'RE FULLY COMMITTED?

Commitment is one of the most critical ingredients required to improve business performance. It requires obligating oneself to a course of action and then diligently following through on that decision until the required actions have been completed.

Commitment allows you to overcome the second and third highest killers of small businesses: complacency and procrastination. Overcoming these business killers begins with your personal commitment and that of your management team before this same commitment finally manifests in your employees.

When people are committed, they fully intend to do what they have promised to do. You can recognize a committed person, because they will fight through many obstacles and challenges to accomplish their goals.

Committed people take unwavering, earnest, and decisive actions. They focus on completing the "critical few" things they need to do to experience better results in their commitment to follow through on promised actions.

They have moved beyond "I'll consider it," which often fades into complacency, to "I want it," which propels them forward all the way to "I did it!" Their accomplishments are the result of a commitment to themselves and those who are depending on them to follow through. And none of this is possible without discipline.

BEING ACCOUNTABLE FOR RESULTS BEGINS WITH DISCIPLINED FOLLOW-THROUGH ON *YOUR* COMMITMENTS

I've come to appreciate the discipline that allows people to truly manifest through their actions, what is most important to them. If delivering on their commitment is highly important to them, they will accomplish this goal; if it isn't, the odds of them following through on the required action is highly unlikely. This is particularly true when the actions they need to take grow increasingly difficult to complete.

Consider the smoker who has been told he or she needs to quit smoking. The challenge the smoker must overcome first is making the move from a soft to a hard agreement to commitment as shown below:

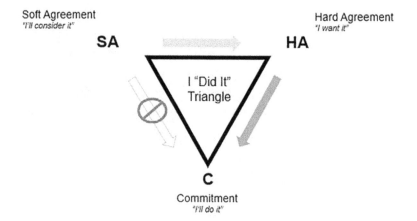

Soft Agreement
"I'll consider it"

SA

Hard Agreement
"I want it"

HA

I "Did It" Triangle

C

Commitment
"I'll do it"

The hard reality is most people resist change, particularly change that is forced on them. In the case of the smoker, this is particularly difficult.

As I was writing this section of the book, I recalled my dad's amazement as he told me about a coworker's wife who had just had both of her feet amputated because she didn't want to quit smoking. Her doctor had seen signs of worsening blood flow throughout her body and had warned her months earlier that this would happen if she didn't quit smoking. He tried in vain to convince her to stop, yet she chose to give up walking over smoking.

A very different case is my colleague, Mike, who I worked with at PPG. He too was a heavy smoker who had always smoked as we traveled together. On one of our road trips, I observed that he hadn't smoked since I'd joined him, even though he had an unopened pack of cigarettes in his cup holder. When I asked if he'd quit smoking, he told me that his grandson had learned about the health problems tied to smoking at school and had asked "Papa" to stop smoking so that he wouldn't die. Mike told me that he had stopped that very minute and he continued to be a nonsmoker during the next several years that we worked together.

Mike told me that he carried the unopened pack of cigarettes as a reminder of his commitment to his grandson. He also said that he enjoyed smoking and that if he were ever diagnosed with terminal cancer, he would light up again enthusiastically. Yet, he wasn't going to smoke any longer, because he had promised his grandson that he wouldn't.

ACTIVE COMMITMENT MOVES ITS POSSESSOR TO PHYSICAL AND MENTAL ACTION

It is rare for people with even the best intentions to sustain changes they embark on to please someone else. In Mike's case, it had worked, because Mike wanted to be there for his grandson. Yet, it is my recommendation to never commit to doing anything that you don't want to do, no matter how persuasive the invitation is presented to you. Failure to follow through hurts you and those depending on you, even more than simply saying "no;" you *won't* do what's being asked of you.

The most effective commitment always moves its possessor to some form of physical and mental action. Commitments based on true principles are more likely to produce desired results.

Any desire to implement change originates through your aspirations for things to improve. By following through on specific actions, you will realize the fruits of your change. First, you will see blossoms come through your leading metric results established in Step 3—Confirm the Quality of *Your* Profits. Before long, the actual fruits of your efforts to change will show up in new, healthier habits and, ultimately, healthier financial statements.

WHY DO APPLE FARMERS PLANT AND CARE FOR APPLE TREE SEEDLINGS?

An apple farmer would be unlikely to plant a seedling apple tree nor care for each tree in her orchard until it matures and bears fruit without the expectation that each tree will someday produce bushels of apples that the farmer could sell at a profit for years to come.

The hope of a better tomorrow is a powerful motivator for change. Step 2—Plan for *Your* Profits of *B-CPR* is designed to awake and arouse your faculties and lead you to think about what needs to be done differently in your business. Your profit plan shapes the changes necessary to help you realize your goals. Soon, you will begin to have faith that your business *can* do better.

MAKE *YOUR* BUSINESS GENERATE *YOUR* DESIRED RESULTS BY BEING ACCOUNTABLE

Being accountable for your results is easier when you understand the essential *principles, practices,* and *processes* that create effective managers and management teams. The management techniques used to make an organization work efficiently are not rare, unique, or even new. What makes them "work" is *your commitment* to seeing them through until you achieve your desired result.

Mastering these principles comes down to how much control you want over your business. *Profit,* in one word, is *action; management,* in one word, is *control.* Over the years, I have learned that the best way for a company to make more money is for each person in the business to hold themselves and each other accountable for achieving the planned-for results. This comes down to being accountable for agreed-upon actions as individuals, as a team, and as a company.

Develop personal accountability by becoming clear on *what* needs to be done, both by you and by those on your management team. To realize your profit plan goals, learn to be clear on what actions need to be taken within a specific time frame.

BEING ACCOUNTABLE FOR RESULTS, OR NOT, TOUCHES EVERYONE

Every employee, regardless of title or function, has a responsibility to be accountable for themselves and the activities they have been assigned to complete. Each person in your employ must complete the work they are accountable for performing if you are ever to earn profits. Failure to complete assigned work will almost always lead to losses.

In its most basic form, effective management should focus on achieving personal and business goals through planning, organizing, leading, and controlling the actions carried out individually and collectively across your business.

SEVEN FOUNDATIONAL BUSINESS MANAGEMENT SKILLS

Managing a business is a continually evolving process. And it requires a continuous repetition of each management phase. As a result, the tasks of management are never "finally" completed. This is why continuous follow-through is critical to your personal and business success.

Anytime a resource is wasted, profits are lost. What further complicates wasted resources is how high the odds are that your employees are growing increasingly frustrated because they see this waste happening. You correct for this by developing the following seven foundational skills of effective business management. The consistent application of each of the seven skills involving assessment, strategy, planning, organizing, leading, controlling, and rewarding the actions that produce the results in your business is how you generate predictable cash flow from higher profits.

1. Determine where you are: This is your starting point = *Assessment*

2. Establish goals and objectives. These define what your desired destination looks like = *Strategy*

    Next, define the desired outcome that sets your direction or the pathway you will follow to reach it. Prepare for the future by setting goals, which represent what needs to be done to realize your strategy. Your stated objectives will tell all those involved how you will collectively determine when you have realized your goal.

3. Make a plan to attain your goals and objectives. This plan directs the course you'll follow to reach your desired destination = *Plan*

    Your plan is the roadmap you'll follow to achieve your goals. For each objective, there are five items to be addressed:

    a. What actions need to be completed to achieve the objective?
    b. Who will be accountable for its completion?
    c. Who will be involved in doing the work?
    d. What will be the cost?
    e. When will it be completed?

4. Allocate and organize your resources. This is how you position the business to succeed = *Organize*

    Align the people involved so that their time and effort, supported by money and fixed assets, are well-positioned to execute the plan.

5. Make it ALL happen through leadership. You must direct these organized resources to achieve the goal = *Lead*

    Leadership involves the ability to diagnose a situation, understand what is needed, translate what needs to be done into a realistic vision and goal, and communicate everything in a way that people can understand and accept. Ideally, effective leadership also inspires others to want to perform the actions that the plan has identified and to which you have committed.

6. Make sure it's happening as planned and measure the results of your efforts concerning your goals = ***Control***

    Your plan charted your route, your organization mobilized your resources to allow you to proceed down the route, and your leadership moved you forward. Now it's about measuring your progress towards your desired destination (or goal). Accurate measurement is the only way to know whether you are progressing forward, and the only way to determine when you have reached your desired destination (achieved your goal). Without this step, you will never know if you are on track, behind, off-course, or even ahead of your plan.

7. Recognize, express appreciation, and reward those responsible for contributing the most toward your progress = ***Reward***

    There will always be obstacles and constraints that hinder your success. Benefiting from others who can help identify and find solutions to these obstacles and constraints is the KEY to achieving your stated goals. As you make progress toward and ultimately achieve your goals, a strong leader will recognize, thank, and even reward all of those who contributed to its accomplishment.

MANAGEMENT TRUISMS THAT SHAPE DISCIPLINED FOLLOW-THROUGH

Truisms are encapsulated words of wisdom gathered from the experience of those who have traveled similar paths before you and me.

- ✓ *Your* efforts as a manager *do* make a difference, some efforts more than others.
- ✓ Information is a valuable tool and is an essential component of the vital work of *planning, organizing,* and *measuring* results.
- ✓ You cannot *manage* what you cannot *measure.*
- ✓ You must *decide* or the world will decide for you.
- ✓ *Organized* chaos is better than complete chaos.

✓ A manager is an *enabler*. If you cannot tell someone *specifically* what you expect from them, then you cannot *expect* a specific performance from them.

✓ *Developing the skills and assets of employees* is the responsibility of every manager. It is also the easiest way to achieve higher profits.

✓ Specific and individual *performance recognition*, if fair and true, is very effective.

QUALITIES OFTEN SEEN IN PEOPLE WHO HOLD THEMSELVES ACCOUNTABLE FOR RESULTS

Beyond the minimal requirements of technical proficiency and an understanding of job requirements, the credible leader must be an effective manager. This role can be defined by the ability to consistently manage diverse individuals who perform dependably on a daily basis. Effective managers have the following qualities:

1. They are skilled in working with information. They can recognize patterns and trends in data and use them to make informed conclusions.

2. They are open-minded and alert to new ideas. An open-minded person has greater flexibility in facing the varying situations that must be faced daily.

3. They possess emotional stability. An effective manager can control his or her temper under all conditions. Even when the going gets tough, they will follow an orderly, well-planned procedure that is flexible enough to permit changes when necessary—all without coming unhinged.

4. They are impartial and fair. An effective manager does not allow personal likes and dislikes to influence decisions.

5. They handle decision-making positively, quickly, and with confidence; shaky and uncertain decisions cost indecisive managers the respect of both other managers and subordinates.

6. They understand the personalities of their subordinates in order to obtain the best work and cooperation from them. Subordinates must feel understood, and they must know

they are under the steady and dependable direction of a manager they trust.

7. They take advantage of opportunities to show the way, rather than simply dictating every move. Subordinates should feel that they are doing worthwhile work that they can see value in completing. This helps them to have a sense of accomplishment in their work.

8. They communicate a feeling of confidence in their subordinate's ability to do what's asked. If a subordinate's confidence is lacking, an effective manager must be able to properly train that subordinate in his or her task.

9. They know when to praise and commend a subordinate for work well done as well as to correct or criticize a subordinate, *privately,* for unsatisfactory work performance.

10. They anticipate changes in the business environment. The best managers continuously scan the horizon and formulate proactive strategies to improve productivity. They don't wait to be blindsided; rather, they take the initiative to discover what's around the next corner so they can be ready when it comes.

CRITICAL SUCCESS FACTORS SHARED BY THOSE WHO HOLD THEMSELVES ACCOUNTABLE FOR RESULTS

Effective managers ensure that planning, organizing, leading, and controlling both their employees and their fixed assets combine to cost-effectively deliver on the accountabilities set in their profit plan. In the simplest terms, *effective managers hold themselves accountable for their results.* The following responsibilities are among the critical success factors common to every effective manager:

1. Be a role model in your observance and practice of company policies and procedures.

2. Accept and understand all duties, standards, and responsibilities delegated to you.

3. Faithfully attend to all assigned duties, and when necessary, take the initiative within your authority to act on unanticipated matters as they arise.

4. Have the confidence to take the initiative in developing recommendations for improvements or modifications within the authority delegated to you without being told.

5. Cultivate the ability to establish cooperation, coordination, and discipline among subordinates and peers.

6. Develop sufficient knowledge to train subordinates at all levels and the desire to develop select individuals to become leads, then supervisors.

7. Simplify all activities to the essential tasks by eliminating marginal work and nonproductive effort.

8. Maintain operating records of the quality and quantity of work performed, planning and rescheduling work to achieve improved workflow and increased production as needed.

9. Remain personally accountable for the proper performance of all duties assigned to the position and the organizational unit supervised.

10. Be willing to honestly evaluate the performance of all subordinates, particularly those who may be in need of progressive discipline.

MANAGERS MUST HAVE THE AUTHORITY AND RESPONSIBILITY TO BE ACCOUNTABLE FOR RESULTS

There is a very common hindrance to people being truly accountable for results. And that is a failure to delegate to them the necessary authority to accomplish what you are holding them accountable to achieve.

Another common problem is the direct issuance of instructions to personnel under that manager's span of control. Doing so undermines the manager and effectively destroys their authority; simultaneously, it diminishes their own feeling of responsibility for achieving results. Rank often matters less than you might think. Accountability, or *who owns the results*, rests with the person issuing the direct orders.

It's a sticky situation whenever you feel you have to step in to direct the subordinates of another manager. In my opinion, you would be better off to remove this person from a management role if you are not prepared to extend them the following considerations:

1. Each manager must have defined accountability and authority over all personnel, equipment, and facilities for which he or she is accountable for achieving specific results.
2. Each manager must have the full support of his or her manager whenever an employee is judged unsatisfactory and must be transferred or terminated.
3. Each manager is expected to develop and maintain a high standard of morale and production. Consequently, he or she must be fully familiar with all company policies and feel they will be supported when they correct for policy and practice infractions as they arise.
4. Each manager is expected to make recommendations concerning subordinate employees. Be clear with them who has the authority to hire, promote, demote, discipline, or terminate any employee under their authority so that there is no confusion.

IMPROVING *YOUR* ACCOUNTABILITY FOR RESULTS

The discipline of personal accountability for results comes down to achieving defined goals within an established time frame through the seven steps identified on pages 156–157.

Step 3 of *B-CPR* involves monitoring the *actual* performance being achieved compared with *planned* performance through both leading and lagging metrics. The difference between actual and planned results is measured, and the causes contributing to these differences are identified. This allows corrective actions to take place sooner rather than later to eliminate or minimize the difference in results.

Neglect or unskilled handling of your profit plan variances will inevitably result in you losing control over your business. Every business will either move forward or regress as results change. Failure to monitor actions and measure results through each day, week, month, quarter, and year results in losing control over your business and your future. *Failure to act* is the number one cause of business cardiac arrest. Ultimately, this is the purpose of Step 5— Be Accountable for *Your* Results.

If you desire to be a more effective manager, particularly of your people assets, then become more skilled in the following twelve practices of highly effective managers. Each skill area has a direct impact on the efficiency, effectiveness, and quality of the work performed.

Management skills one through four provide the mechanics for establishing objectives and standards.

1. *Gather Information:* Information gathering occurs when managers speak with people and read reports, mail, and other publications. It occurs more formally whenever a manager purposefully seeks to collect data pertinent to a problem with which he or she is concerned. Information gathering is an essential preliminary step to making informed decisions that lead to intelligent actions.

2. *Synthesize Information Gathered:* When enough information has been collected and deemed sufficient to support quality decision-making, managers must use the best available information to form an honest picture or judgment of the situation and use it as the basis for taking action.

3. *Create a Plan:* As each situation is considered, the objectives to be attained are thought through and the critical actions identified. Possible alternatives and courses of action are defined and weighed so that the best path forward, and its associated actions can be determined.

4. *Make an Informed Decision:* Weigh your options, then make a choice. Your informed decision is the result of having thoroughly completed these first three steps. Your informed decision means selecting the particular course of action that seems to offer the best likelihood of meeting the planned objective or solving the specific problem.

Failing to decide or act is still a decision. While people often delay acting as they wait for more information to come in before making a decision, this is frequently a mask to hide behind. And it is often the worst action to take because it paralyzes everyone on the team and prevents them from moving ahead. Even a bad decision is sometimes better than no-decision.

The good news is once the decision has been made, and you see things begin to go the wrong way, you can quickly admit the error and take corrective action. In contrast, the "no decision" alternative means you and your team are "stalled" in place, resulting in a traffic pile-up effectively blocking the path to your desired destination.

Management skills five through nine are the action steps of management, ensuring that work gets done as planned.

5. *Organize Your Resources:* This step consists of determining the people, money, and equipment that will be required to accomplish your objectives. Once these resources are determined, your team must be assigned to the task at hand. Then the effective manager organizes the activity or project so that the objectives are accomplished through the targeted efforts of the people he or she manages. The manager decides who is to complete each phase of the required work. The goal is to maximize these resources with efficiency and within the allotted amount of time, or even better, in the shortest amount of time possible.

6. *Communicate Clearly:* The manager directs their subordinates in what to do and in what sequence. He or she explains the objective and describes the actions necessary to realize the objective. They make sure that everyone understands the work that has been assigned to each of them individually. Directions are typically put in writing to ensure that the message is both understood and preserved so that the quality of employee performance can later be evaluated.

Clear communication is a must to maximize the value of your invested resources. It only happens after the manager is sure that there is a complete understanding by those being communicated with what is to be done, how it is to be done, and who is to complete each part of the task, even if gaining this understanding requires repetition. Failure to put directions in writing is frequently the single greatest reason tasks are not completed correctly or on time.

Don't forget the written instrument. People that are verbally told will often forget what was decided, assume that no decision was made, or think that a different decision was made. If an employee does not understand his or her assignment, then it is the manager's fault, and the manager, not the employee, must accept responsibility. This is because we can only reliably change our behavior; we can't change the behavior of others. So if you want a different result, then you need to change your behavior by putting it in writing to obtain the desired result.

7. *Encourage:* A manager cannot motivate people; he or she can only create an environment in which the team will be inspired to do what needs to be done. The understanding of "why" by everyone involved is necessary to gain "buy-in," skillfully. If each member of your team, individually, can identify himself or herself with the "why" of the project, you will see an increased desire to contribute to the project's success.

When encouraging people, the two most commonly used terms are the "carrot" and the "stick." Be careful in your use of these "motivating tools;" they cause severe problems within an organization when mishandled. The better approach is to emulate what drives an athlete to the point of perfection, almost beyond their natural ability. This motivation comes from the gut: it's the personal pride of accomplishment.

8. *Direct, Guide, and Counsel:* This step is concerned with the "how" stage or "doing the work." It consists of guiding progress via instructions, suggestions, and providing additional data. Occasionally, this step involves teaching your team, precisely how the defined objective can be accomplished more efficiently.

   The best managers ensure that each person under their direction knows what is expected of them, how their assignment fits into the whole operation, and how their performance will be measured. Each team member has a set of specified goals that he or she is expected to accomplish within a specific time frame so that there is no misunderstanding about what they are supposed to do. Actual performance compared against expected performance is how the manager and they're subordinate know the difference between exceeds, achieves, and does not meet.

9. *Measure, Evaluate, and Control:* Performance measurement is necessary to determine the effectiveness with which the planned work is being carried out. Through performance measurement, managers discover any impediments to progress. This discovery process creates information that is understood by the team—seeing how actual results compare to plan is how individual and team performance adjustments are made.

Management skills ten and eleven ensure the future success of your company.

10. *Develop Your People, Individually, and as a Team:* The responsibility of every manager is to develop through training. A Manager is no stronger than the weakest person on his or her team. A manager's results are obtained by effectively directing the work of others. It necessarily follows that if subordinates are adequately qualified, through proper development, the results obtained by the manager's efforts will continuously improve. The manager must

encourage the development of his or her successor so that when they need to move, there will be a qualified replacement to step in and continue the work.

11. *Promote Innovation:* The manager must be a steady force supporting innovation. If the manager wants the business to progress forward, he or she must never permit anyone on the team to become satisfied with "the way things are." Managers must always strive to stimulate subordinates to seek better ways of doing their jobs.

    The constant search for continuous improvement should influence every phase of the management cycle. The best managers continuously encourage their people to express themselves and then listen to their team's ideas with an open mind. Encourage your staff when faced with a problem, to come up with three to five solutions, then ask them to recommend which solution they think is best, with an explanation of why they would choose this solution.

Management skill twelve reinforces what works, so it keeps on working at its best.

12. *Recognize and Reward Results, not Efforts:* This step is about more than encouraging. In any competitive environment, "trying hard" is not enough. Achieving results is what counts, and it's often the difference between winning and losing. Results will always be the final judge. When any behavior, task, or particular performance is repeated at or above standard, you must recognize, praise, and reward the performance.

    If you can't recall recognizing or rewarding an employee for favorable results, then either you are failing in the first eleven management practices, or you may need to end the employment relationship with the marginal or poor performer. The most effective form of recognition is done in public. Make it public to reinforce the positive practice to the individual and others on the team. Most people want to do a good job, and they like to be recognized for doing so. Public recognition and praise are the most economical tools used to encourage employees to be their best; all it takes is awareness and a little extra time.

If you aren't comfortable recognizing or rewarding an employee, you can at least stop tolerating marginal performers. The most frequent and insidious personnel mistake managers make is to live too long with marginal or poor performers. The best managers are tough-minded yet fair and objective in all performance evaluations. They are unemotional in their decisions regarding who is performing and who is not. Finally, the best managers are eminently fair and decisive in the way they carry out these vital people decisions.

It's essential to follow through on these twelve practices for establishing objectives and standards and then ensure that the designated work is completed as planned. On the other hand, any failure to being an effective manager will lead your business to experience restricted cash flow and poor profit performance. Ultimately, failure to follow through hinders your ability to ensure the future success of your company and will result in your business failing. The bottom line is that you will never obtain the profits you need to keep your business alive or fund your lifestyle if you and the managers who work for you aren't accountable for their results.

COMMIT TODAY TO BE ACCOUNTABLE FOR *YOUR* RESULTS

The management principles, practices, and processes outlined in this chapter are closely followed by those who consistently hold themselves accountable for results. I invite you to reflect on your personal strengths and weaknesses. Through honest reflection, consider your own role in the business you own. Where would you like to play more to your strengths? Or if you play a management role, how you would like your senior manager to help you improve? Once you gain clarity, consider sharing your personal development plan with your manager or your significant other.

Your goal through this exercise is to achieve confirmation in the following areas:

1. Become clearer on what areas of personal effectiveness you want to build on.
2. Determine what you want to experience more of and where you want to change and/or improve to experience better results.
3. Recognize where you need help and what you believe you can achieve through your personal self-development efforts.
4. Invite your manager to help you play to your strengths while helping you shore up where you have room for growth in order to be more effective.

Use the following exercise or one of your own choosing to help you address these areas of development as you continue your journey to becoming more accountable for your results.

HOW I SEE MYSELF BECOMING A MORE ACCOUNTABLE PERSON

1. Go back to pages 156-158 and identify which out of the ten qualities and ten critical success factors considered common among accountable people is your greatest source of strength and which area you would like to improve on.

My Source of Greatest Strength	My Area to Improve

2. Do I feel that the required authority and responsibility for being accountable for my results have been extended to me? _____ Yes or _____ No; What circumstances lead you to feel this way?

3. On pages 160-165 involving the twelve principles for improving your personal accountability effectiveness, where do you see yourself being in a position to coach others? And where would you like to receive coaching?

I Definitely Could Coach Others At	I Would Like Help Getting Better At

4. Now confirm what area of strength you want to build on and what area you want to change and improve so that you can experience better results.

My Strength to Build On	My Skill to Further Develop

5. What are you going to do differently today to help you become a more accountable person?

6. How can your manager help you follow through on your desired change?

7. Communicate your personal development plan to your superior: "I will share my responses from this exercise with my manager by _____."

CONCLUDING THE IMPORTANCE OF STEP 5—
BE ACCOUNTABLE FOR *YOUR* RESULTS

The step that holds the *B-CPR* system together is Step 5—Be Accountable for *Your* Results. Without deliberate action on the critical few things needing to get done, you will never produce your desired results.

Knowing what to act on to get the planned results is identified through each of the first four steps of the *B-CPR* system shared in order of importance to the survival of your business. If you can't identify the new actions needed, then *start, change,* or *stop* something you're already doing in order to produce superior profits and protect cash flow. If you don't like feeling out of control—or worse yet, you are running out of cash—then follow-through on the action(s) you *must* take through the other four steps. It's up to you to decide *which B-CPR* step is the essential step for you to take today to avoid business cardiac arrest.

AUTHOR'S SIDE NOTE—HOW THE GAME OF BUSINESS
IS MORE CHALLENGING THAN A ROUND OF GOLF

In my view, the greatest game played around the world is the game of business. It's exciting to see business owners put themselves out there every day. I love studying the different ways in which business owners play their game of business, taking the required actions their businesses need them to deliver on. Yet, ultimately, they are all playing the *same* game of business involving *sales, gross profit, operating income,* and *net profit.*

At its core, all business comes down to satisfying customer needs or wants at a profit. Many business owners play this game at a high level, while a significant number of others are struggling because they fail to master the basic elements of the game of business. I liken mastering the basics in the "game of business" to mastering the basics in the "game of golf." Some golfers learn to shoot low rounds and come in winners. In comparison, most golfers never master the basics at all; they simply grow frustrated with the game and give up.

There's an old saying that "business is like golf—you have to play it as it lays." Playing a golf ball well where it lays begins with mastering your swing over many years of practice and play, continuously refining how you approach each shot.

In golf, you have to pull everything together at the same time—your ball's lie, its target, club selection, posture, the strength of your swing, distance, wind, and so forth to produce the desired outcome.

The only way to excel at golf is to hit a lot of golf balls with different clubs and taking a variety of shots. You have to hit thousands of balls over and over until you build muscle memory through your hands, arms, back, and legs. And then you have to do it over and over to maintain that muscle memory. Most of us don't commit at this level, and that is why, despite all of the technology and equipment advancements in golf, the average score for even the best-equipped golfer never drops below a certain level.

I find it interesting that golf is a linear game, involving eighteen holes, played independently in sequence. And each golf hole has some mix of the following elements:

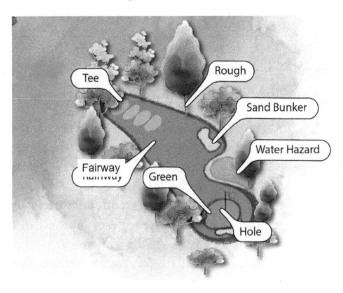

The only thing that you do consistently from the first hole to the second and on through a round of golf is to carry your score for that hole forward. As you move through the course, what you scored on the previous hole no longer matters; your only concern is how you are going to perform on the current hole. The score you earned on the hole you have just completed is the score you will carry with you to the next hole. You might get lucky and shoot a hole-in-one on hole eight, but that doesn't matter on hole nine.

A round of golf is the *cumulative score* of the eighteen individual holes, each played consecutively. If you think about the game of golf in business terms, it might resemble the following:

Mission	Play eighteen holes in the fewest number of strokes.
Vision	A mental picture of the mission successfully being accomplished.
Objectives	Eighteen of them ranging from Par 3 through Par 5.
Strategy	Each hole requires its own strategic plan for attacking the hole.
Tactics	Execution specific to the variables required to play the shot.
Scorecard	Where the golfer records their score for each hole.
Golf Score	Represents the score shot in total from a round of golf.

Nevertheless, there is a difference between playing the game of golf and the game of business. In the game of business, you are required to play the equivalent of all eighteen holes at once! Plus your game of business involves multiple forces in simultaneous play amid fluid objectives, depending on your near, short, and long-term strategic priorities. This is why I consider the game of business to be the best game I've ever played. Every day, it's as if you are standing in the middle of the following golf course, having to play every hole at the same time:

In golf, fortunately, you *do* have the luxury of playing one hole at a time. Unfortunately, in business, you are constantly bouncing from decision to decision and action to action, never getting the chance to play a true linear game.

And this is why Step 5—Be Accountable for *Your* Results is so important. You rarely get to see an action through from tee-shot to picking the ball up out of the cup to recording your score for that hole. You constantly have to go backward to advance an action, then move on to another action before either action is fully seen to completion. This is why business owners who want to master the game of business must become masters of follow-through. And they must hold themselves accountable for completing necessary actions, because without a completed action, they can't create their desired results.

My hope is that you will slow down and take a measured approach. I hope you will methodically build the muscle memory you need to play the game of business and play it well. I hope you'll follow the proven system I've laid out to begin managing your cash and planning and executing for higher profits with the help of accurate, plus timely reports. Ultimately, I hope your score at the end of a week, a month, a quarter, and a year, exceeds your expectations.

Turn the page to see all of the key principles taught through *B-CPR* pulled together for your immediate use, beginning today.

8

PULLING IT ALL TOGETHER—HOW EACH *B-CPR* STEP IS ESSENTIAL TO *YOUR* BUSINESS SUCCESS

If you accept that in business, Control = Income and Actions = Results, then it follows that having *control* over your *actions* is the key to realizing your desired results. You also know you won't have real control over your actions unless you can start, change, or stop whatever you and your employees are doing whenever you are dissatisfied with your results.

I recently resumed work with one of the smartest clients I had ever worked with back in 2017 that owns a demolition company. Since I had worked with them they had been awarded some impressive work that was projected to continue into 2020. We resumed working together because ownership was feeling overextended. What I quickly confirmed as we started out was how they had entered the "perfect storm" in their business that was about to get much worse.

Their problems began to multiply when the Army Corps of Engineers suspended work on an army hospital demolition project in the fall of 2018. They had already done most of the prep work for tearing down the old hospital when the Army Corps of Engineers decided they didn't want to spend the extra $11 million dollars required for asbestos removal. They preferred to "kick the can" down the road and let someone else deal with this environmental issue. So the Corps mothballed the entire hospital, rather than proceeding to finish the project.

The reason for the higher-than-expected asbestos abatement costs stemmed from its 1950s architecture. To ensure that the buildings many windows were properly insulated, each concrete block-encased window had been wrapped thoroughly in asbestos. In terms of its demolition, this meant that every window had to be taken out by hand and the asbestos removed before the excavators could make quick work of the remainder of the building. Due to the Army Corps' decision, this five-story, sixty-year-old hospital now sits, rotting away.

This abrupt contract termination by the government meant that my client had to idle their site management, key operators, and laborers needed on their next major projects. The problem was these upcoming projects weren't set to begin for another six months. This resulted in them burning through their cash reserves holding onto needed talent faster than they fully grasped.

The next bombshell was that the large demolition project their new Hawaii division was supposed to land never materialized. Apparently, that division's manager had overpromised and under-delivered. In coming in to assess this operation, we quickly learned that this division manager saw his operation primarily as a labor company, not an equipment-driven demolition company.

His goal was to keep his "buddies" in the labor union busy, so he lined up a number of small low-priced jobs so they had ongoing work. Before my client knew it, their new Hawaii operations had burned through a million dollars in cash, acquiring assets for work that never came. Couple the Hawaiian losses early in 2019 with the never-ending jobsite issues at a state transportation job on the East Coast, and a slowdown on a federal job on the West Coast things became dire. By May of 2019, my client was hemorrhaging cash as if an artery had been cut. Running through cash at this pace put them into business cardiac arrest.

The first thing we did was to cut office staff immediately, reducing cash outflows for office payroll. Next, we took a close look to see if there were any profits to be generated by the Hawaiian division in the near-term. When it was confirmed that the balance of 2019 was not looking any better than the beginning, we immediately suspended operations there in order to stop uncontrolled cash outflows.

As the company's president began selling the underutilized Hawaiian assets to free up cash, its owner focused on stopping the bleeding on the East Coast. Another issue with the state transportation project was its degree of difficulty. The bridge demo happened to be right over an environmentally protected marsh. Its proximity to sensitive wetlands required the capture of all concrete slurry and debris as each span of the bridge was removed. Unfortunately, my client's site team got off to a slow start due to a high number of petty issues triggered by the State Department of Transportation. These issues were further complicated by the general contractor on-site.

Because they didn't have a well thought-out demo plan going in they kept encountering issues that should have been thought through before beginning the job. As a result, they never worked the job as estimated. This led them to absorbing higher costs while simultaneously generating lower revenue than expected. While the owner worked to get things back on track on the East Coast, he failed to pick up that the team running the West Coast aerospace building demolition project had slowed its work pace. They had slowed the work because they weren't clear on their next job assignment so they weren't in any hurry to finish this project. Unfortunately for the client this led to direct costs exceeding sales on both coasts.

Let's look at a couple of areas where we might find fixes: First, my client was not using accurate and timely reports that provided insight into how the work was being done in their three large jobsites: Hawaii, California, and North Carolina. They were overtrusting in their people on-site, and they were failing to verify the quality of their results. Before they knew it, they'd burned through their sizeable cash reserves, because they did not have sufficient profit *quality* in their cash. They were, in essence, trading four quarters for three quarters and a nickel.

Failure to confirm the quality of their profits hindered their ability to recognize where the most pressing issues lay. They had at least one manager who was clearly in over his head and two others who were mismanaging their accountabilities. To make matters worse, when confronted with the facts and shown their actual results, these managers were quick with excuses. The hard reality is that it's never helpful to blame others and avoid taking personal ownership of the profit losses occurring in one's respective area of accountability.

Using the power of *B-CPR,* this client *stopped* their profit losses, *increased* their cash velocity, and *improved* their profit quality. Today, their demo business is stable, yet it remains at high risk because the company still has a ways to go in digging itself out of the hole that snuck up on them. The key to this business's survival is the owner's high degree of resolve and that of his president to fix their profit losses by changing how they manage their business. Today, they are more vigilant in managing their cash flow velocity and more comfortable using daily, weekly, and monthly reports to confirm the quality of their results across their various jobsites.

EMBRACE THE BEST WAY TO GAIN AND MAINTAIN CONTROL OVER *YOUR* BUSINESS

If you can't identify the right actions needed to produce higher profits and protect cash flow, then you need to identify what you must *start, change,* and *stop* or you will never have the desired profits and cash flow. If you don't like feeling out of control—or worse, you're running out of cash—the best thing to do is build up your cash reserves through disciplined actions easily identified through the following five-step model:

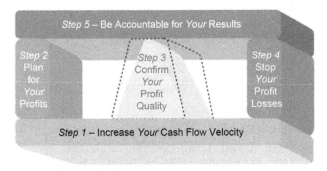

The goal of this proven system for controlling your business is grounded in its strategic intent. It's essential to position your management structure like a solid roof *over* your business. This is the only way to ensure that your business does what *you* want it to do. Below is a high-level overview that pulls *B-CPR* together by step offering a succinct breakdown of its most foundational components:

HOW YOU GAIN CONTROL OVER YOUR BUSINESS IN FIVE "MUST DO" STEPS...

Step 1	*Step* 2	*Step* 3	*Step* 4	*Step* 5
Cash = C	Profit = P	Reporting = R	Control = Income	Actions = Results
Manage *Your* Weekly Cash Velocity	Build *Your* Twenty-Four-Month Profit Plan	Confirm the Quality of *Your* Profits	Stop the Losses that Keeps *Your* Business at Risk	Be Accountable for *Your* Results

WHAT IS THE OUTPUT OF EACH STEP THAT MUST BE DONE...

Project *Your* Weekly Cash Flow	Realize *Your* Monthly Profit Plan Targets	Use *Your* Weekly KPIs + Monthly Variance Reports	Stop *Your* Most Costly Profit Losses	Control *Your* Business to Get *Your* Results

WHY EACH STEP MUST BE DONE...

Protect *Your* Cash Outflows From Ever Exceeding *Your* Cash Inflows	Know Whether *Your* Actions Hit or Missed *Your* Profit Plan Targets	Know Where You are Winning and Losing Through *Your* Measures of Success	Stop Wasting *Your* Cash That Drains *Your* Bank Account and Costs You Profit Dollars	Complete *Your* Critical Few Actions By Not Getting Distracted by *Your* Relevant Many To Do's

WHEN EACH STEP MUST BE DONE THROUGHOUT THE YEAR...

Every Monday Establish *Your* Cash Projections For the Next Four Weeks	Ideally in Month Eleven For Next Year Or This Week If It Doesn't Exist	Distribute *Your* Results the Day Before Each Management Meeting	Quantified and Prioritized Based on *Your* Most Costly Metric Misses	*Your* Daily Actions Shaped by *Your* Profit Plan Desired Results

Fundamentally, *B-CPR* is a management process designed to help you run a more profitable business, according to proven principles, brought together in five easy-to-follow steps. As established, the keys to protecting your business from suffering the effects of business cardiac arrest start and end with avoiding failures in **c**ash management, **p**rofit generation, and basic management **r**eporting.

An effective way to appreciate the importance of each *B-CPR* step to your business success is to look at the consequences that arise when that step is *missing*. Below is a high-level review of "what gets lost" when a *B-CPR* step is *skipped, missed,* or *fails in its execution*.

> Step 1 – Increase *Your* Operating Cash Flow Velocity

Anytime you fail to do Step 1—Increase *Your* Operating Cash Flow Velocity, you are at increased risk of *cash outflows* exceeding *cash inflows*. Allowing this to happen means you will go out-of-business whenever there is insufficient cash available to operate your business. Always remember, the velocity of your cash flow from operations sets the pace (pulse) for your business.

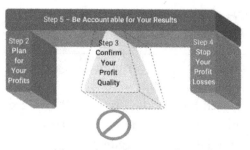

Forecasting your weekly cash inflows and outflows protects your business through this first *B-CPR* step. Consistent action applied here allows you to recognize and stop unnecessary cash outflows currently depleting your cash reserves.

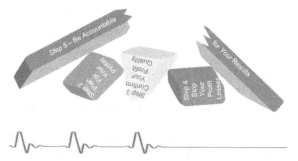

When cash outflows exceed cash inflows, you are in cardiac arrest, because you are out of cash to fund your operations. The five most significant complications from cash outflows exceeding cash inflows are listed below:

1. The owner is continually *seeking* cash versus *controlling* cash and, as a result, has no cash reliably on hand.
2. A/R aging is more heavily weighted on the greater-than-sixty-days past due than on current receivables.
3. Calls from vendors looking for their money inevitably increase in frequency and hostility.
4. The business begins "borrowing from Peter to pay Paul" and, as a result, has zero cash reserves. Every dollar coming in is going out to pay others, usually the same day.
5. The owner sees an increasing amount paid in NSF bank fees, because they fail to understand how to manage their business through accurate and timely management reporting.

The "C" in *B-CPR* stands for Cash. Always protect your cash by building cash reserves through weekly management of cash inflows so that they never exceed cash outflows. By projecting your cash position every Monday afternoon for at least the next four weeks, you can determine where immediate action needs to be taken. Your primary action from Step 1 is to increase your cash velocity by collecting on the monies owed to you for the work you have performed *when* the money is due to you.

Anytime you fail to do Step 2—Plan for *Your* Profits, you have *no* guide to help you make decisions nor a clear line of sight to what *is* and what isn't important.

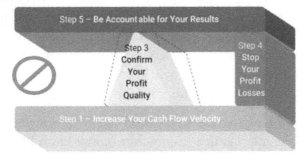

Your profit plan sets the direction for your business. Here is where you define your targets to be realized by month and year for net sales, gross profit, operating income, and net income.

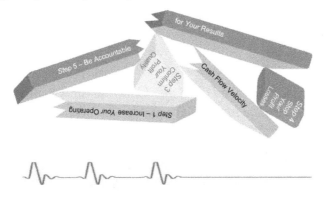

Without a profit plan, *your* decision quality is always at risk, because it isn't framed in by what success and failure look like. This exposes your business to the following cardiac arrest risks:

1. The overwhelmed owner is always fighting daily fires because they lack a well-developed profit plan that prevents them from decisively executing their monthly money-making plan.
2. Low probability of being awarded higher cash quality sales, because your sales efforts aren't targeted where you have the best chance to make the most money.
3. There are no monthly targets to be realized. As a result, you and those in your employ never know whether you are accomplishing your goals or not.
4. You have poor cash quality because you aren't efficient in your material purchases and direct labor management, because no one is clear on *who* is accountable for *what*.
5. Your business is worth less today than it was last year or the year before, because there is no plan stating what you plan to do differently to improve the coming year's results.

The "P" in *B-CPR* stands for Profits. The remedy to any of the above cardiac arrest risks lies in a twenty-four-month Profit Plan that sets clear targets and guides wise decision-making. This includes committing to the necessary actions that will help you to realize the plan. Ideally, your Profit Plan is put in place the month before the start of your next year or this week if it doesn't exist for the next month.

Anytime you fail to do Step 3—Confirm the Quality of *Your* Profits, you have *no* line of sight to what *is* and what *isn't* working as planned in your business. Your profit plan is only as good as the quality of the actual profits being produced each month. In the illustration reflected above, the dotted line represents what you spent; the solid triangle represents what you had *planned* to spend with the difference between the two representing the profit you failed to generate.

Confirming the quality of your actual month-to-month gross and operating profits against your planned sales and profits is the only way to know where you are tracking better than planned. Knowing this information allows you to confidently focus on fixing the areas that are worse than the plan.

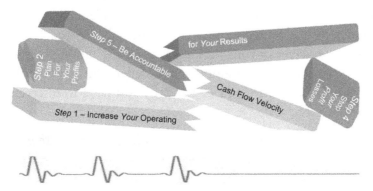

Similar to the importance of consistently monitoring your pulse and blood pressure in your quest for heart health, failure to monitor your profit quality prevents you from recognizing what you need to start, change, or be stop before your business suffers full-blown cardiac arrest. Below are some of the consequences to your business that result from not confirming your profit quality on a monthly basis:

1. Lack of timely financial reporting means you never know for sure if you are winning or losing in your game of business.

2. COGS and SG&A expenses are growing faster than sales, because there is no budget with which to manage them and no variance report to monitor their trending.
3. The business owner is likely working harder today than ever before while paying themselves less because cash quality (profits) is not being produced.
4. Employees are increasingly frustrated, because management is more worried about money than about their well-being or their productivity.
5. Odds are near 100 percent that failing to use financial reporting to confirm the quality of your profits means you won't have control of your cash (Step 1) or a well-developed profit plan (Step 2) to manage your business.

The "R" in *B-CPR* is for Reporting. Avoiding the above business risks starts with *your* Weekly KPIs and Monthly Variance Reports. Monitoring these reports ensures that your planned actions are producing your desired results. This is the only way to know, with confidence, *where* in your business you are performing better and worse than planned. Without this knowledge, you will never know with confidence *where* and *how quickly* you need to intervene to stop your profit losses.

Anytime you fail to do Step 4—Stop *Your* Profit Losses, you place *your* business at risk through costly profit losses as you run out of cash from operating your business at a loss.

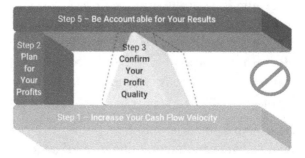

No matter how thoughtfully it is constructed, no plan is perfect, because the people executing it are human. You can compensate for human mistakes by decisively attacking your most unwanted profit losses. Failure to stop your biggest profit losses keeps your business at risk, and it's the leading contributor to coming up short of your profit plan targets.

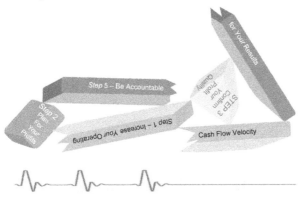

Slow cash flow from operations at low gross and operating margins puts you at immediate risk of cardiac arrest as seen in the following negative scenarios:

1. You'll have less money today for the bills you're already past due in paying.
2. You'll waste too much time trying to collect monies owed to you while holding off those to whom you owe money.
3. You'll see sales are suffering, because it's hard to source materials and keep up with COGS and SG&A expenses.
4. Your employee's uncertainty is high with no one taking any initiative to improve results.
5. Your equity as a business owner is diminishing, because losses from the P&L Statement are transferring to the Balance Sheet.

As you can see, these are problems related to cash flow. You can be certain that there will *never* be enough cash from profits whenever there are profit losses. There is no "C" or "P" in CPR if there are losses, unless you find a way to stop these unwanted cash drains.

Protect yourself from running your business out of cash by acting on the quantified leading and lagging metric "misses" that are most impacting your cash quality (heart rate) and cash velocity (pulse). Taking these actions ensures that your business is making the money it should as confirmed by the weekly cash on hand (Step 1) and monthly change in profit levels (Step 3).

Anytime you fail to complete Step 5—Be Accountable for *Your* Results, you rob yourself of the ability to control the actions of *your* business. You also disrupt any rhythm you are building through Steps 1 through 4 in an effort to realize your desired results set in Step 2.

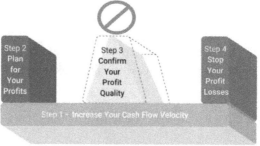

Prioritizing and eliminating activity based on what needs to be capitalized on or fixed in your business is an essential step. But it requires a disciplined follow-through to achieve your desired cash position from your growing business profitability.

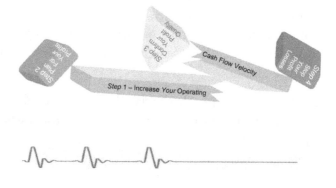

Without action on the "critical few" things needing to be completed each week, you will end up wasting time and money on the "relevant many" things that are easy to do but can and should be ignored for the moment. Lack of priority focus is a quick way to begin feeling the following business cardiac arrest effects:

1. Stuff happens, but no one is sure if it's the *right* stuff to do, because there is no monitoring of actual performance results through recognized metrics.

2. No one is clear on *who* is accountable for *what* nor are they clear on what's expected of them in their individual roles.

3. Employees are more worried about whether their payroll checks will clear than they are about producing quality output and efficiently serving customers.

4. Any work getting done is the result of efforts by the critical few in your employ; the rest of your employees have given up or checked out.

5. The above four conditions result in the *owner* either checking out or doing even more work for little to no pay. There is no organized, consistent process for effectively managing others in an effort to maximize profits.

When you are stressed about cash or worried about profits, you know with 100 percent certainty that the *right* actions have not been taken. You know this definitively based on the poor results produced. Every time you are left with less cash and smaller profits at the end of a month, quarter, or year, you know your actions—even if they involved a lot of hard work—weren't what they needed to be.

The best way to realize your monthly sales and profit goals, identified in Step 2, is through disciplined action *every day*. The key is to focus on the "critical few," not the "relevant many" things needing to get done. *Prioritize* your weekly actions according to Step 1—Cash Velocity, Step 3—Cash Quality, and Step 4—Stop the Losses. These three steps of the *B-CPR* model combine to help ensure that your planned actions are producing your desired results.

CONCLUDING THE IMPORTANCE OF EACH
B-CPR STEP TO *YOUR* BUSINESS SUCCESS

Never lose sight of the following essential truth in business:

> The true lost income of any business is not the actual money lost but the difference between the money made and the money that should have made but wasn't.

Disciplined use of the *B-CPR* management process will protect your business from failing, and it's the surest way to realize your sales, profit, and wealth creation goals. Cash flow from your operations sets the foundation for the business you are building, while your profit plan provides your monthly and annual targets.

Your profit plan is only as good as the accurate and timely monitoring of your *actual* results against your *planned* results throughout any given time period. This is the *only* way to know *where* your business is comfortably exceeding your expectations so that you can fix any areas in which your business is performing less optimally.

As stated previously, no plan is perfect, because the people executing it will never perform perfectly 100 percent of the time. You compensate for human imperfection by decisively attacking unwanted cash drains and profit losses. Failure to stop your most costly profit losses is the difference between ending the year in a better position than you had planned or coming up short of your profit plan targets. Come up short and you will have less money in the bank than you expected.

Remember, no plan will be successful if there isn't enough *cash available* to operate your business. Always protect your business by protecting your cash—the lifeblood of any business—first through forecasting weekly cash *inflows* and *outflows*, and second, by stopping unnecessary cash outflows that drain cash reserves and contribute to profit leakage. You must follow through on these actions month-to-month in order to achieve your annual business goals and objectives. As you prioritize and eliminate unnecessary activity through disciplined follow-through, you will experience better results and work fewer hours.

AUTHOR'S SIDE NOTE—THE *B-CPR* MANAGEMENT PROCESS INCLUDES AN OPTION TO USE AN ONLINE TOOL TO HELP YOU WORK THROUGH EACH STEP IN THE MODEL

An accompanying tool to help you realize the multiple benefits provided by the consistent application of the *B-CPR* management process is available at www.mybpisite.com. This exclusive "business planning and intelligence" tool has been designed to fill a void in reporting cash and profits—one that QuickBooks, Sage, and other accounting software packages fail to address. It has the ability to easily produce *actionable management reports* that shed light on *where* your business is performing as you intend it to and *where* it isn't.

The good news is that *every* accounting software system is designed to account for all of your different business transactions throughout the year and assist your accountant in efficiently filing your taxes. The problem is that *none* of these popular accounting systems are intended to be used as management tools to help you plan, organize, lead, and manage your business more efficiently.

Over the years, I have redesigned and restructured my clients' charts of accounts (COAs) to allow their accounting software to provide more accurate managerial reports. I have made this effort, because it's critical to show my clients precisely *where* they are making money and *where* their business profits are turning into losses. My goal was to provide these individuals with a P&L Statement that accurately reflects their true COGS and SG&A expenses. Only with accurate information can they identify, with confidence, their true gross profit and operating income.

I have also learned that while fixing the COAs helped, it was never enough to produce the desired managerial reporting structure my clients needed to more efficiently and effectively manage their businesses. My goal then became the creation of a system that worked efficiently for everyone who desires to see higher profits and more cash in the bank this year.

It's important to know that the *B-CPR* tool does not *replace* your existing accounting software. You still need whatever accounting software system you are currently using to record your business transactions. What you will begin to do, going forward, is to update the *B-CPR* online tool each month with the numbers drawn from your P&L Statement and Balance Sheet. The *B-CPR* management process only requires that you load these numbers into the BPI Management Tool. Then you will have readily available, current management reports that enable you to confirm how you are doing across your business.

Within Appendix A, you will find the exact series of steps that the *Business Planning and Intelligence (BPI) Management Tool* follows to help you gain control of your business. Your work with this tool will provide you with management control that is not available in any existing accounting software program. Your use of this tool will guide you in easily producing the critical information your business needs, even if you do not currently have an accurate chart of account.

CONCLUSION

Before I end this book, let me share with you the key paragraph from my first book, *Owning a GREAT Business*, found at the top of page 18.

> Once you know *who* your customer is, *what* problem they are trying to solve, *when* they are most likely to need your help, and *where* they will want to transact business; you can define *why* and *how* they should value what you are offering, at a profitable price point. While this concept may seem simple on the surface, it amazes me how many business leaders fail to grasp these business fundamentals clearly, and

apply them to the small to large decisions they
make every day.

Since writing this book, I've realized through my continued business studies that before you can confidently apply the 7-P Framework to your business, you need to effectively manage the relationship between your **c**ash flow and **p**rofits through your business **r**esults **r**eporting.

The goal of this book is straightforward: to present an easy-to-apply five-step management system to mastering the relationship of cash to profits through your business's financial reports. Understanding this relationship with confidence is the best way to avoid business cardiac arrest. Hopefully, you have found the content in this book helpful to seeing how *you* can easily apply the five steps to *B-CPR* to revive *your* business should you need it as well as to help you achieve greater levels of financial success.

Adoption of this proven system for controlling YOUR business so it does what YOU want it to do will help you continuously improve the value of your business. Simply knowing the relationship of cash to profits through understanding your financial reports will keep you from ever asking why your bank balance is different from your reported profits on your P&L Statement. The long-term viability of your business is dependent on the consistent application of the principles of *B-CPR* as long as your goal is to have a profitable business with a predictable cash flow.

Never lose sight of the simple truth that Step 5—Be Accountable for *Your* Results is the *B-CPR* step that will most effectively help you to avoid business cardiac arrest altogether. Without deliberate action on the critical few things needing to be done, you will never produce your desired results. Every business starts with cash, which is invested in various ways to generate revenue. Ultimately, the revenue is turned back into cash, and the cycle begins anew.

Each completed business transaction produces data that forms the financial reports used by your accountant to calculate your financial position for tax liability purposes. Those who choose to play the game of business to win recognize that these *same* financial reports can be used for so much more. They know that to win in the game of business, they must use their financial data to help build and maintain positive operating cash flows and a sustainable net income.

Playing the game of business to win starts with knowing the core elements of the game and how well you score on the quality of your play. Without this understanding, it's hard to know, with certainty, the next smart move to make in your business. Your financial statements give you everything you need to play your game of business smarter today than you ever have before. The key is to recognize *what* to act on to achieve your planned results. Follow the *B-CPR* system through each of these first four clearly determined steps given in order of importance to the survival of your business.

Step 1—Increase the velocity of *your* operating cash flow today in order to fund your way into next week.

Step 2—Build *your* twenty-four-month profit plan to set your direction and guide your decisions.

Step 3—Confirm the quality of *your* profits to identify what you need to start, change, or stop, in your business.

Step 4—Stop the losses that keep *your* business at risk; begin by quantifying your losses so you can easily prioritize which issues to fix first.

Business CPR not only protects your business from failing; it's the surest way to realize your sales, profit, and wealth creation goals. As I have said multiple times throughout this book, if you can't identify the actions you need to start, change, or stop to produce superior profits and protect cash flow, then you won't have control over your business. If you don't like feeling out of control—or worse, you're running out of cash—then take action through this five-step system to avoiding business cardiac arrest.

Thank you for investing your time to read this book. I hope that you have found the thoughts, observations, insights, and simplicity of ideas helpful. My contact information is listed below. Feel free to share your stories on how this book has helped you or ask me any questions. I'm happy to help as part of your success team.

To your continuously improving profits and cash flow,
Lorin Young
lyoung@keystonetoprofits.com

APPENDIX A

STEP-BY-STEP GUIDE TO THE *B-CPR* MANAGEMENT SYSTEM.

Below is the step-by-step guide through the *B-CPR* management system that is available at www.mybpisite.com. As you follow through on the actions required at each step, consistent use of this tool will position you to realize better business results. Simultaneously, you will be laying and maintaining a sure foundation for greater success and superior control over your business.

STEP 1—INCREASE THE VELOCITY OF YOUR OPERATING CASH FLOW TODAY

Without cash, you are out of business. This unbreakable rule of any cash management plan, intended to protect you from running out of cash, is pretty simple: cash *outflows* can never be greater than cash *inflows*. Everything your business does depends on having an *available* and *predictable* flow of cash.

The cash management tool included with Step 1 will convert your twelve-month profit plan into fifty-two-week cash management projections once you have built your profit plan. This integrated worksheet will help you confirm whether your cash reserves exceed your week-to-week projections. If yes, you're on track to realize your profit goals. If no, you're likely burning through *more* actual cash than projected. Allowing these missed cash projections to continue will increase your risk of failing to deliver on your profit plan as you face an even greater risk of running out of cash.

STEP 1.1—CONFIRM THE URGENCY OF YOUR CURRENT CASH POSITION TODAY

Before you begin Step 2—Build *Your* Twenty-Four-Month Profit Plan, you first need to confirm your current cash position relative to cash in the bank. Take a close look at your most recent Balance Sheet: What does it say about your accounts receivable, accounts payable, current assets, and current liability values?

Frequency = Revisit every month as part of Step 3—Confirm the Quality of *Your* Profits through the process of assessing your cash velocity.

STEP 1.2–PROJECT YOUR ACCOUNTS RECEIVABLES FOR THE NEXT FOUR TO EIGHT WEEKS

This worksheet auto-reports your projected cash collections through the year based on the sales plan you create in Step 2.3. You can also pull down the A/R aging data from your accounting software into Excel, then copy it into this section of the cash management system for more precise cash inflow projections. I recommend that you try, at a minimum, to be as precise as you can be in projecting your cash inflows for the next four weeks.

Frequency = Update every Monday.

STEP 1.3–PLAN YOUR ACCOUNT PAYABLES BASED ON PROJECTED AVAILABLE CASH

This worksheet reports your projected COGS projections by week, throughout the year, based on the gross profit plan you created in Step 2.4. You can also pull down the A/P aging data from your accounting software into Excel, then copy it into this section of the cash management system for more precise cash outflow projections. I recommend that you try, at a minimum, to be as precise as you can be in projecting your cash outflows for the next four weeks.

Frequency = Update every Monday.

STEP 1.4–PROJECT YOUR ENDING CASH ON HAND, AS A PERCENT OF TARGET

This worksheet brings it all together, beginning with your cash inflow projections from Step 1.2 and your cash outflow projections from Step 1.3. Included below these data are your payroll expenses based on your profit plan and your recurring SG&A expenses from your operating income plan (created in Step 2.5.)

Your next goal is to use this worksheet to dial in your cash forecast for at least the next four weeks. This is the only way to know where you need to make any immediate adjustments based on your projected ending cash balances in the near-term.

Frequency = Review every Monday.

STEP 1.5—CONFIRM WHETHER YOU'RE IMPROVING IN YOUR ABILITY TO PROJECT AND HOLD ONTO CASH

Remember the first law of business: When you're out of cash, you're out of business. The unbreakable rule of any cash management plan, completed in Step 1.4, is to ensure that cash outflows never exceed cash inflows. The specific moments when you're most at risk of violating this rule are more easily seen in a "trend line"—a graphic that shows *up* or *down* movement over time.

Graphing data allows you to quickly see which numbers are trending up or down. Graph direction tracking means that you don't have to "interpret" the future direction of the numbers. This worksheet enables you to monitor your cash projected as well as actual cash inflows and outflows by aligning your profit plan into a week-to-week view. This allows your eye to quickly pick out any pattern inconsistencies in the number sequencing as they appear in the table below your cash management chart.

Frequency = Look at this table weekly to confirm that your cash trend is continuously moving in the right direction throughout the year.

GAME CARDS—KNOW WHAT YOUR FINANCIAL STATEMENTS ARE TELLING YOU

Playing the game of business to *win* starts with two critical factors; everything else is a means to that end:

1. Generate sufficient CASH to survive through the next day, week, month, and year.
2. Produce appropriate PROFITS to make money, so that you earn a return on your Investment.

When you transfer your financial statements into this business control tool, you're creating a *personalized scorecard*, which shows you whether your business is winning, or losing, over its years of operation:

- Remember, your Balance Sheet is your company's personalized health metric.
- Your Income Statement tells you whether the health of your business may be in decline and, if so, precisely what you can do about it.

Your personalized business game cards detail the core elements of the game you're being scored on. Without this understanding, it's hard to know your "next best move (you would only be guessing)."

Each "Monopoly"-like card provides you with a summary explanation of each of the components of your P&L Statement and Balance Sheets, the same numbers that you entered into the data worksheets. On each finance card, you will see actual numbers by year as well as targeted questions that will help you if you get stuck completing your profit planning worksheets.

The plan and projection years will populate after you have completed Step 2—Build *Your* Profit Plan. These cards have been structured to print with "cut marks" so that you can easily work with the individual "cards" to improve your play in the great game of business. See Appendix B to fully appreciate the power available to you through the use of these Game Cards.

Frequency = Each company-specific card is automatically created from your data loading and profit planning outputs. Revisit these cards anytime you have questions on key financial statement terminology using your data.

GAME CARD CHARTS—WHAT ARE YOUR FINANCIAL STATEMENT CATEGORIES TELLING YOU?

To help you realize your cash flow and profit goals, the Game Card Charts provide you an isolated view of your financial statement results by category relative to Net Sales. This view will help you to more clearly understand how well your business is performing and where it specifically needs to improve, based on your actual-to-plan trending.

Use the actual results of your financial position and performance versus plan to identify what company strengths you should be building on and what weaknesses you need to fix, improve, or ignore.

Frequency = Use this step if you are stuck trying to determine the *best* area to fix next.

KEY CHARTS—LOOK FOR PATTERN INCONSISTENCIES AND TREND DIRECTIONS IN YOUR CHARTS

Working with numbers is not intrinsic to the human race. Our ancestors were hunters or gathers who survived by recognizing *patterns* and *trends,* not by working with numbers like accountants and mathematicians.

By learning how to use pattern recognition and trend tracking, you don't have to be an accountant to know when a number is out of sequence or whether the trend is positive or negative. You'll simply "see" it: this pattern recognition occurs when we notice what "stands out" by looking for inconsistencies.

Aligning month-to-month next to each other and year-to-year on top of each other allows your eye to quickly pick up any patterns of inconsistency in number sequencing. Try using pattern recognition in Steps 2.3 through Step 2.6 worksheets to help you refine and dial in your Profit Plan.

In business, trends show movement, either up or down, over a period of time. These company-specific charts provide you with isolated views segregated by each financial statement category so you don't have to be an accountant to see if an actual or planned number is out of sequence. Or whether the year's trend is positive or negative. Included below each chart are key questions to ask yourself if you have trouble completing Steps 2.1 through 2.6 in building your Step 2—Profit Plan.

Frequency = Each chart will print to its own page. Look at your charts every time you update your P&L Data to confirm how your Profit Plan numbers are trending.

STEP 2—BUILD AND USE A MONTHLY PROFIT PLAN TO GUIDE YOUR DECISION-MAKING

Without targets to be realized, by month, it's impossible to know if you are accomplishing your goals. Ideally, it's best to finalize your Profit Plan in December for the following year or the first week if your Profit Plan doesn't extend into the following month.

Your Profit Plan is more than planning for profit on your P&L Statement; it involves considering this implication on your Balance Sheet. Too many business owners pursue a healthy profit that looks attractive on a financial statement. But they fail to account for capital expenditures or receivables collection issues that may be draining cash and putting their business at increased risk.

STEP 2.1—JUMP START YOUR PROFIT PLAN THINKING

Your goal in completing Step 2—Build *Your* Twenty-Four-Month Profit Plan is to establish performance targets by month, which you will use to manage your business through at least the next twelve months. To help you jump-start your thinking when setting objectives, you'll have access to five potential business scenarios. These scenarios are built from the historical data you've already populated, and they should help you to determine if you should focus on improving sales, ops, or overhead management in the year ahead.

Each scenario takes your "Best Case," "Worst Case," and "Most Likely" assumptions from Net Sales impact through Operating Income (EBITDA Earnings) through the projected result. Your goal is likely to have your business succeed and be worth more next year than this year. Using the EBITDA multiplier value range to gain a sense of what your business *could* be worth at different EBITDA multiples can be helpful.

Once you're clear on which scenario you are going to pursue in the coming year, you'll be prepared to make your first at pass setting your P&L Success Targets—in Step 2.2 for your P&L Statement and Step 2.3 for your Balance Sheet.

Frequency = Revisit anytime you are rethinking your "critical few" success targets throughout the year as circumstances change.

STEP 2.2—SET YOUR P&L SUCCESS TARGETS

Set the core P&L measures that will quantify your definition of business success at least for the year ahead, particularly as they relate to sales growth, targeted gross profit, and operating income percentages.

The targets set in Step 2.2 expressed as percentages are used to initiate your Profit Plan Projections for the next twenty-four months. If you have trouble setting your core P&L targets, refer to Step 5 to dial in the action steps you are considering in the coming profit year. Step 5.4 helps you think through sales, 5.5 covers operations, and 5.6 reinforces what you have to do to collect payment and hold onto cash.

Frequency = Revisit your "critical few" success targets anytime throughout the year as circumstances change.

STEP 2.3—SET YOUR BALANCE SHEET SUCCESS TARGETS

Define the Balance Sheet measures that will quantify your definition of business success at least for the year ahead, particularly as they relate to accounts receivable, accounts payable, current assets, and current liabilities. The values set in Step 2.3 are used to establish the key leading metrics used in Step 3.1.

Should you not be happy with any of the calculated profit planning results as you move forward, go back, and change the assumptions you established in Steps 2.2 and 2.3. These Profit Planning worksheets are dynamically linked so that you can dial in what you specifically plan to accomplish in the year ahead by month.

Frequency = Revisit your "critical few" success targets anytime throughout the year, as circumstances change.

STEP 2.4—CONFIRM YOUR REVENUE OBJECTIVES, BY PRODUCT

Project your monthly sales by first entering the number of units or orders sold by each core product line by month. The tool will automatically calculate the rest of your sales projections based on your historical seasonality by month; it will also load your income into the first section of each profit level setting (Step 2.5 through 2.7).

Frequency = Revisit your sales targets anytime throughout the year, as circumstances change.

STEP 2.5—ALLOCATE YOUR COGS
AS A PERCENT OF SALES

Establishes your Cost of Goods Sold by COGS category, based on the percent of revenue you want each direct expense category to represent—by gross profit planning year and by COGS category.

Changing sales in Step 2.4 won't help you, because your COGS are planned as a percent of sales. The only way to improve your planned gross profit as reflected in Step 2.5 is to reduce the percentage of direct expenses allocated to the individual costs of goods categories. See Steps 4.2 and 4.3 for ideas on where to focus.

Frequency = Revisit your planned Sales and COGS thinking anytime you are dissatisfied with your Gross Profit results.

STEP 2.6—SET YOUR SG&A EXPENSE
CATEGORY BUDGETS

This step establishes your Sales, General, and Administrative Expenses that you are building into your Step 2—Profit Plan. Here, enter the total dollars you are planning to invest by overhead expense category. Your results will confirm your Operating Income Plan by month.

If you don't like the way the numbers are adding up, you can increase your net sales projection in Step 2.4 so that you have more revenue to cover your fixed costs. Or you can reduce COGS to improve your Gross Profit from Step 2.5 to generate more gross profit to cover your overhead expenses. Your third option in improving your operating income number is to reduce the SG&A Expenses budgeted for in this operating profit planning worksheet.

The SG&A expense projections will automatically populate, by month, based on a monthly average of the total. In reviewing the gray-shaded historical numbers by month and their corresponding averages (found below the gray-shaded area), you can improve the accuracy of your SG&A projections. Using the tool, you'll be able to adjust them throughout the individual months versus allocating funds on a straight-line average.

Frequency = Revisit your planned overhead expense thinking anytime you are dissatisfied with your Operating Income results.

STEP 2.7–ESTABLISH YOUR NON-OPERATING EXPENSE AND INCOME

Confirm your Net Income Plan by Month based on the Sales Plan in Step 2.4, using the Gross Profit planned in Step 2.5, and Operating Income in Step 2.6. Then be sure to subtract your "other non-operating" expenses. Also, include the non-operating income you are planning for in Step 2.7.

If you don't like how the numbers are adding up, you can either change your nonoperating expense and income projections in Step 2.2; or go back to Step 2.4 to increase your sales targets. Two additional options are to go back to Step 2.5 to reduce your cost of goods sold or return to Step 2.6 to lower your overhead expense plans. Changing any one of these four areas will increase your bottom-line net profit.

Frequency = Revisit your planned non-operating expense and income thinking anytime you are dissatisfied with your Net Profit results.

STEP 2.8–QUALITY CONTROL YOUR TWENTY-FOUR-MONTH PROFIT PLAN

Now that you have completed your Sales (Step 2.4), Gross (Step 2.5) Operating (Step 2.6,) and Net (Step 2.7) Profit Planning, you are ready to quality control your Profit Plan Objectives and Targets. Start with the summary table comparing your plan to your historical numbers supported by Key P&L number graphs. As you look at your four historical and two plan years, look for any pattern inconsistencies.

Your Key P&L numbers are also shown in two different views by year on an Annual, Quarterly, Monthly, Weekly, and Daily basis. These separate views allow you to appreciate what you have done in the past and what you are planning to do over the next twenty-four months. Keep an eye out for big leaps in results that aren't consistent with past experience nor supported by planned changes in sales or ops performance for the planned years.

Frequency = Revisit your Profit Plan Quality Control sheet anytime you change a projection or an assumption.

STEP 2.9—USE YOUR TOP-DOWN PROFIT PLAN TO CONFIRM WHAT YOU NEED TO SELL

The results of completing Step 2—Build *Your* Monthly Profit Plan, driven by targets set in Step 2.1, involving Step 2.3 through Step 2.6, are summarized in Step 2.9. Combined, these worksheets guide you through Sales by Product, COGS, Gross Profit, SG&A Expense, and EBITDA Earnings by month.

This is your *top-down* view of what you have to *sell* by month and what you can afford to *spend* each month in COGS and SG&A in order to generate those sales if you are to hit your operating income number by month.

Frequency = Revisit your Profit Plan top-down summary anytime you change a projection or an assumption.

STEP 2.10—USE YOUR BOTTOM-UP PROFIT PLAN TO CONFIRM WHAT YOU CAN AFFORD TO SPEND

The results of completing Step 2—Build *Your* Monthly Profit Plan driven by targets set in Step 2.1, and also involving Step 2.3 through Step 2.6, are summarized in Step 2.10. These results range from planned EBITDA Earnings by month, through SG&A Expense, to Gross Profit, to COGS, to Sales by Product.

This is your bottom-*up* view of what you can *afford* to do if you want to hit your operating income goal by month. Anything *greater* than planned, in SG&A or COGS, will undermine the top number represented in this *bottom-up* view of your Profit Plan.

Frequency = Revisit your Profit Plan bottom-up summary anytime you change a projection or an assumption.

STEP 3—CONFIRM THE QUALITY OF *YOUR* PROFITS THROUGH WEEKLY KPIS AND MONTHLY VARIANCE REPORTS

This business-critical step is founded on the truism that you can't *control* what you can't *manage*, and you can't *manage* what you can't *measure*. Anytime you want to improve something, start by *measuring* it to confirm how you are doing relative to your established goals. Where are you doing better and worse than you planned to be?

Consistent action throughout the year on Step 3 is critical to your business success. This is because every profit dollar you earn is the result of past actions. The sooner you identify exactly *where* corrective action is needed, the sooner you will see improvements in your actual results.

STEP 3.1—KNOW WHETHER YOUR KEY WEEKLY ACTIVITIES ARE HELPING YOU TO ACHIEVE YOUR GOALS

Weekly "Key Performance Indicators" (KPI) reporting is the measurement of weekly progress toward your planned goals by measuring current results against identified "critical success" activities. A quality weekly KPI metric is an effective outcome predictor of your planned results. If your action to directly influence a key activity results in improvement, you have a *quality* KPI metric.

The Weekly KPI Dashboard in Step 3.1 is a foundational leading metrics measurement system built around the core business functions of *sales, operations,* and *finance.* The purpose of this first dashboard is to measure the key activities necessary to achieve your goals.

If you are missing any *one* of these leading indicator goals for a week, you have identified an area for considering corrective action. Deciding *what* corrective action needs to be taken, *who* is responsible for accomplishing it, and *when* it needs to be completed will keep you from falling short of your goal. Any KPI metrics miss, if not corrected, will prevent you from meeting your monthly and, ultimately, your annual goals.

Frequency = Update and use every week.

STEP 3.2—CONFIRM YOUR BUSINESS'S PERFORMANCE ACROSS SALES, OPS, AND FINANCE

The preloaded Monthly KPI Dashboard in Step 3.2 is a foundational lagging metrics measurement system focused on *sales, operations,* and *finance.* These preloaded measures of performance are the most common sales, ops, and finance-lagging metrics to consider when monitoring each critical part of your company. Focus on ensuring that your actions are producing the desired results month-to-month.

If you are missing any one of these lagging-indicator goals for a month, you have identified another area to consider for taking corrective action. Choosing *what* corrective action needs to be taken, *who* is responsible for accomplishing it, and *when* it needs to be completed helps you avoid falling short of a goal. Over time, these lagging-metrics misses by core business function will also cause you to miss your monthly and, ultimately, your annual goals if they are not corrected.

Frequency = Use this automatically populated worksheet every month when you update your P&L and Balance Sheet Data to identify where you are leaking cash and profits.

STEP 3.3—KNOW WHETHER YOU ARE DOING BETTER THIS YEAR THAN LAST YEAR

Your first variance assessment in Step 3.3 involves your monthly Profit & Loss statement comparing actual versus previous for the same period. Make sure that the results being reported for the current year are relatively consistent with the same period in the previous year. If the results are *widely different* and you don't have a ready explanation as to *why* you likely have a data-entry error, these variances by major sources of revenue and expense categories should be relatively easy to explain, based on known changes in the business this year compared to last year.

If you *can't* explain the variance this year versus previous year, then you have another area where corrective action needs to be taken. Again, any corrective action involves identification of *what* needs to be done, *who* is responsible for accomplishing it, and a *deadline* for completion completed. Avoid falling short of your profit goals by making sure you follow through on each assigned corrective action.

Each month is set up to print on its own page with a notes section to record anything significant that you might want to recall at a later date. There is also a variance action plan tracker, included in Columns BQ through BT for use in your weekly Return + Report Accountability Meetings. This information is useful, should the need for corrective action be assigned to another employee based on this variance report.

Frequency = Use this automatically populated worksheet every month when you update your P&L and Balance Sheet Data to identify *where* you are leaking cash and profits.

STEP 3.4—CONFIRM YOUR BUSINESS'S ACTUAL PERFORMANCE VERSUS ITS PLANNED PERFORMANCE

Your second variance report in Step 3.4 helps ensure that your business is on track to achieve your planned profits built during Step 2—Build *Your* Twenty-Four-Month Profit Plan.

Confirm your actual performance against your planned performance by month and by year-to-date. A positive variance indicates that actual performance is exceeding planned. A negative variance tells you *where* you are falling short relative to your profit plan.

Any negative actual-to-planned variance will cause you to miss that planned number unless a corresponding positive variance in another area is correcting for the miss. You can prevent this from happening by identifying *what* corrective action needs to be taken, *who* is responsible for accomplishing it, and the specific deadline for completion. Timely follow-through on each assigned corrective action is the best way to avoid falling short of your profit goals.

Frequency = Use this automatically populated worksheet every month you update your P&L and Balance Sheet Data to identify where you are leaking cash and profits.

STEP 3.5—MONITOR YOUR FINANCIAL RATIO RESULTS

The variance reports you reviewed monthly in Step 3.3 and 3.4 are your foundational managerial accounting tools. Step 3.5 offers you a view of your business results through the lenses of financial ratios. Each ratio provides a mathematical comparison of financial statement accounts that are most commonly used by finance professionals. These dynamic comparisons, based on decision science, help to determine how well a business is performing and where it needs to improve.

Interestingly, financial ratios don't take into consideration the *size* of a company or industry. Each ratio in Step 3.5— Monitor *Your* Financial Ratio Results is a simple raw computation of *your* financial position and performance; use these results to identify *your* company's strengths and weaknesses. These are provided in a summary view in Step 4.3, should you be ready to attack your next largest Profit Loss.

Each "Monopoly"-like card provides you with a summary explanation of each financial ratio. You'll see actual numbers by year as well as targeted questions that will help you if you're stuck looking for a starting point for attacking profit losses. These cards have been structured to print with "cut marks" so that you can easily work with the individual "cards" to improve your play in the great game of business. See the second half of Appendix B to appreciate the power that is available to you when you use these financial ratio game cards.

Frequency = Use these automatically populated ratio cards every month as you update your P&L and Balance Sheet Data to identify where you are leaking cash and profits.

STEP 4—STOP THE LOSSES THAT KEEP *YOUR* BUSINESS AT RISK

The key to profit growth is resolving the #1 constraint impacting business profitability—*costly profit leaks*. Step 4 is the process for stopping your business from unnecessarily forfeiting, cash and, ultimately, losing profits. Profit Losses include any business issue, waste, poor productivity, missed profit opportunity, or failed actions.

The goal of this important step is to identify and quantify the annual problem costs and opportunities lost, in your business, based on their calculated profit impact. You will know the "Stop Your Losses" process is working when you see positive changes occurring. This is not simply an accounting exercise. Its real behavior change that results in your business performing differently through your continuous execution of Step 4—Stop *Your* Losses That Keep *Your* Business at Risk.

Ending unnecessary profit losses that cause cash to drain from operations constantly is the most effective way to ensure that your business makes and holds onto more money. And the tangible benefits of stopping these losses are easily confirmed by positive changes in monthly profits and weekly cash on hand.

STEP 4.1–SUMMARY CHART VIEW
OF *YOUR* FINANCIAL RATIOS

It's possible that you may still have difficulty identifying the costliest Profit Losses that are holding your business back from realizing your cash flow and profit goals. If so, Step 4.3 provides a summary view of your financial ratios to help you more clearly understand how well your business is performing and where it needs to improve.

Look at your business through the eyes of financial ratios, used by the pros, to identify what company strengths you should be building on and what weaknesses you need to either fix or choose to ignore.

Any red-shaded cells are "Profit Losses" based on the result of the financial ratio calculation. Refer to Step 3.5 for more information about a particular financial ratio.

Frequency = Use whenever you are stuck trying to determine the best area to fix next.

STEP 4.2–HOW WELL IS *YOUR*
BUSINESS PERFORMING, AND WHERE
DOES IT NEED TO IMPROVE?

To help you realize your cash flow and profit goals, Step 4.2 provides a summary view of your financial statement results. A close look at this summary will help you to more clearly understand how well your business is performing and where it needs to improve.

Use the actual results of your financial position and performance versus plan to identify what company strengths you should be building on and what weaknesses you need to fix, improve, or ignore.

Frequency = Use this step whenever you are stuck trying to determine the best area to fix next.

STEP 4.3—BUILD A PLAN FOR STOPPING *YOUR* LOSSES

Based on the corrective actions to be taken as identified in Step 3—Confirm the Quality of *Your* Profits, at the end of Steps 3.1 through 3.4, you identified the areas where you want to intervene to improve your financial performance. Use the planning form loaded into Step 4.1 to follow the five steps required to stop any size profit losses completely.

This planning form will guide you through the critical few steps you need to think through before building your profit loss attack plan. Successful use of this tool will result in rapid improvement in your month-to-month profit levels and week-to-week cash on hand. It's easy to see positive results when you stop wasting money!

Frequency = Use anytime you are tired of losing money in a given area.

STEP 4.4—USE A DASHBOARD TO MONITOR *YOUR* PROGRESS IN STOPPING PRIORITIZED LOSSES

Once you have defined the "fix" elements of your profit losses using Step 4.1, you are now ready to populate your Profit Loss Dashboard in Step 4.4. This tool is designed to help you track your progress in resolving each prioritized profit loss.

Frequency = Weekly, if you are taking daily actions to stop a profit loss; monthly, if you need weeks to resolve an issue concerning losses.

STEP 4.5—CAPTURE THE VALUE OF A STOPPED LOSS IN *YOUR* PROFIT PLAN

You'll know you've successfully stopped a profit loss when you see the value reflected in your weekly use of Step 1—Increase the Velocity of *Your* Operating Cash Flow; you will also see improved Profit Plan projections based on reflecting the value of your stopped profit loss in Steps 2.3 through 2.6.

This management page is used to capture the value of a successfully stopped profit loss. When you are ready to reflect the improvement in your Profit Plan projections, enter the Stopped Profit Loss value by core planning element in the space provided. For stopped losses *not* reflected by P&L line item use the open space as appropriate.

Frequency = Update monthly to keep track of your wins.

STEP 5—BE ACCOUNTABLE FOR *YOUR* RESULTS

The biggest difference between success and failure is following through on the actions you must take by their specific deadlines. Be sure to prioritize by determining what tasks you and those who work for you will and won't take on. And communicate these accountabilities clearly.

The worksheets in this portion of the tool are designed to help you better plan, organize, and control your business by knowing with confidence where disciplined action is needed and where the action isn't a top priority. The goal should never be to "work harder" by working more hours but to "work smarter" by focusing your actions on the "critical few" actions you need to complete. Don't be distracted by the "relevant many" actions that you could take on (they will *always* exist.) Prioritizing and eliminating nonessential activities are the best strategies for achieving your desired results without doubling the number of hours you or your team members work each week.

STEP 5.1—KNOW *YOUR* CLEAR PATH TO SUCCESS THROUGH STRATEGIC PLANNING

Strategic planning is defined as "determining your path to success" in the planned period ahead. This planning process helps you define the strategies, tactics, and actions you'll use to reach your short and long-term profit plan objectives.

A well thought-out profit plan forces you to think about the future and the challenges you will face. It forces you to consider your financial needs, your sales, ops, and management plans; it even forces you to take a look at your competition and develop your overall strategy. You'll know you have a viable business plan when you can use it to focus your goals and your vision and then see a clear path that will help you realize them.

Managing this process is one of the most important duties of every business owner. Through the strategic planning process, you not only verify what you plan *to do*, you become clearer about what you *don't want to do*. Successful business leaders are masters at knowing how to use their employee talent, company assets, and resources to their best advantage. And Strategic Planning is the essential process that helps them do this.

Frequency = Formalize during the initial Profit Planning process, and then update anytime you change your strategic priorities.

STEP 5.2—*YOUR* PROFIT PLAN SUCCESS STARTS AND ENDS WITH *YOU*

Your disciplined action every day on the "critical few" versus the "relevant many" actions you commit to completing enables you to realize your sales, profit, and wealth creation goals, all without working more hours each week. Step 5.2 lists "MY weekly Step 5 'Must Dos' for Controlling MY Businesses." This dashboard is designed to help you recognize *what you did well* as the leader of your company, *where you got stuck*, and *what you now intend to do differently* to achieve superior results for your hard work and sacrifice.

Frequency = Complete weekly, either before you head home for the week or before you start the week ahead.

STEP 5.3—*YOU* CAN ONLY DO SO MUCH WITHOUT A TEAM *YOU* TRUST

Without a *team* working together, you can only do so much. And it is this team's responsibility to manage the company. Assembling this "framework" can help learning, developing, and implementing controls, reporting structural-mechanisms to manage the "ACTIONS" of the company; utilizing the institution of effective management team meetings focused on relevant metrics and related "return + report" accountability.

This management page provides a sample of an effective agenda for your weekly "action accountability" meetings. Each agenda should be reflective of what the meeting leader has decided to discuss and has distributed at least forty-eight hours before the scheduled meeting. This provides each participant with the opportunity to come to the meeting prepared to report on their relevant accomplishments.

Frequency = Weekly; distribute at least forty-eight hours before Management Accountability Meeting.

STEP 5.4—*YOU* WILL NEVER EARN PROFITS WITHOUT GENERATING SALES

The overriding objective of sales is to persuade a sufficient number of people to pay enough money to buy your products and services to enable you to realize your planned gross profit number. While the total amount sold matters, of course, the most important number in your business is "what it *cost* you to convert a dollar of sales into a profit." Without a strong *Gross* Profit number, it is impossible to have a strong *Net* Income number.

Your actual sales are the best reflection of how well you are utilizing your capital, capacity, and other resources to generate the top line of your business and that funds everything else in your business.

Frequency = Review and update monthly and as required, based on your sales plan variance results.

STEP 5.5–*YOU* MUST PRODUCE AND DELIVER WHAT *YOU* SOLD AT A PROFIT

You will never have a strong gross profit if it's a struggle to keep your sales greater than the cost of producing the goods (COGS) and the services you sell. Failure to see sales greater than COGS results in having no money left over to pay for operating expenses, let alone provide the owner with profits.

Your gross profit percentage is the best determiner of how efficient your operations are in converting sales into profits. If your percent of gross profit earned on every dollar sold isn't noticeably improving, year-over-year, then your business operations aren't becoming more efficient. You *need* your gross profit percentage to be continuously improving if you expect your business to be worth more this year than it was last year.

Frequency = Review and update monthly and as required, based on your gross profit plan variance results.

STEP 5.6–EVERY PROFIT DOLLAR EARNED REFLECTS THE QUALITY OF PAST MANAGEMENT DECISIONS, LUCK, OR BOTH

Throughout a year, every viable business is earning revenue and incurring expenses in fulfilling its purpose. Whether this occurs by strategic intent or by happenstance, the work will be accomplished by those employed in the business. Your profits are the ultimate measure of how well this work is being done.

Every profit dollar you earn reflects the quality of past management decisions. Profits are a *lagging* indicator, whereas customer loyalty, employee engagement, and operating-cycle times are core *leading* indicators of your profit quality and cash flow velocity.

Frequency = Review and update monthly and as required, based on your operating profit plan variance results.

The sub-steps to *B-CPR* identified above will help you protect your business from failing. Adherence to this process is the surest way to realize your sales, profit, and wealth creation goals. Disciplined use of each of these steps enables you to *gain and maintain control over your business today and into the future.*

Go to www.business-cpr.com\bpitool to see how easy this online tool is to use and how effectively it will help you to gain and maintain control over your cash flow and realize your desired business profits.

APPENDIX B

GAME OF BUSINESS PLAYING CARDS

Game of Business

Every business starts with cash, which is invested in various ways to generate revenue. Ultimately, the revenue is turned back into cash, and the cycle begins anew.

Each completed business transaction produces data that forms the financial reports used by your accountant to calculate your financial position for tax liability purposes. Those who choose to play the game of business to win recognize that these same financial reports can be used for so much more. They know that their financial data can help them build sustainable operating cash flows and higher profits.

You best play the Game of Business to win, starting with knowing the core elements of the game and how the quality of your play is scored. Without this understanding, it's hard to know what the next smart move is if you don't know where you are in the game. Your financial statements give you what you need to play your game of business smarter today than you have ever before.

Balance Sheet Retained Earnings on 12-31 by					Plan	Projected
2016	2017	2018	2019	Jan-00	2020	2021

What do you love most about your business play today?

What would you like to be different?

Step 1 - Increase the Velocity of *Your* Operating Cash Flow
Step 1 – Manage Your Weekly Cash InFlows to be Greater than Your OutFlows

When you are out of cash, you are out of business. This is the #1 law of business. To prevent cash outflows from ever exceeding cash inflows, always maintain at least a four-week rolling cash forecast to confirm how much money you are holding onto through your business operations.

Establish Cash Flow projections for at least the next four weeks every Monday afternoon, based on your projected accounts-receivable collections, and your planned recurring expense and accounts-payable payouts for the week.

Weekly cash flow projections are the only way to know precisely where you need to focus your business efforts when you have low cash on hand as a percent of your cash reserve target for the weeks ahead.

Ending A/R - A/P from Balance Sheet					Plan	Projected
2016	2017	2018	2019	Jan-00	2020	2021

Do you have an issue with A/R collections? ___ Yes ___ No   If yes, what needs to be done this week to improve your Accounts Receivable collections?

Who is the best person to be accountable for getting this action done?

STEP 2 – Build *YOUR* 24-month Profit Plan
Step 2 – Use Your Monthly Profit Plan to Guide Your Decision-Making

Profit is what's leftover after employees, suppliers, lenders, and the government has been paid. The amount remaining represents the business's return for the capital put at risk to produce this income. In business, as in most games, the objective is to win. In business, the equivalent of the 'games' final score is your Net Income, the last number on your P&L Statement. Without a profit goal—and targets to be realized by month—it is impossible to know if your business is winning or losing.

First, you need to be able to identify what your "winning score" should look like based on the time, money, and risk you are incurring. In business terms, this is your planned Net Income number. Ideally, your monthly Profit Plan is finalized in December for the next year, or this week if it doesn't exist for the next month. Without a defined monthly Profit Plan, you will never know, for sure, if you are failing or succeeding in your business month-to-month.

P&L Net Income					Plan	Projected
2016	2017	2018	2019	Jan-00	2020	2021

What's the #1 action you must take to realize your stated Net Income Goal?

Who is responsible for determining this number?

STEP 3 - Confirm the quality of *YOUR* profits
Step 3 – Monitor Your Results with Weekly KPIs and Monthly Variance Reports

Consistently monitoring the results of your business is the best way to know if your business is succeeding, week-to-week, and month-to-month. To protect your business from losing money and running out of cash, you must be able to instantly identify where you are performing better and worse then what you planned in your Step 2 - Profit Plan

Use KPIs to measure your WEEKLY progress towards your planned goals, by quantifying current results against identified "critical success" activities. Misses to target results indicate where corrective action should be taken. You do KPIs weekly because the sooner you intervene, the better you position your business to get back on track to realizing your profit goals. Use monthly Variance Reports during your second weekly management meeting each month to look back at your reported financial results. Do this to identify what new actions need to be taken to improve your prospects for achieving your profit plan.

P&L Net Sales					Plan	Projected
2016	2017	2018	2019	Jan-00	2020	2021

What is the #1 action you must take to realize your Net Sales Goal?

Who is the best person to be accountable for achieving it?

Step 4 - Stop the Losses That Keep *Your* Business at Risk
Step 4 – Stop Your Most Costly Profit Losses that are Wasting Cash

All wasted or lost cash costs you both cash reserves and profits. Every profit failure drains your bank accounts and puts your business at increased risk each time you fail to make money on a sale. Ending unwanted cash drains is essential to making money throughout the year, as confirmed by your monthly profit levels and weekly cash on hand as a percent of your cash reserve target

Your profit losses are easily identified and quantified through leading and lagging metric "misses," identified through Step 3 - Confirm the Quality of Your Profits. When prioritizing which profit loss to fix first, consider each loss impact on cash quality and cash velocity. Doing so enhances your ability to make money while protecting your business from missing your Step 2 - Profit Plan.

P&L COGS + SSG&A Expense					Plan	Projected
2016	2017	2018	2019	Jan-00	2020	2021

Where is your business spending more than it should? _____

How much cash is being lost from your business as a result? $ _____

Who is the best person to be accountable for stopping this loss?

Step 5 - Be Accountable for *Your* Results
Step 5 – Commit to Acting on the Less than Satisfactory Results from Steps 1 – 4

You control your business through disciplined actions. In every business, there are always more smart actions one could take than time available to do so. The hard reality is that not every activity you complete will produce the results you lay out in your Profit Plan.

Instead of committing to work more hours to achieve the results you desire, focus your time each day on those "critical few" actions that only you can accomplish. And, in exchange, decide which of the 'relevant many' actions you will put on hold, not do, or delegate to others. The key to your success and quality of life is to focus on what matters most.

If your disciplined actions aren't creating the intended results, then change your actions to ensure that you realize your desired results. Prioritizing and eliminating activity through disciplined follow-through helps you to achieve your desired results.

P&L Operating Income Percent Change (YTD is % of Plan)					Plan	Projected
2016	2017	2018	2019	Jan-00	2020	2021

Who in your business do you spend the most time cleaning up after?

What can you do differently to help this person get done what they commit to do?

Financial Statements

Data from your revenue production efforts are used to create financial summary reports on the results of operations for any period you have recorded the transaction data in your accounting software. Each available financial statement represents different roll-ups of your business transactions. The reason why most business owners struggle with holding onto cash is that they are inconsistent in recording their business transactions into their accounting software. Use your financial statements to forecast your cash position or stop your profit losses by understanding how the funds entrusted to management by the owners (stockholders) and lenders led to the current financial position, through the following three primary financial statements:
1. The P&L (also called income) statement shows how the net income of your business is determined over a stated period by subtracting expenses from revenues.
2. The Balance sheet shows your assets, liabilities, and net worth on a stated date
3. The Statement of Cash Flows shows the sources of cash utilized by your business activities during a stated period

Profit Plan	Revenues	Expenses	Assets	Liabilities	Owners' Equity
% of Revenue					

Which of the five basic units of accounting for your business transactions represented by revenues, expenses, assets, liabilities, and owners' equity is most concerning to you, and why?

Who is the best person to be accountable for correcting the financial reporting concerns you may have?

P&L, or Income Statement

The best summary of management's performance is your P&L Statement, which, as the name indicates, reflects either profitability or the lack of profits from business operations through each year.

Your P&L Statement itemizes the revenues and expenses that led either to your current profit or loss. By looking at the actual numbers produced through your business, you can compare the planned versus actual numbers. The variance, or gap between actual and planned, is the best way to identify where you need to take action to improve future results.

Your Profit Plan establishes what you should make, and your P&L shows you what you did make. A positive difference between actual and plan indicates that you made more money than you planned to make. A negative difference, even if you showed a profit, shows what you lost money by failing to meet your profit plan.

Profit Plan	Sales	- Expenses	= Net Inc
% of Revenue			

With a check mark, identify which of the following two areas will be your biggest profit plan challenge in the coming year: ___ sales generation or ___ expense management

If sales, determine if your problem stems from:___ lead generation; ___ lead conversion ___ average transaction value or something else?
If expense management, where are your expenses most out of control? _____

Balance Sheet

The Balance Sheet lists company assets, how it paid for them, what it still owes (its liabilities). The difference between what it paid after depreciation, and the amount left goes to the owners after satisfying the liabilities. The purpose of this financial statement is to list, at any point in time, your company's measurable resources in:

1. Assets – Your capacity to produce revenue.
2. Liabilities – Your borrowings to acquire these assets and pay your bills.
3. Equity – Your investment as the owner representing the claim you have against your assets.

Remember, the owner's equity is not the same as the owner's piggy bank; it represents the owner's claim on the company assets leftover after all liabilities have been paid off.

	Assets	- Liabilities	= Owners' Equity
Profit Plan			
% of Assets			
% of Sales			

What portion of your Asset base is failing to produce revenue?

Who is the best person to implement changes that enable this Asset to produce better?

Statement of Cash Flows

A business's Statement of Cash Flows provides a comprehensive picture of the company's cash flows, beyond operations. Use this financial statement to follow how cash changes from the beginning to the end of a period.

Banks like to see this statement to see both the actual and projected incomings and outgoings of cash over an accounting period. This statement answers the following questions:

1. Where did the money come from, or where will it come from?
2. Where did the money go, or where will it go?

Operating cash flow is the best method for generating cash in a business, and it's the most cost-effective way to make new investments in your business, repay financial debt, or return capital (money) to the owners.

	Cash from Operations	+ Investment Money	+ Financed Money
Profit Plan			
% Total Cash			
% of Sales			

What action can you take today to hold onto more of your cash from operations?

Who is the best person to ensure these cash savings actually occur?

Gross Sales

The topline view of the P&L Statement that establishes how well or poorly your company is utilizing its capital, capacity, employees, and other resources, to generate business. This is the topline number for your P&L Statement that every subsequent revenue and expense transaction during the accounting reporting period reduces.

The amount shown represents the total amount of money that should be collected for goods or services sold before any production costs (cost of goods sold), and expenses (SG&A and Other) are subtracted, during that accounting period. This number can only be improved by selling more, raising selling prices, or reducing discounts and bad debt write-off. Every dollar of Gross Sales has the potential to be a full dollar that you can use to pay expenses with what's left after paying ALL expenses being your profit.

Year-to-Date P&L Actuals & Percent of Net Sales					Plan	Projected
2016	2017	2018	2019	Jan-00	2020	2021

Do your gross sales basically equal your net sales? ___ Yes ___ No. If yes, are you writing off A/R as bad debt within your 4000 COA series? If no, you may be over-stating net sales, and over-stating the expense category you've recorded your bad debt within. If needed, who is responsible for making these corrections, and when would you like them completed?

Total Expenses

Any cost (expense) incurred in a company's efforts to generate revenue needs to be a contributing cost of doing business, or it should be eliminated. Expenses are summarized and charged on the income statement as deductions from sales income, before assessing income tax. Each business expenses is allocated to one of the following three expense categories.

Direct Expenses are always related to producing the goods sold by a business and are often referred to as Cost of Goods Sold or COGS.
Indirect Expenses represent the fixed expenses or overhead of the business that cannot be directly assigned to a particular job or product. Most often referred to as SG&A Operating Expense.
Other Expenses represent costs incurred that are not directly attributable to the company's core business operations and are considered unusual, infrequent, or extraordinary business expenses.

Year-to-Date P&L Actuals & Percent of Net Sales					Plan	Projected
2016	2017	2018	2019	Jan-00	2020	2021

Are you satisfied with what is left over after Total Expenses are subtracted from Net Sales? ___ Yes ___ No. If no, what are you going to do differently today to 1) either increase sales while holding expenses steady, or 2) to decrease expenses across your business until you can grow sales?

Net Sales

After you deduct sales discounts, returned merchandise credits, and write-offs for a bad debt from Gross Sales, you are left with Net Sales. These Gross Sales reductions should not be buried way down in your expense accounts. Accounting for these negative sales impacts outside of gross sales overstates what cash you brought into your business from your marketing and sales efforts.

Your net sales represent the total amount of money collected for goods or services sold before any expenses are subtracted during that accounting period. It is the best reflection of how well you are utilizing your capital, capacity, and other resources to generate the top-line of your business, which funds everything else in your business.

Accrued net sales do not represent cash flow, nor does cash sales represent profit. Net sales only represent what your sales transactions reflect, in total, for that period, as the

Year-to-Date P&L Actuals & Percent of Net Sales					Plan	Projected
2016	2017	2018	2019	Jan-00	2020	2021

Is there a significant difference between your Gross Sales and your Net Sales? ___ Yes ___ No. If yes, what needs to be done differently today to hold onto more of your Gross Sales, and who is accountable for making these corrections?

Cost of Goods Sold

One reoccurring business goal is always to be reducing your direct expenses related to producing the goods and services bought by your customers within your cost of goods sold or COGS.

When accounting for COGS, consider what is being recognized as a direct expense in what is being produced. COGS are considered variable expenses because they vary with sales.

If an expense accounted for here doesn't change as sales levels change, then it's a fixed, not a variable, expense. It's difficult to calculate an accurate gross profit if you have variable costs sitting in SG&A and fixed costs sitting in COGS.

The most common COGS are Direct Labor, Subcontractors, Materials, and Equipment.

Year-to-Date P&L Actuals & Percent of Net Sales					Plan	Projected
2016	2017	2018	2019	Jan-00	2020	2021

What variable expenses are failing to decrease by a similar percent when sales decreases? _____ Why aren't these expenses lowering at a comparable percent to your sales decreasing?

Who should be accountable for fixing this problem?

Sales Commission

Sales commissions involve a mutually agreed upon percent, or fixed fee, accruing to an agent, broker, or salesperson for facilitating, initiating, and executing a commercial transaction. For salaried sales employees, the sales commission is the additional amount these employees receive over and above their salary, often for exceeding sales performance expectations.

The upside of sales commissions is when they are paid, they are paid for results through pay at risk tied to sales incentives paid for sales produced instead of getting a guaranteed hourly, or weekly pay is the better sales compensation model. This means the amount of commission earned by sales talent varies depending on how much sales success they have. Monies accounted for here are sales commissions or bonuses paid based on actual sales results for a stated goal or target by an employee or representative of your company. Guaranteed wages and employee bonuses not tied to a specific sale should be accounted for where that employee's wages are recorded, not here.

Year-to-Date P&L Actuals & Percent of Net Sales					Plan	Projected
2016	2017	2018	2019	Jan-00	2020	2021

Are you concerned about meeting your revenue goal? ___ Yes ___ No. If yes, how do you believe incentivizing people to generate new sales will help you achieve your Profit Plan sales goal?

Who is accountable for designing your sales commission plan?

Direct Labor Costs

Direct labor costs are the direct worker wages paid associated with the manufacture of a product, a particular work order, or delivery of a service. When possible, these costs should include direct labor benefits, payroll taxes, and worker's comp insurance. If you can't easily segregate these additional payroll costs from the costs included in your SG&A salaries, then you must include them in your overhead absorption rate, if you can't include them with your direct labor wages paid.

If sales decreases and your direct labor costs don't proportionally drop, then you are most likely "creating work" for your direct employees. This means that you are paying your direct workforce to do work that you aren't being paid to perform. Every time you do this, you are turning a variable cost into a fixed cost. Do this for very long, and you will see a rapid erosion in your gross profit. Never a wise move.

Year-to-Date P&L Actuals & Percent of Net Sales					Plan	Projected
2016	2017	2018	2019	Jan-00	2020	2021

When sales decreases, do direct payroll costs decrease by a similar percent? ___ Yes ___ No. If no, is this because you are paying your direct labor to do work that you are not getting paid by your customer to complete? ___ Yes ___ No. If no, what has caused you to turn this variable cost into a fixed cost for your business?
Who is accountable for correcting this problem?

Subcontractors

A subcontractor is an individual or company not in your direct employ, who you hire to help complete a specific task or project tied to helping you deliver your products or services. A subcontractor's work is usually overseen by a member of your operations management team to ensure that it's executed and completed as specified.

The most common use this expense category for work requiring seldom-used skill sets that you should only pay for when needed. Other common uses for subcontractors is for labor augmentation during peak sales cycles, and for any recurring work that you don't want to take on the risk and liability to do yourself.

Direct subcontractor, or temporary employee, costs are directly attributed to operations in support of future sales. If these costs can't be attributed to a job, a product, or a service, they should be included in SG&A or indirect expenses.

Year-to-Date P&L Actuals & Percent of Net Sales					Plan	Projected
2016	2017	2018	2019	Jan-00	2020	2021

Do you use your accounting software or some other tool to help you keep track of subcontractor bonding and "other named insured" on their liability insurance? ___ Yes ___ No. If no, who is accountable for managing your Subcontractor documentation records?

Material Costs

Material costs encompass any purchased materials used to make something else, or, which you resell with a markup. Material costs include, but are not limited to, raw and processed material, components, parts, assemblies, and sub-assemblies that are consumed directly in the production of a product or the delivery of a service.

"Net" material costs represent the total material cost after returns, and vendor discounts are deducted from the material purchases. Any material cost cash paid or payable offsets must be accounted for in your material sub-accounts to give you the most accurate picture of your actual material costs.

Year-to-Date P&L Actuals & Percent of Net Sales					Plan	Projected
2016	2017	2018	2019	Jan-00	2020	2021

If material costs represent a large direct cost, what can be done to reduce this cost by at least 5%? $_____ Reducing material costs is most likely to occur when people are directly accountable for generating these material cost savings.

Who in your business should be accountable for realizing material cost reductions?

Equipment Costs

Fixed assets, other than land, buildings, and vehicles owned or rented by the company, and used in the operations of a business is equipment. Examples include devices, machines, and tools.

Equipment costs included within COGS are the direct operating costs of the equipment attributed to the manufacturing of a product, delivery of a service, or completion of a job. These costs include fuels, lubricants, coolants, cleaning agents, small tools, and equipment accessories that are directly charged to the production of a product, the completion of a job, or fully allocated in direct costs.

Year-to-Date P&L Actuals & Percent of Net Sales					Plan	Projected
2016	2017	2018	2019	Jan-00	2020	2021

Are your equipment costs rising and falling with sales? If no, your equipment costs represent a fixed not a variable cost for your business.

Who is the best person to be accountable for managing these costs down?

ABC - Additional Large COGS Area

The direct costs represented within this data card is of significant size, frequency, and impact on your direct operations to warrant a unique direct expense category.

Use this data card to pull related expenses into a unique subcategory for better cost management and more accurate product and service pricing. This is how you ensure you are fully covering your direct expenses at a profit to you.

A business that finds itself with shrinking gross profit has likely lost track of expense groupings that are not segregated together for easier expense management and cost control.

Year-to-Date P&L Actuals & Percent of Net Sales					Plan	Projected
2016	2017	2018	2019	Jan-00	2020	2021

Are you satisfied with the level of spend occurring here? ___ Yes ___ No.

Would a 10% reduction in this expense category significantly change your total gross profit dollars? ___ Yes ___ No. If no, do nothing.

DEF - Additional Large COGS Area

The direct costs represented within this data card is of significant size, frequency, and impact on your direct operations to warrant a unique direct expense category.

Use this data card to pull related expenses into a unique subcategory for better cost management and more accurate product and service pricing. This is how you ensure you are fully covering your direct expenses at a profit to you.

A business that finds itself with shrinking gross profit has likely lost track of expense groupings that are not segregated together for easier expense management and cost control.

Year-to-Date P&L Actuals & Percent of Net Sales					Plan	Projected
2016	2017	2018	2019	Jan-00	2020	2021

Are you satisfied with the level of spend occurring here? ___ Yes ___ No.

Would a 10% reduction in this expense category significantly change your total gross profit dollars? ___ Yes ___ No. If no, do nothing.

HIG - Additional Large COGS Area

The direct costs represented within this data card is of significant size, frequency, and impact on your direct operations to warrant a unique direct expense category.

Use this data card to pull related expenses into a unique subcategory for better cost management and more accurate product and service pricing. This is how you ensure you are fully covering your direct expenses at a profit to you.

A business that finds itself with shrinking gross profit has likely lost track of expense groupings that are not segregated together for easier expense management and cost control.

Year-to-Date P&L Actuals & Percent of Net Sales					Plan	Projected
2016	2017	2018	2019	Jan-00	2020	2021

Are you satisfied with the level of spend occurring here? ___ Yes ___ No.

Would a 10% reduction in this expense category significantly change your total gross profit dollars? ___ Yes ___ No. If no, do nothing.

Other Direct Costs

If an expense varies with the volume of sales, or if it goes away entirely if a product or service is discontinued, then this is a direct cost. "Other" direct costs involve those costs directly attributable to operations but are not of significant size, or frequency of purchase, to warrant a unique direct expense category.

It is always better to allocate other direct costs directly to a specific job or product cost code. If not directly assignable, then other direct costs must be included in the direct expense allocation percent used to derive your sales price.

Avoid frequently occurring, and high dollar values in this subcategory—these should be in an individual sub-account. The purpose of accounting for Other Direct Costs is to group small and infrequent direct costs that should be tracked with COGS in this subcategory to establish an accurate picture of your gross profit generated.

Year-to-Date P&L Actuals & Percent of Net Sales					Plan	Projected
2014	2015	2016	2017	Jan-00	2018	2019

Do you have costs assigned here that should be managed within its own subcategory? ___ Yes ___ No. If yes, who is accountable for adjusting your chart of accounts to improve your ability to manage these direct costs?

Gross Profit

Gross Profit measures your first level of profit contribution that comes from transforming a dollar of sales into a profit. Without a strong gross profit in your business operations, it is impossible to have a strong Net Income number.

Gross profit is calculated by subtracting the direct costs incurred to produce a product, complete a job, or deliver services, from Net Sales. Your gross profit percent is the best determiner of how efficiently your operations convert sales into profits. If your percent of gross profit earned on every dollar sold isn't improving noticeably, year-over-year, then your business operations aren't becoming more efficient. A gross profit that is continuously improving is the best reflection of a well-managed business.

An unhealthy gross profit results in a continuous struggle to keep sales greater than the cost of production. If sales are not greater than COGS, there will never be money left over to pay operating expenses and provide the owner with profits.

Year-to-Date P&L Actuals & Percent of Net Sales					Plan	Projected
2014	2015	2016	2017	Jan-00	2018	2019

If you reduced the most expensive area of your operations by 12% how much more Gross Profit dollars would your direct operations produce? $_____
If you reduced this area by 5%, how much more Gross Profit dollars would you have to pay your overhead expenses, leaving you a profit? $_____
Who is the best person to be accountable for lowering costs identified above?

Selling, General, and Administrative Expense

SG&A Expense represents the overhead of the business—fixed expenses that can't be directly assigned to a job, product, or service bought by a customer.

Because these expenses don't fluctuate with sales, production, or the market, they should be relatively consistent in their amount from month-to-month and year-to-year.

If you are accounting for an expense involving an item on which a sale depends, and which is necessary to complete an order, then you have a direct expense. Account for a direct expense here, you will overstate your SG&A expenses and understate your COGS.

The most common SG&A expenses for small businesses include office salaries, rent, professional fees, insurance, and the like.

Year-to-Date P&L Actuals & Percent of Net Sales					Plan	Projected
2016	2017	2018	2019	Jan-00	2020	2021

Do you have expenses reported here that should be accounted for in COGS?
___ Yes ___ No. If yes, who is accountable for adjusting your chart of accounts to improve your ability to account for these direct costs?

Marketing Investments

The primary purpose of investing money in marketing is to create awareness and interest in your business. Typical marketing costs include everything involved with the execution of the 4 P's of marketing

1. Product – the identification, selection, and development of a product or service
2. Price – the determination of what you will charge to deliver a product or service
3. Place – the distribution channel you will use to connect the customer with your business, and
4. Promotion – the development and implementation of how you create awareness and interest in what you do.

Year-to-Date P&L Actuals & Percent of Net Sales					Plan	Projected
2016	2017	2018	2019	Jan-00	2020	2021

Do you have more leads to follow-up or customers to serve than you can keep up with?
___ Yes ___ No. If the answer is yes, than this expense category should be close to zero.

Travel & Entertainment Expenses

T&A expenses are those costs of doing business incurred by a non-operating employee while he or she is traveling for business purposes or entertaining a business customer or client.

Examples of traveling expenses include money spent on lodging, transportation, and meals. Entertainment expenses include taking a client to dinner, to a theater, show, concert, or a sporting event.

Any meal, lodging, and travel expenses that are directly assigned to a job are to be included in COGS, and should not be accounted for here.

Year-to-Date P&L Actuals & Percent of Net Sales					Plan	Projected
2016	2017	2018	2019	Jan-00	2020	2021

Do you have a travel expense policy in place? ___ Yes ___ No. Answering no to this question is acceptable if T&E is a small expense.
Does your accounting processes give you clear expense visibility by category of expense and by the individual? ___ Yes ___ No. Answering "no" to this question is never acceptable, no matter how small the expense.

Office Expenses

Office expenses represent any expense related to office consumables and equipment regularly used in the office to keep the business running.

Typical expenses include postage, printer ink, paper clips, paper, and staples. Electronic equipment, such as a computer, printer, fax machine, and furniture, such as a desk or chair, are considered office expenses if the item is used solely for the business.

Year-to-Date P&L Actuals & Percent of Net Sales					Plan	Projected
2016	2017	2018	2019	Jan-00	2020	2021

Given the size of this expense, should you centralize office supply purchasing? ___
Yes ___ No. If yes, who should the person accountable for managing office related purchases?

Office Payroll

Office payroll is the amount paid out to employees for the services they have done for the organization during that pay period. The office payroll expense category represents the amount your business spends paying its office workers and non-operating (direct) employees in salaries and wages, bonuses, benefits, payroll taxes, and payroll processing fees. It should not include direct payroll costs that vary with operations.

Employees who don't contribute directly to gross profit are an additional expense that must be worth more than the cost being incurred, or they cost you money.

Year-to-Date P&L Actuals & Percent of Net Sales					Plan	Projected
2016	2017	2018	2019	Jan-00	2020	2021

Do you have people taking more money out of your company than the value they are creating? ___ Yes ___ No. If yes, what are you going to do to help the employee contribute more than they cost you?

Insurance Expenses

Insurance expense is the cost that has been incurred, has expired, or has been used up during the current accounting period to protect the nonmanufacturing functions of a business. The insurance costs incurred for manufacturing operations are allocated to the cost of goods produced.

Typical insurance expenses are Business Liability Insurance, Property Insurance, Vehicle Insurance, Product Liability Insurance, Medical, Dental, and any other related premiums paid for transferring the risk of loss from one party to another.

Year-to-Date P&L Actuals & Percent of Net Sales					Plan	Projected
2016	2017	2018	2019	Jan-00	2020	2021

How much property damage or liability claim could you afford to pay out-of-pocket for if damage or legal claim was filed against your company? $_____
When was the last time you completed an insurance coverage audit to confirm that you have the right levels of insurance ___/___/___ ? Do this to make sure you aren't overpaying for the coverage and risk profile that your business represents and that you are prepared to live with?

Professional & Outside Fees

Professional and Outside Fees are indirect costs incurred in the purchase of non-operating outside services and fees associated with running your business. Every outside fee paid is overhead that is only incurred to help you manage your business better, or because it is a hard indirect cost of doing business.

Typical expenses in this category range from professional fees paid to accountants, bookkeepers, and lawyers, to bank fees, business licenses, and any other expense you pay to an outside entity for services and business support.

Remember, every dollar you spend is a dollar on which you need to generate a return, or you will lose money. In taking on outside fees, the first question to ask is: is the cost I am taking on something my customers will pay for?" The second question is "will my employees be willing to work with the outside people I bring in? If the answer to both questions is "no," you are at risk of wasting money on which you won't make a return.

Year-to-Date P&L Actuals & Percent of Net Sales					Plan	Projected
2016	2017	2018	2019	Jan-00	2020	2021

Do you treat the hiring of outside advisors who work with your company the same way you treat an employee? ___ Yes ___ No. Do you vet hiring an outside service provider with the same rigor that your customers use to vet you before they elect to buy from you? ___ Yes ___ No.
If the answer is no to these questions, then you are likely wasting money on professional fees.

Property Expenses

Property expenses include all costs related to the occupancy and use of any property, including land and buildings, in which you conduct your business. Your business facilities must perform the following key functions for this to be a wise use of your money.

1 Foster efficient business operation
2 Present your business in a good light
3 Allow for future business growth
4 Accomplish these objectives at an economical cost

The start for determining your business facility needs is figuring out what is required to foster an efficient business operation.

Typical property expenses include rent or mortgage payment, property association fees, building repairs, cleaning, and maintenance.

Year-to-Date P&L Actuals & Percent of Net Sales					Plan	Projected
2016	2017	2018	2019	Jan-00	2020	2021

Do you believe your current business property is contributing to or detracting from your profitability?
___ Contributes ___ Detracts
Are you able to answer 'yes' for your current property to each of the four key functions of a facility?
___ Yes ___ No. If no, can you adjust your current facility layout and appearance to meet your business needs better? ___ Yes ___ No. If yes, who is accountable for doing this?

Utility Expenses

Utility expenses range from electric, gas, water, sewer, garbage, and security—to internet service providers, cell phones, and landlines. These expenses are not easily allocated to a product or job, and, as a result, are considered "overhead" to the business. These expenses can also be difficult to project when problems occur with a needed utility that requires out-of-pocket payment to repair.

Utility expenses may also fluctuate widely during the year. If this is the case, it's important to explore with your utility providers the options of flex-pay, competitive rates, or budget billing. Energy audit programs can also help improve your business's energy efficiency resulting in you a more accurate prediction of these month-to-month expenses.

Lastly, utility costs do add up, and they are difficult to reduce in the short-term, so, be very careful in every contract you sign, because you can't quickly pull these costs down once you've committed.

Year-to-Date P&L Actuals & Percent of Net Sales					Plan	Projected
2016	2017	2018	2019	Jan-00	2020	2021

Do you have utility expenses that fluctuate widely during the year? ___ Yes ___ No
If yes, who is the person accountable for managing your utility expenses down?
Do you have a 'rainy day' fund of monies set aside to pay for unexpected business costs? ___ Yes ___ No. If yes, how much cash do you have set aside?
$_____ If no, how much cash should you set aside? $_____

ABC - Additional Large SG&A Area

Other indirect costs and overhead expenses that do not change with the volume of sales and are not directly attributable to operations yet represent a significant spend warrants a unique SG&A expense category.

Year-to-Date P&L Actuals & Percent of Net Sales					Plan	Projected
2016	2017	2018	2019	Jan-00	2020	2021

Are you satisfied with the level of spend occurring here? ___ Yes ___ No.

Would a 10% reduction in this expense category significantly change your total operating income dollars? ___ Yes ___ No. If no, do nothing.

DEF - Additional Large SG&A Area

Other indirect costs and overhead expenses that do not change with the volume of sales and are not directly attributable to operations yet represent a significant spend warrants a unique SG&A expense category.

Year-to-Date P&L Actuals & Percent of Net Sales					Plan	Projected
2016	2017	2018	2019	Jan-00	2020	2021

Are you satisfied with the level of spend occurring here? ___ Yes ___ No.

Would a 10% reduction in this expense category significantly change your total operating income dollars? ___ Yes ___ No. If no, do nothing

Miscellaneous Expenses

The miscellaneous expense category is used to account for indirect costs and overhead expenses that do not change with the volume of sales, are not directly attributable to operations, and are not of such a significant size or frequency of purchase to warrant their own SG&A expense category.

The word "miscellaneous" comes from the Latin word "miscere," meaning "to mix." Use this general ledger account to record minimal amounts that occur from time to time. If you find the amount or frequency of an item, you're reporting increasing; then, you should create a new general ledger account to report on these as a selling, general, or administrative business expenses.

Year-to-Date P&L Actuals & Percent of Net Sales					Plan	Projected
2016	2017	2018	2019	Jan-00	2020	2021

Are you satisfied with the level of spend being recorded here? ___ Yes ___ No. If yes, do nothing.

Would a 10% reduction in this general ledger account significantly change your total operating income dollars? ___ Yes ___ No. If no, do nothing

Operating Income

Your second most important number from your P&L Statement measures what it cost you to support your operations out of every dollar of gross profit earned. Operating Income or EBITDA earnings are calculated from the company's Gross Profit, less SG&A, or overhead expenses.

The profit view reflected in your EBITDA earnings is used to determine how profitable a company is concerning operations, and it's a more accurate picture of a company's success than gross sales, gross profit, or net income. This profit number represents the income or profit resulting from your primary business operations, excluding interest, taxes, depreciation, amortization, extraordinary income, and other income.

Year-to-Date P&L Actuals & Percent of Net Sales					Plan	Projected
2016	2017	2018	2019	Jan-00	2020	2021

What is the biggest drain against your operating profits ?- Is it that you aren't producing enough gross profit to fund your overhead? Or, are your SG&A expenses too high? I have a ___ gross profit or ___ overhead expense problem?
Who is the best person to be accountable for fixing the problem area you have identified above?

Interest Expense

Interest expense is the cost of money a company pays for borrowing from a bank or other lending institution to buy an asset of any kind. For example, when you buy a piece of equipment using a bank loan, you must pay not only the amount you borrowed you will also pay interest based on the interest rate being charged on the amount you borrowed.

It is the interest paid, not the principal amount, that is included in this non-operating expense. Including interest expense within SG&A Expenses understates Operating Income.

Year-to-Date P&L Actuals & Percent of Net Sales					Plan	Projected
2016	2017	2018	2019	Jan-00	2020	2021

Are you fully accounting for the interest expense you are paying across all of your short-term liabilities? ___ Yes ___ No. If no, what accounting process do you have in place to record the interest expenses you are incurring and paying?

Who is accountable for ensuring that these costs are being recorded properly?

Taxes Paid

Any charge levied by a governmental entity for income, consumption, and wealth. Taxes paid expenses that should be included here involve Federal, State, City, and Property taxes.

Sales tax should be included in your COGS because it is a sales expense that is only incurred if a taxable sale occurs. As a result, it is a direct cost that will vary with sales.

Year-to-Date P&L Actuals & Percent of Net Sales					Plan	Projected
2016	2017	2018	2019	Jan-00	2020	2021

Are you behind on any tax payments that are due? ___ Yes ___ No. If yes, paying this expense is a high priority area and should be reflected in your cash management plan.
Are you expecting any large tax bills that you need to be setting aside funds to pay? If yes, how much money should you be setting aside to meet your tax obligations? $_____

Depreciation & Amortization Expense

Depreciation expense is an allowance made for wear and tear on an asset over its estimated useful life. Amortization is a gradual and periodic reduction of the cost of an intangible asset. Both depreciation and amortization expenses are non-cash expenses. They do not represent a cash outflow on the P&L Statement since you do not write a check for either of these costs of doing business. This is because the relevant cash outflow happened at the time the asset was purchased. When reported on the P&L Statement, this expense will reduce Net Income. It should never represent the total amount of depreciation and amortization that is reflected on your Balance Sheet. Depreciation reported on the balance sheet is the accumulated or the cumulative total amount of depreciation that has been reported as expensed on the income statement. The Balance Sheets Accumulated Depreciation amount is from the time the assets were acquired, until the date of the balance sheet. Depreciation represents the cost of capital assets used over time and is a contra asset account that offsets the fixed asset account. Any time a depreciated asset is sold, the accumulated depreciation reported is removed from the Balance Sheet.

Year-to-Date P&L Actuals & Percent of Net Sales					Plan	Projected
2016	2017	2018	2019	Jan-00	2020	2021

Are you accurately reflecting the portion of the fixed and intangible assets that should be considered consumed in the current period? ___ Yes ___ No.
Are you setting aside a portion of depreciation expense in a savings or money market account for necessary asset repair and replacement? ___ Yes ___ No. If no, you should reconsider not setting aside necessary monies required to maintain your revenue-producing assets.

Owners' Compensation

While knowing how much a business earns in profit is vital knowledge for every business, no matter its size—many small business owners fail to account for the value of their time adequately in their costs of doing business. Most often, this occurs through a failure to account for the personal labor they put into providing their customers with a service or product at a reasonable price. They neglect to place a cost per hour on the value they should be paid for their time. The wages, benefits, bonus, and payroll taxes a business owner pays themselves for the work they perform in the business should be reported as W-2 income. This is separated from Direct and Office Payroll because you are the last "employee" to get paid. Put another way, if there is no operating income, there is no money to pay yourself. As a result, the wages paid to owners should be included after reporting Operating Income.
Owners' Compensation does not include equity distributions or owners' draws. These are Balance Sheet transactions reflective of the business owner, whereas the wages they take for the work performed should be treated as a cost of doing business.

Year-to-Date P&L Actuals & Percent of Net Sales					Plan	Projected
2016	2017	2018	2019	Jan-00	2020	2021

Are you factoring in a fair wage for your time in the prices you set for your products and services? ___ Yes ___ No. If no, fix this mistake immediately.
What is the dollar difference between what you consider a fair wage for the work you do, and what you are paying yourself? $_____ Do you find this amount acceptable? ___ Yes ___ No. If no, what are you going to do differently to pay yourself the money you should be paid?

Other Nonoperating Expenses

Other Nonoperating Expenses often referred to as extraordinary expenses are those not directly attributable to the company's core business operations. Any nonoperating or extraordinary (one-time) expenses that are considered unusual or infrequent should be reflected here, and not reflected in COGS or SG&A. You account for these expenses here because they aren't a part of your on-going business operations.

Year-to-Date P&L Actuals & Percent of Net Sales					Plan	Projected
2016	2017	2018	2019	Jan-00	2020	2021

Are you satisfied with the level of spend being recorded here? ___ Yes ___ No. If yes, do nothing.
Would a 10% reduction in this general ledger account significantly change your Net Income dollars? ___ Yes ___ No. If yes, what are you going do to about it, and who is accountable for getting it done?

Other Nonoperating Income

Any inflow of monies from earnings or payments received that is not directly attributable to the company's core business operations are accounted for here as "non-operating income or other income" on your P&L Statement.

Nonoperating income usually does not occur on an ongoing basis and is examined separately from operating income. Income reported here includes gains or losses from investments, property or asset sales, currency exchange, and other atypical gains or losses that are not reflected in gross sales.

Any income generated through the sale of a subsidiary or division would also be accounted for here since the company won't be able to resell that division again. Such income is a one-time occurrence, and therefore, categorized as nonoperating income.

Year-to-Date P&L Actuals & Percent of Net Sales					Plan	Projected
2016	2017	2018	2019	Jan-00	2020	2021

Do you have non-operating inflows of money recorded in your gross sales? ___ Yes ___ No. If yes, who is accountable for recording them in the correct income category?
Do you have reoccurring operating income flows being recorded here? ___ Yes ___ No. If yes, you need to adjust how you are accounting for this income and any associated expenses.

Net Income

In any accounting period, Net Income is the end financial result. Net Income is referred to as the Bottom Line of the P&L Statement; after all, expenses are deducted from net revenues earned during that same period. This number represents your business's profit after employees, suppliers, lenders, and the government has all been paid—the amount left over goes to the business owner(s) in return for the capital they put at risk to produce this income. Net Income is also called earnings, net earnings, or net profit.
Net income is the owners' return from operations, and it should represent an increase in the value of their business investment if the business is profitable. If the business is operating at a loss, this number represents excess business spending in that accounting period. It is the only number that transfers from your P&L Statement to your Balance Sheet. Yet, it's your fourth most crucial number from business operations, because it is considered a "lagging number," generated after every expense has been deducted from Net Sales.

Year-to-Date P&L Actuals & Percent of Net Sales					Plan	Projected
2016	2017	2018	2019	Jan-00	2020	2021

Are you on track to realize your Net Income goal? ___ Yes ___ No. If no, what is the #1 action you must take to realize your Net Income goal?

Who is the best person to be accountable for getting this action done?

Assets

Assets represent the capital deployed to generate profits and cash flows. Asset values are shown on the Balance Sheet, classified according to the ease with which each asset can be liquidated or converted into cash.

Current assets include cash, inventory, marketable securities, and enforceable claims against others, such as accounts receivable.
Fixed assets include furniture, equipment machinery, vehicles, land, and building. They can also be a right to use, such as copyright, patent, trademark, or an assumption, like goodwill.

When people talk about asset values, particularly as it relates to purchasing them, it is vital to confirm if they are talking about asset cost, book value, market value, or residual value for the asset.

Balance Sheet on 12-31 by & Percent of P&L Net Sales					Plan	Projected
2016	2017	2018	2019	Jan-00	2020	2021

Is the value of your Balance Sheet total assets value increasing or decreasing this year over last? ___ Yes ___ No. If no, how many of the assets do you own are failing to produce value for your company? ___
Who is the best person to ensure that your core assets are producing value for you?

Current Assets

Current assets are the resources you have available to run your businesses on a short-term basis. Current assets are essential—you can't run a business without them. These assets are continually flowing in and out of your business through the ordinary course of business operations. For example, cash is converted, first into goods, and then back into cash.

Current assets are used to fund day-to-day operations and pay ongoing expenses. On the Balance Sheet, current assets are generally displayed in order of liquidity: that is, the ease with which they can be turned into cash in less than one year. These assets include petty cash, checking, savings, prepaid expenses, accounts receivable, marketable securities, inventory from raw materials, WIP, to finished goods.

Balance Sheet on 12-31 by & Percent of P&L Net Sales					Plan	Projected
2016	2017	2018	2019	Jan-00	2020	2021

Are most of your Current Assets tied up in Accounts Receivable? ___ Yes ___ No. If yes, how confident are you that you will collect on ALL of you're A/R? ___ Confident ___ Concerned. If concerned, what are you going to do to get paid what you are owed?
How much more do you have in current assets than in current liabilities? $_____ If current liabilities exceed current assets, you have a serious problem.

Cash

Cash is a current asset reported on your Balance Sheet that represents ready money which you have on deposit or in petty cash. These "cash assets" include money in hand, petty cash, bank account balance, customer checks, marketable securities, and the unutilized portion of a line of credit.

The key to cash as an asset is that, when you are out of cash, you are out of business. It's critical to maintain some cash balance reflective of your cash on hand target, the amount that you never intend to dip below for peace of mind.

Carry too much of a cash balance, you lose the opportunity to put your cash to work for you in short to near-term marketable securities. Fail to carry enough cash, and you are at risk of going out of business because you ran out of cash.

Balance Sheet on 12-31 & Percent of P&L Net Sales					Plan	Projected
2016	2017	2018	2019	Jan-00	2020	2021

What is the minimum amount of cash you want to have on hand at any time throughout the year? $_____ Divide this amount into how much cash you are reporting on your Balance Sheet – is the result of the math greater than 1? ___ Yes ___ No. If yes, then your business is performing better than the target. If no, what are you going to do today to improve your cash on hand ratio?

Accounts Receivable

Accounts Receivable, also referred to as A/R, consists of sales made but not yet paid for by the customers (trade debtors). This number represents the amount of money still owed to you by customers after they have received the goods or services you've delivered.

Accounts receivables are shown as current (short-term) assets on the Balance Sheet. The represent unsecured promises by your customer to pay you in the future. These sums must be accurate, as they are a critical factor in determining business liquidity.

Balance Sheet 12-Month Average & Percent of P&L Net Sales					Plan	Projected
2016	2017	2018	2019	Jan-00	2020	2021

Is your A/R Aging current amount (less than 30-days) greater or less than the monies owed you that are greater than 30-days? ___ Yes, the current A/R is higher than past due or ___ No, the current A/R is less than what's past due.
Do you have an A/R collections strategy in place? ___ Yes ___ No. If you answered no to both of these questions, then you need to address your approach to collecting the money that is owed to you.

Inventory

Cash is a current asset reported on your Balance Sheet that represents ready money which you have on deposit or in petty cash. These "cash assets" include money in hand, petty cash, bank account balance, customer checks, marketable securities, and the unutilized portion of a line of credit.

The key to cash as an asset is that, when you are out of cash, you are out of business. It's critical to maintain some cash balance reflective of your cash on hand target, the amount that you never intend to dip below for peace of mind.

Carry too much of a cash balance, you lose the opportunity to put your cash to work for you in short to near-term marketable securities. Fail to carry enough cash, and you are at risk of going out of business because you ran out of cash.

Balance Sheet on 12-31 by & Percent of P&L Net Sales					Plan	Projected
2016	2017	2018	2019	Jan-00	2020	2021

Do you have materials, component parts and WIP sitting in your facility that you have an intent to resell? ___ Yes ___ No. If yes, it is advisable that you properly account for the value of this inventory.
Do you consider the inventory you are reporting as salable at a price greater than the amount paid for the goods originally? ___ Yes ___ No. If no, unload it.

Other Assets

Accounts Receivable; also referred to as A/R, consists of sales made but not yet paid for by the customers (trade debtors). This number represents the amount of money still owed to you by customers after they have received the goods or services you've delivered.

Accounts receivable are shown as current (short-term) assets on the Balance Sheet. They represent unsecured promises by your customer to pay you in the future. These sums must be accurate, as they are a critical factor in determining business liquidity.

Balance Sheet on 12-31 by & Percent of P&L Net Sales					Plan	Projected
2016	2017	2018	2019	Jan-00	2020	2021

Do you have current or fixed assets within Other Assets that you consider core to successfully operating your business? ___ Yes ___ No. If yes, there is probably a better asset classification you should be using. If no, why are you holding onto this asset?
When are you going to deal with your Other Assets issue?

Fixed Assets

A Fixed Asset is an asset that is not consumed or sold during the ordinary course of business. These assets include land, buildings, equipment, machinery, vehicles, leasehold improvements, and other such items.

Fixed assets enable their owner to carry out operations. These assets are not immovable, but they are expected to last or to be in use for more than one year. The value of a fixed asset is calculated by deducting depreciation from the purchase price.

As any fixed asset with long-term value is used, the value of that asset decreases. The annual decrease in value is expensed as "depreciation," so that the current estimated value of each fixed asset as an accumulated depreciation offset on the Balance Sheet.

Balance Sheet on 12-31 by & Percent of P&L Net Sales					Plan	Projected
2016	2017	2018	2019	Jan-00	2020	2021

What planned Fixed Asset purchases do you intend to acquire in the next 24-months?

How will these fixed asset investments impact your sales production and cost structure?

Accumulated Depreciation + Amortization

Accumulated depreciation represents the expired value of an asset. It is neither cash nor any other type of asset that can be used to buy another asset. Its purpose is to spread the cost of a fixed asset over its useful life to accurately match the cost of the asset with the revenue it generates. Accumulated depreciation is calculated by dividing the asset's cost by its useful life.

Accumulated amortization of assets refers to allocating the cost of an intangible asset over a period of time. These amounts recorded on the Balance Sheet reflect the total allowed accumulated amortization over the life of the asset. Once the asset is removed from the balance sheet, the equivalent depreciation or amortization is removed as well.

The expensed portion of depreciation and amortization is recorded on the P&L Statement, after Operating Income. Each time depreciation or amortization is expensed, the amount expensed is added to the accumulated amounts reflected on the Balance Sheet.

Balance Sheet on 12-31 by & Percent of P&L Net Sales					Plan	Projected
2016	2017	2018	2019	Jan-00	2020	2021

What fully depreciated assets do you have that remain key to your long-term business success? Should any of these assets be replaced? ___ Yes ___ No. If yes, when?

If no, are you budgeting appropriate repair and maintenance costs for your aging assets?
___ Yes ___ No.

Liabilities

A liability is defined as a company's legal, financial debts or obligations that arise during business operations. It is a claim against the assets of a business, as a result of past or current third-party financing transactions or actions.

Liabilities require a mandatory transfer of assets, or provision of services, at specified dates. They are recorded on the right side of the balance sheet as follows

Current Liabilities include trade debt (accounts payable), wages payable, accrued expenses, taxes, short-term loans, customer deposits, and unearned revenues.

Long-term Liabilities represent monies owed at a future period more than twelve months from the Balance Sheet date for loans accrued by a business to acquire an asset on credit.

Balance Sheet on 12-31 by & Percent of P&L Net Sales					Plan	Projected
2016	2017	2018	2019	Jan-00	2020	2021

Are you "borrowing from Peter to pay Paul?" ___ Yes ___ No. If yes, you are in serious problems because your assets aren't generating sufficient return to meet your financial obligations.
Do you have underperforming assets that you can convert to cash so you can retire the debt you must pay others? ___ Yes ___ No. If yes, free up the cash.

Current Liabilities

Current liabilities are a company's debts or obligations due within one year. They are settled by the use of a current asset, such as cash, or by creating a new current liability.

Current liabilities appear on a company's balance sheet and include short-term debt, accounts payable, accrued liabilities, and other similar debts. They can represent a significant impact on your ability to manage your cash flow generation.

Your business is at risk anytime Cash OutFlows, associated with your Current Liabilities, are close to exceeding your Cash InFlows, associated with your Current Assets. You protect your business by avoiding any additional debt that you are not adequately capitalized with cash reserves to meet should a business downturn or emergency arise.

Balance Sheet on 12-31 by & Percent of P&L Net Sales					Plan	Projected
2016	2017	2018	2019	Jan-00	2020	2021

Are your current liabilities of $_____ greater than your current assets of $_____ ___ Yes ___ No. If yes, you have a serious problem than needs to be addressed immediately.
Who is the best person to ensure that your current assets are greater than your current liabilities?

Accounts Payable

Accounts Payable (A/P) represents the amount of money a company still owes creditors (suppliers, etc.) in return for their goods and services. This value includes unpaid bills owed to suppliers (trade creditors) as distinguished from accrued interest, rent, salaries, taxes, and other such accounts.

Accounts payable are shown under current liabilities in the Balance Sheet. Lenders and investors typically examine the relationship of these accounts to judge the soundness of a business's day-to-day financial management.

When processing A/P, avoid transposing errors or failing to record the expense in the right GL account. It is also important that you are timely and disciplined in matching delivery receipts with invoices. This business practice is the best way to detect fraudulent activity from either employees or vendors.

Balance Sheet on 12-31 by & Percent of P&L Net Sales					Plan	Projected
2016	2017	2018	2019	Jan-00	2020	2021

Are your current accounts payable ($_____) greater than your current accounts receivable ($_____)? Is your cash on hand as a percent of target less than 1? If yes, you have a serious problem than needs to be addressed immediately.
What expenses can you end immediately to prevent further increases in A/P?

Long-term Liabilities

Long-Term Liabilities are financial obligations or debts incurred during business operations that are payable over a period greater than one year from the date of the Balance Sheet.

Long-term debt restricts your monthly cash flow in the near term. The higher your debt balances, the more you have committed to paying on them each month. This means you have to use more of your monthly earnings to repay debt rather than encourage new investments to grow. It also limits your ability to build up a safety net of cash savings to cover unexpected business costs.

The other challenge with long-term debt is tied to collateral. Using personal and business assets as security to gain financing at reasonable interest rates puts you at risk of losing the asset through repossession if you get into a cash flow crisis and fall behind in your payments.

Balance Sheet on 12-31 by & Percent of P&L Net Sales					Plan	Projected
2016	2017	2018	2019	Jan-00	2020	2021

Are your long-term liabilities of $_____ greater than your fixed assets after depreciation worth $_____ ___ Yes ___ No. If yes, you owe more than your core assets are worth.
What underutilized assets can you sell immediately to free up cash to pay down your long-term liabilities?

Equity

Equity is represented at the bottom of the Balance Sheet, after the reporting of assets and liabilities. It represents the capital used by the business owners to generate income. The amount is calculated by deducting the book value of the liabilities from the book value of the assets.

This third category on your balance sheet represents the amount of the funds contributed by the owners or shareholders, plus any additional investments by owners, into the business—less any amount that the owner draws, plus the net income or losses of the business recorded as retained earnings. Put more simply, the accounting equation: equity (or owners' equity) is the difference between the value of the assets, and the value of the liabilities of the business.

Subtract Liabilities from Assets, you get owners' equity. If this final number is increasing year-over-year, then you are building the value of your equity. If it's declining, then you are destroying equity. Mathematically, its as simple as that.

Balance Sheet on 12-31 by & Percent of P&L Net Sales					Plan	Projected
2016	2017	2018	2019	Jan-00	2020	2021

Over the last three years, has the equity value reported on your balance sheet been increasing or decreasing? ___ Increasing ___ Decreasing. If decreasing, you are failing to own a business that is worth more today than it was in previous years. Would you be better served placing your money with a bank to invest for you? ___ Yes ___ No. If yes, then it's time to explore selling or closing your business.

Owners' Equity

Owners' Equity is the amount of money invested in the company by its owners to start the business. It represents the initial ownership interest or claim of a holder of common stock (ordinary shares), and some types of preferred stock (preference shares) of a company. Ultimately, owners' equity represents the monies available for the owner(s) after everyone else has been paid. It is termed a liability, because it is an obligation of the company to its owners, for their investment in the business—minus the owner's draws or withdrawals from the business, plus the net income (or minus the net loss) since the businesses launch.

Mathematically, the amount of owners' equity is the amount of assets, minus the amount of liabilities. Another way to consider owners' equity in a business is is the financial value of the business to a prospective buyer. Viewed in this way, owners' equity would not be considered a recordable value until the business has been sold—yet, ultimately, this value helps determine what the business is worth to you, based on what the buyer is prepared to pay. Unfortunately, this amount is rarely what you think your business is worth.

Balance Sheet on 12-31 by & Percent of P&L Net Sales					Plan	Projected
2016	2017	2018	2019	Jan-00	2020	2021

What was your initial investment in your business $_____? Is this amount larger or smaller than what is reported as Total Equity? ___ Larger ___ Smaller. If the initial amount invested is less than what is reported as Total Equity, than you have lost money on your investment. What are you prepared to do differently today so that by the end of the year you have increased the value of your Total Equity?

Owners Draw or Distribution

An Owners' Draw or distribution is money taken from a company's revenue by the owner for their personal use. The amount of an owners' draw is not reported as an expense on the income statement of the business. Instead, the owners' draw is considered to be a direct reduction of the owners' capital reducing the amount of total equity.

If the business owner is withdrawing profits generated by the business, this is viewed as taxable income on the owners personal tax return. If the owner is taking out funds previously contributed to operate the company, then it must be made clear in your financial statements that the owners' draw is from capital contributed, not profits generated.

Balance Sheet on 12-31 by & Percent of P&L Net Sales					Plan	Projected
2016	2017	2018	2019	Jan-00	2020	2021

Are you satisfied with the amount of money you are taking out of your business? ___ Yes ___ No. If no, what will you do differently today to create more income from the business to pay you your desired earnings?

Retained Earnings

Retained Earnings represent the profits a company has earned as of the date of the Balance Sheet, less any dividends or other distributions paid to investors. This amount is adjusted whenever there is an entry to the accounting records that impacts a revenue or expense account. It is the most important balance sheet number signifying the 'sum of all profits' retained since the company's inception less reported losses. Mathematically, it is the accumulated undistributed earnings of a company retained for future needs, or for future distribution to its owners, from profits generated by a company that is not distributed to stockholders (owners) as dividends. These earnings do not represent surplus cash. Instead, retained earnings demonstrate what a company did with its profits—the amount of profit that the company has reinvested in the business since its inception. Retained earnings are not an asset. They are considered a liability to the business—money that has been set aside to pay stockholders in the event of a sale or buy-out of the business. Consequently, retained earnings are part of stockholder's equity. They are also referred to as accumulated earnings, accumulated profit, earned surplus, or undistributed earnings.

Balance Sheet on 12-31 by & Percent of P&L Net Sales					Plan	Projected
2016	2017	2018	2019	Jan-00	2020	2021

What is the #1 action you must take to realize your Net Income Goal?

What are the consequences to ownership for failing to realize your Net Income Goal?

Financial Ratios

Financial ratios are mathematical comparisons of financial statement accounts used to understand how well a business is performing, and where, exactly, it needs to improve. A significant benefit of financial ratios is that they are agnostic relative to the size of a company, or the type of industry.

Each ratio is simply a raw computation of financial position and performance used to identify a company's strengths and weaknesses. The most common categories of financial ratio groupings include the following:

Profitability Ratios verify how well the company uses its resources and assets to generate profits.

Efficiency Ratios analyze the time that it takes a company to convert a sale into cash.

Liquidity Ratios are used by creditors to measure a firm's ability to meet its short-term obligations by turning liquid assets into cash.

Solvency Ratios measure a company's ability to sustain operations by comparing debt levels with equity, assets, and earnings.

Coverage Ratios measure how easily companies can afford to meet the interest payments associated with their debt.

Profitability Ratios

Business profitability is critical to the concept of business solvency and in determining the probability of a business to remain a "going concern." Profitability Ratios compare P&L Statement categories to show a company's ability to generate profits from its operations by calculating a company's return on its investment in assets. Profitability ratios closely relate to Efficiency Ratios that too, show how well a company uses its assets to generate profits. The most common profitability ratios are the following:

Gross Margin Ratio
Contribution Margin
Operating Margin Ratio
Profit Margin Ratio
Return on Assets Ration
Return on Capital Employed
Return on Equity
DuPont Formula

The above ratios are used to judge how well a company uses its resources and assets to generate profits from operations.

Gross Margin Ratio

(Net Sales - COGS) / Net Sales

Gross Margin represents the percentage of pure profit from the sale of the cost of goods sold that remains to pay the balance of operating costs. A falling gross profit shows that costs of production are rising faster than the selling price, or that inventory is shrinking due to fraudulent activity or product spoilage. A higher Gross Margin Ratio is achieved in two ways:

1. Reduce costs by buying materials or labor at a lower price
2. Sell your products at a higher mark-up.

A high Gross Margin Ratio means stability in times of economic downturn because the company can afford to cut prices. A low gross margin may mean low creditworthiness, or the inability to fight off competition.

Year-to-Date P&L Acutals					Plan	Projected
2016	2017	2018	2019	Jan-00	2020	2021

Higher is Better	Lower is Worse
More money for the company to make a profit after paying direct costs.	Company is likely operating at a loss with less money to pay other business expenses.

A 40% gross margin means that for every dollar of sales, 40 cents remains from that sales dollar after the cost of goods sold is paid to cover the non-operating or fixed expenses before a profit is realized.

Contribution Margin Ratio

Net Price per Unit - Cost per Unit - Variable Operating Expenses per Unit

The Contribution Margin equation is dependent on the difference between fixed and variable costs. It represents the distinction between a product's sales revenue, and the variable costs calculating the amount of sales that exceed variable costs.

The Contribution Margin Ratio measures how efficiently a company can produce products while maintaining low levels of variable costs. Managers use this calculation to help improve internal procedures in the production process.

Year-to-Date P&L Acutals					Plan	Projected
2016	2017	2018	2019	Jan-00	2020	2021

Higher is Better	Lower is Worse
Products being produced and sold are contributing to covering other business expenses.	You should question the value of selling a product if it fails to contribute margin to cover other expenses.

A 40% contribution margin per unit means that for every dollar of unit sales, 40 cents remains from that sales dollar to cover other expenses. A 25% contribution margin per unit means that product sales contribute 15 cents less for every dollar sold than the higher margin product.

Operating Margin Ratio
(Gross Profit - Depreciation - Amortization) / Net Sales

Operating Margin Ratio represents what's leftover from a dollar of sales after subtracting all costs associated with producing, acquiring, and selling your products and services. It represents what is available from each dollar of sales to pay the company's fixed expenses, capital providers, and its taxes after subtracting depreciation and amortization from net sales.

The Operating Margin Ratio is the best measure of operations managerial performance relative to how much revenue is left over after all operating costs have been paid. This number reveals what proportion of revenues is available to cover non-operating costs.

	Year-to-Date P&L Acutals				Plan	Projected
2016	2017	2018	2019	Jan-00	2020	2021

Higher is Better	Lower is Worse
The more money from operations to pay for its fixed costs, the more stable the company.	Using non-operating income to cover operating expenses shows operations that are not sustainable.

A 20% operating margin ratio means that for every dollar of sales, only 20 cents remains to cover the non-operating expenses of a business before a profit can be realized.

EBITDA Earnings Ratio
(Gross Margin - G&A Expenses before Interest, Taxes, Depreciation, Amortization) / Net Sales

The EBITDA Earnings Ratio, as a percent of Net Sales, is a top-level indicator of the current operational profitability of a business. As such, it's often used to set performance standards.

The EBITDA Earnings Ratio is used to determine the profitability of a business's operations before interest, taxes, depreciation, and amortization expenses are factored in. It is a more accurate picture of a company's success than gross sales and a better proxy for cash operating profit.

	Year-to-Date P&L Acutals				Plan	Projected
2016	2017	2018	2019	Jan-00	2020	2021

Higher is Better	Lower is Worse
Means more money for the Owners to pocket or reinvest after paying COGS + SG&A Expenses.	Means less money for the Owners to work with after paying COGS + SG&A Expenses.

A 15% EBITDA earnings ratio means that for every dollar of sales, only 15 cents of operating profit remains to cover interest, taxes, depreciation, and amortization expenses, and only what is left over can be paid out as dividends or reinvested into the business.

Net Income Margin Ratio
(Operating Income - ITDA - Other Expenses + Other Income) / Net Sales

Net Income Margin Ratio measures how effectively a company can convert sales into net income. Also called the net profit ratio or the return on sales ratio. It validates a company's pricing policies and its ability to control variable, fixed, and nonoperating costs. A low-net profit margin indicates high risk, with the possibility that a decline in sales will erase profits and result in loss.

Indirectly, Net Income Margin Ratio measures how well a company manages its expenses relative to its net sales by showing what percentage of sales are left over after all expenses are paid. A business earns a higher Net Income Margin Ratio by generating more revenues while keeping expenses constant; or, by keeping revenues constant and lowering expenses.

	Year-to-Date P&L Acutals				Plan	Projected
2016	2017	2018	2019	Jan-00	2020	2021

Higher is Better	Lower is Worse
Company is running efficiently, creditors will get paid, and owners will get a return on their investment.	Indicates expenses are too high; management needs to tighten its budget and reduce expenses.

A 10% net income or profit margin ratio means that for every dollar of sales only 10 cents remains as profit to be paid out as dividends or reinvested into the business.

Return on Asset Ratio
Net Income / Total Assets

Since the sole purpose of assets is to generate revenues and produce profits, the Return on Asset Ratio (ROA) ratio shows how well the company can convert its investments in assets into profits—whether funded by equity or debt.

ROA measures how efficiently a company is managing its current and fixed assets to produce profits during a given period. The return is measured in "net profits earned" from all of the company's assets, regardless of whether they were funded with debt or equity—whereas ROE (see below) is focused only on the owner's investment (equity).

	Year-to-Date P&L Acutals and Ending Balance Sheet				Plan	Projected
2016	2017	2018	2019	Jan-00	2020	2021

Higher is Better	Lower is Worse
A positive ROA is usually an indicator of an upward profit trend.	Any ratio below 1 indicates that assets are not efficient in producing sales.

A ratio of 1 means that the net profits of a company equals the average total assets for the year. In other words, the company is generating $1.00 dollar of profit for every dollar invested in assets.

Return on Equity Ratio
Net Income / Owners' Equity

The Return on Equity Ratio (ROE) reflects how much money is made based on the investors' investment in the company, not the company's investment in assets, or something else. ROE measures the ability of a company to generate profits from its shareholder investments by showing how much profit is generated by each dollar of common stockholders' equity.

ROE is especially important for potential investors, who want to know how efficiently a company will use their money to generate net income. ROE also indicates how effectively management uses equity financing to fund operations and grow the company.

	Year-to-Date P&L Acutals and Ending Balance Sheet				Plan	Projected
2016	2017	2018	2019	Jan-00	2020	2021

Higher is Better	Lower is Worse
Indicates that the company is using its investors' funds effectively.	Means that the company isn't growing and owners aren't receiving a return on their investment.

A ratio of 1 means that every dollar of equity generates a $1.00 dollar of sales. A 1.8 ROE means that every dollar of equity earned $1.80 or 180% return to owners on their investment.

Return on Capital Employed
Operating Income / (Total Assets - Current Liabilities)

The Return on Capital Employed (ROCE) refers to the total assets of a company, less its current liabilities. ROCE is also viewed as stockholders' equity, less long-term liabilities. Both equal the same figure, which shows how efficiently a company generates profits from its capital employed, by comparing operating income to capital employed.

ROCE is more useful than ROE in evaluating the longevity of a company. This is because ROCE shows how many dollars in profits are generated by each dollar of capital employed. ROCE also considers long-term financing in looking at asset performance—to confirm whether the assets are generating returns at a higher rate than what it costs to borrow funding to secure these assets. To put it simply, if a company borrows at 10% and can only achieve a return of 5%, they are losing money.

	Year-to-Date P&L Acutals and Ending Balance Sheet				Plan	Projected
2016	2017	2018	2019	Jan-00	2020	2021

Higher is Better	Lower is Worse
Means that more dollars of profits are generated by each dollar of capital employed.	Management is inefficient at using capital employed. A real problem if ratio is lower than the borrowing rate.

A ratio of 1 means operating income equals the capital employed by that company to produce that income. i.e., the company is generating 1 dollar of profit for every dollar of capital employed. A 0.2 return indicates that for every dollar invested in capital employed, the company made 20 cents of profits.

Dupont Formula
(Net Income/Sales) X (Sales/Total Assets) X (Total Assets/Owners' Equity)

While ROE shows the percentage of capital returned to the owners of a business, it does not provide insight into how the return was earned. The Dupont Formula is not about looking for large or small output numbers. It is about analyzing what is causing the current ROE. To measure the performance of a company, use the following ratios:
1. Profit Margin (Net Income / Sales) helps you to quantify operating efficiency as determined by profit margin and shows you the quality of earnings that result from each dollar of sales.
2. Asset Turnover (Sales / Total Assets) measures asset use efficiency by total asset turnover, showing how well the business uses its assets to generate sales.
3. Financial Leverage (Total Assets/Owners' Equity) measures financial leverage by the equity multiplier, showing how much debt the firm has used to acquire the assets necessary to generate sales or provide services.

	Year-to-Date P&L Acutals and Ending Balance Sheet				Plan	Projected
2016	2017	2018	2019	Jan-00	2020	2021

Increasing any one of these three levers will increase the owners' return. The first two are closely related to the company's operations, while the third (financial leverage) is the way the company has been funded.

Based on these three performance measures, the model illustrates whether a company can best raise its ROE by maintaining a high profit margin, increasing asset turnover, or leveraging assets more effectively.

EFFICIENCY RATIOS

Efficiency Ratios like Profitability Ratios measure how well companies utilize their assets to generate income. They are also called Activity Ratios. They analyze the time that it takes a company to collect cash from its customers, or the time it takes the company to convert inventory into cash—in other words, make sales.

Most often, when companies are efficient with their resources, they will be more profitable. The most common Efficiency Ratios used are the following:

Accounts Receivable Days
Accounts Receivable Turnover Ratio
Working Capital Ratio
Total Asset Turnover Ratio
Fixed Asset Turnover Ratio

The above Efficiency Ratios go hand-in-hand with the Profitability Ratios since company profits are derived from the efficient use of company resources.

Accounts Receivable Days
(Net Accounts Receivable / Net Sales) X 365

Accounts Receivable Days (ARD) is the average number of days a company takes to collect payments on goods sold. Also called "days sales" in receivables or "debtor days." It represents the length of time it takes to clear all Accounts Receivable, or, how long it takes to receive the money for goods sold. This is a useful number for determining how efficiently the company collects the money owed to them by their customers.

Year-to-Date P&L Acutals and Ending Balance Sheet					Plan	Projected
2016	2017	2018	2019	Jan-00	2020	2021

Shorter is Better	Longer is Worse
Lower than 30-days may indicate credit policies are too strict that hold business back from making higher revenues.	An ARD of 50-days or more indicates collection problems, which place significant pressure on cash flows.

A/R Days of 45 establishes that the average days it takes to collect payment from your customers is 45-days. Customers taking longer to pay may represent bad debt, whereas customers who pay on time are more valuable and should be retained.

Accounts Receivable Turnover Ratio
Net Credit Sales / Average Accounts Receivable

Accounts Receivable Turnover Ratio (ARTO) shows how efficiently a company collects its credit sales from customers, and it's an indication of the quality of credit sales and receivables. The more quickly a company can collect cash from its customers, the faster they can use that cash to pay bills and meet other obligations.

ARTO measures how many times a business can turn its accounts receivable into cash during a given period. The greater the turnover, the shorter the period between sales and collections.

Year-to-Date P&L Acutals and Ending Balance Sheet					Plan	Projected
2016	2017	2018	2019	Jan-00	2020	2021

Higher is Better	Lower is Worse
This means that the company is collecting its receivables more frequently throughout the year.	Indicates difficulties collecting monies owed to the company by its customers.

A receivables turnover of 8 signals that, on average, receivables were fully collected eight times during the period or once every 46 days (365 ÷ 8).

Total Asset Turnover Ratio
Net Sales / Total Assets

The real value of any business is not in the assets it owns, but in the profits and cash flows generated by those assets. Value is a function of the returns to the owners, after accounting for the costs of acquiring and maintaining the business's assets. The Total Asset Turnover Ratio (TATR) the value of the investment or money tied up in a business waiting to become throughput. This ratio measures how efficiently a company uses its assets to generate sales from each dollar of company assets.

Since the assets of a business equate to a business's capacity to earn money from its resources, TATR also measures how well a company is managed and how it uses its assets to produce products and sales. Adding assets requires capital, which means those new assets need to earn a return to cover the cost of this additional capital.

Year-to-Date P&L Acutals and Ending Balance Sheet					Plan	Projected
2016	2017	2018	2019	Jan-00	2020	2021

Higher is Better	Lower is Worse
This means that company is better at using its assets to generate sales.	The company isn't using its assets efficiently, and most likely, that it has management or production problems.

A ratio of .5 means that each dollar of assets generates 50 cents of sales.

Inventory Turnover Ratio
COGS / Average Inventory

Inventory Turnover Ratio (ITR) shows how easily a company can turn its inventory into cash through projected sales. If the inventory can't be sold, it's worthless to the company. ITR depends on purchasing efficiency and sales velocity. Ideally, sales must match inventory purchases; otherwise, the inventory will not turn over efficiently.

High inventory turns mean better liquidity from superior merchandising, or, can also mean a shortage in needed inventory for sales. Low inventory turns mean poor liquidity, possible overstocking, obsolescence, or a planned inventory buildup. Zero is the best possible ITR ratio.

Year-to-Date P&L Acutals and Ending Balance Sheet					Plan	Projected
2016	2017	2018	2019	Jan-00	2020	2021

Higher is Better	Lower is Worse
Normally, a high number indicates that inventory is sold at a faster rate and that fewer company resources are tied.	Represents a higher risk of loss through un-saleable inventory (see above.)

An inventory turnover ratio of 4 means that inventory was "turned over" or replenished 4 times during a period of one year. This equates to inventory being turned over once every 91 days, or 365 days ÷ 4.

Day's Sales in Inventory
(Ending Inventory / COGS) X 365

Management wants its inventory to move as fast as possible, to minimize inventory carrying costs, and to increase cash flows. Day's Sales in Inventory measures the number of days it takes to sell all inventory by measuring the inventory value, company liquidity, and cash flows. Day's Sales in Inventory is also called "days inventory outstanding" or "days in inventory."

It's expensive for a company to keep, maintain, and store inventory—and, older, more obsolete inventory is always worth less than current, fresh inventory. Days in Inventory shows how fast the company is moving its inventory, and how fresh the inventory is, by indicating the average number of days merchandise remains in inventory.

Year-to-Date P&L Acutals and Ending Balance Sheet					Plan	Projected
2016	2017	2018	2019	Jan-00	2020	2021

Shorter is Better	Longer is Worse
Shorter days inventory outstanding means the company can convert its inventory into cash much sooner.	The longer inventory sits unused, the longer the company's cash can't be used for other operations.

A days' sales in inventory of 10 tells you that a business has enough inventory to last the next ten days or that you can turn your inventory into cash in the next 40 days if your average A/R Days are 30.

Day's Sales Outstanding
(Accounts Receivable / Net Credit Sales) X 365

Day's Sales Outstanding measures the number of days it takes a company to collect cash from its credit sales. Remember, a completed sale doesn't matter until the cash is efficiently collected.

Days' Sales Outstanding calculates the liquidity and efficiency of a company's collections, by showing how well a company can collect cash from its customers, by measuring the number of days it takes a company to convert its sales into cash.

Year-to-Date P&L Acutals and Ending Balance Sheet					Plan	Projected
2016	2017	2018	2019	Jan-00	2020	2021

Shorter is Better	% Credit Sales	Longer is Worse
This means cash is getting collected from A/R. A lower number also shows that A/R is less likely to be written off as bad debt.		Reveals a problem with collection procedures. Your customers are either unable or unwilling to pay for their purchases from you.

If your payment terms are net 30 and your day's sales outstanding is 50, this means it takes you 50 days, on average, to collect cash from your customers. I.e., you have more delinquent customers than you have prompt payers for the goods and services you sold them.

Day's Payable Outstanding
(Accounts Payable / (COGS-Direct Labor)) X 365

Day's Payable Outstanding measures the average number of days it takes the business to make payments on purchased goods.

The length of time it takes to clear all outstanding Accounts Payable (A/P) is a useful number for determining how efficiently the company is clearing its short-term liability obligations.

Year-to-Date P&L Acutals and Ending Balance Sheet					Plan	Projected
2016	2017	2018	2019	Jan-00	2020	2021

On-Time is Best	Longer is Worse
Numbers lower than 30 days indicate that you are paying your vendors too quickly.	Numbers much higher than 50 days indicate possible payment problems and significant pressure on cash flows.

A/P Days of 35 establishes that the average number of days it takes to pay your vendors is 35-days from the date of invoice.

CASH CONVERSION CYCLE
Days Inventory Outstanding + Days Sales Outstanding - Days Payables Outstanding

The Cash Conversion Cycle measures the amount of time each net input dollar is tied up in production and sales to customers before it is converted into cash. It is the length of time in days that it takes for a company to convert resource inputs into cash flows by selling inventory and collecting receivables. This cycle has three distinct parts.
1. Current inventory level: how long it will take the company to sell this inventory as measured by days inventory outstanding.
2. Current sales: the amount of time it takes to collect the cash from these sales as calculated by days sales outstanding.
3. Current outstanding payables: representing how much a company owes its current vendors for inventory purchases, and when the company will need to pay off its vendors, calculated by days payables outstanding.

Year-to-Date P&L Acutals and Ending Balance Sheet					Plan	Projected
2016	2017	2018	2019	Jan-00	2020	2021

Fewer Days is Better	Greater Days is Worse
A small conversion cycle indicates an ability to buy and sell inventory, and then receive cash from customers in less time.	Means an extended number of days between paying the vendor for the inventory, and receiving the cash from its customers.

A cash conversion cycle of 20 means it takes 20 days from paying for inventory to receiving the cash from its sale.

Fixed Asset Turnover Ratio
Net Sales / (Fixed Assets - Accumulated Depreciation)

The Fixed Asset Turnover Ratio measures the return on investment in property, plant, and equipment. This ratio is obtained by comparing net sales with fixed assets and by calculating how efficiently a company is producing sales with its machines and equipment.

A high or low Fixed Asset Turnover Ratio does not always have a direct correlation with performance. If a company uses an accelerated depreciation method, like double-declining depreciation, the book value of their equipment will be artificially low—which makes their performance look much better than it is. Similarly, a company that is not reinvesting in new equipment will see this metric continue to rise, year over year, because the accumulated depreciation balance keeps increasing, thus reducing the denominator.

Year-to-Date P&L Acutals and Ending Balance Sheet					Plan	Projected
2016	2017	2018	2019	Jan-00	2020	2021

Higher is Better	Lower is Worse
Means assets are being utilized efficiently in generating sales unless the company has sold equipment and is now doing more outsourcing.	Indicates fixed assets are not fully utilized if product demand and machine investments are out of alignment.

A ratio of 5 means that the company generates five times more sales than the net book value of its assets.

Liquidity Ratios

Liquidity is a measure of a company's ability to meet its near-term financial obligations through liquid assets that can be converted to cash. These assets are reported on the Balance Sheet as cash, short-term investments, current A/R, and inventory.

Liquidity Ratios are the second most widely used ratios, coming in at a close second to Profitability Ratios. Creditors use Liquidity Ratios to measure a firm's ability to meet its short-term obligations by turning liquid assets into cash to pay off liabilities and other current obligations. The most common Liquidity Ratios are the following:

- Working Capital or Current Ratio
- Quick Ratio
- Cash Ratio
- Accounts Payable Turnover
- Times Interest Earned Ratio

The above ratios measure how easy it will be for the company to raise enough cash or convert assets into cash to pay off its current liabilities as they become due, as well as their long-term liabilities as they become current.

Working Capital or Current Ratio
Current Assets / Current Liabilities

The Working Capital or Current Ratio is mainly used to gauge the company's ability to pay back its liabilities with its current assets over the next 12 months. This ratio compares a firm's current assets (cash, marketable securities, inventory, accounts receivable) to its current liabilities (short-term debt and accounts payable).

Every business has a limited amount of time to raise funds needed to pay for their most common liabilities. The higher the Current Ratio, the greater the "cushion" to cover its obligations. If the Current Ratio is too high, then the company may not be efficiently using its current assets. In contrast, a low Current Ratio is usually the result of poor collections and accounts receivable processing. It is very unfavorable to run a negative Working Capital Ratio. This ratio also sheds light on the overall debt burden of the company. When current assets exceed current liabilities, there should be enough capital to run day-to-day operations. If a company is weighted down with current debt, its cash flow will suffer.

Year-to-Date P&L Acutals and Ending Balance Sheet					Plan	Projected
2016	2017	2018	2019	Jan-00	2020	2021

Above 1	Less than 1
Means that the company can pay all of its current liabilities and still have current assets or positive working	Shows that the company isn't running efficiently and can't cover its current debt out of its current assets.

If current liabilities exceed current assets, the current ratio will be less than one (< 1), challenging the company's ability to meet its short-term obligations. A current ratio of 4 would mean that the company has four times more current assets than current liabilities.

Quick Ratio or Acid Test
(Cash + Cash Equivalents + Short-Term Investments + Current Receivables) / Current Liabilities

A Quick Ratio, also called the Acid Test, quantifies whether there are enough current assets to cover current liabilities. This ratio indicates a company's capacity to maintain operations as usual with current cash or near-cash reserves in slow periods.

The purpose of the Quick Ratio is to show how quickly a company can convert its "quick assets" (cash, cash equivalents, short-term investments, marketable securities) into cash to pay off its current liabilities within 90-days.

If a company has enough quick assets to cover its total current liabilities, the firm will be able to pay off its obligations without having to sell off any long-term or capital assets. This is the "acid test" for a company, signifying the degree a company's current liabilities are covered by the most liquid of its assets.

Year-to-Date P&L Acutals and Ending Balance Sheet					Plan	Projected
2016	2017	2018	2019	Jan-00	2020	2021

Above 1	Less than 1
Shows that there are more quick assets than current liabilities.	Shows that there are more current liabilities that quick assets.

A Quick Ratio of 1 indicates that quick assets equal current liabilities. This means that the company could pay off its current liabilities without selling any long-term assets. A Quick Ratio of 2 shows that the company has twice as many quick assets than current liabilities.

Cash Ratio
(Cash + Cash Equivalents) / Current Liabilities

The Cash Ratio shows the company's readiness to immediately cover current liabilities by measuring a company's ability to pay off its current liabilities with only cash and cash equivalents as a percentage of current liabilities.

The Cash Ratio is used to confirm that a company maintains adequate cash balances to pay off all of its current debts as they come due, given that inventory could take months or years to sell, and that receivables could take weeks to collect. With a healthy Cash Ratio, cash is guaranteed to be available for creditors.

Year-to-Date P&L Acutals and Ending Balance Sheet					Plan	Projected
2016	2017	2018	2019	Jan-00	2020	2021

Above 1	Less than 1
Means that all the current liabilities can be paid with cash and equivalents.	Means that all the current liabilities can be paid with cash and equivalents.

A Cash Ratio of 1 means that the company has the same amount of cash and equivalents as it has current debt.

Cash Operating Cycle Time
Days Inventory Outstanding + A/R Days Outstanding - A/P Days Outstanding

Cash Operating Cycle Time measures how quickly and efficiently a company can buy, sell, and collect on its inventory. This calculation establishes the number of days it takes a company to receive a final cash payment from a customer to repay its initial cash outlay for inventory. The cash conversion cycle has three distinct stages:
1. The first stage represents the company's current inventory and how long it will take to sell it. This stage is derived using the day's inventory outstanding calculation.
2. The second stage represents the current sales, and the time it takes to collect the cash from these sales. This number is derived using the day's sales outstanding calculation.
3. The third stage is the current outstanding payables, representing the amount a company owes its current vendors for inventory and goods purchased, and when the company will need to pay off its vendors. This is calculated using the day's payables outstanding calculation.

Ending Balance Sheet					Plan	Projected
2016	2017	2018	2019	Jan-00	2020	2021

Shorter is Better	Longer is Worse
Indicates company is quick in converting sales to cash. As a result, has lower working capital needs.	Means that a company's money is tied up in inventory longer waiting for cash to be received.

A cash conversion cycle of 25 means it takes 25 days from paying for inventory to receiving the cash from its sale.

Accounts Payable Turnover Ratio
Total Purchases (Materials + Equip + Subs + End Inv - Beg Inv) / Accounts Payable

Accounts payable represent trade credit that is essentially "free" financing, and it is an essential source of short-term financing. Companies able to pay off supplies frequently throughout the year are seen to have a high probability of making regular interest and principal payments as well.

The Accounts Payable Turnover Ratio measures how many times a company can pay off its average accounts payable balance during a year. This ratio is calculated by adding the ending inventory to the cost of goods sold and then subtracting the beginning inventory. The ratio increases as more purchases are made, or as a company decreases its accounts payable.

Year-to-Date P&L Acutals and Ending Balance Sheet					Plan	Projected
2016	2017	2018	2019	Jan-00	2020	2021

Higher is Better	Lower is Worse
Indicates the company is paying off its creditors. An unusually high ratio may suggest not effectively utilizing the credit available to them.	A low ratio indicates that a company is having trouble paying off its bills or is taking advantage of lenient supplier credit policies.

A payables turnover of 6 suggests that, on average, the company used and paid off the credit extended 6 times during the period or once every 61 days (365 ÷ 6).

Time Interest Earned Ratio
EBIT / Interest Expense

The Time Interest Earned Ratio or Interest Coverage Ratio measures the amount of income that can be used to cover interest expenses and make debt service payments in the future. Its calculation shows how many times a company could pay interest using its before-tax income.

Year-to-Date P&L Acutals					Plan	Projected
2016	2017	2018	2019	Jan-00	2020	2021

Higher is Better	Less than 1
Confirms that the company can afford to pay its interest payments as they come due.	Indicates an existing credit risk

A ratio of 4 means that a company makes enough income to pay for its total interest expense 4 times over.

Solvency Ratios

Financial leverage is the relationship between debt and equity on the right-hand side of a company's Balance Sheet. Solvency Ratios are used to measure a company's ability to sustain operations, indefinitely, by comparing debt levels with equity, assets, and earnings. They are also called Leverage Ratios.

Increasing leverage means increasing the proportion of debt to equity. The most commonly used Solvency Ratios are the following:

Equity Ratio
Debt Ratio
Debt to Equity or Debt to Net Worth Ratio

Equity Ratio
Total Equity / Total Assets

The Equity Ratio measures the amount of assets that are financed by owners' investments (i.e., owned outright by the investors) by comparing the total equity in the company to its total assets. Inversely, it shows how leveraged the company is with debt. In other words, after all of the liabilities are paid off, the investors will end up with the remaining assets.

	Ending Balance Sheet				Plan	Projected
2016	2017	2018	2019	Jan-00	2020	2021

Higher is Better	Lower is Worse
Higher investment levels by shareholders shows investor confidence in financing the company	Lower equity ratios lead to more financing and higher debt service costs.

An equity to asset ratio of 1 means that investors own 100% of the business assets. A ratio of 2-to-1 indicates that more equity funds than credit monies have been used to fund company assets.

Debt Ratio
Total Liabilities / Total Assets

The Debt Ratio measures a company's total liabilities as a percentage of total assets, showing the company's ability to pay off its liabilities with its assets. More simply, this ratio shows how many assets the company must sell to pay off all of its liabilities. It is a measure of the financial leverage of the company.

	Ending Balance Sheet				Plan	Projected
2016	2017	2018	2019	Jan-00	2020	2021

Lower is Better	Higher is Worse
Less than 1 means that the company owns more in assets out-right than it owes its creditors.	Higher levels of liabilities compared with assets are considered highly leveraged and riskier for lenders.

A ratio of 1 means the company would have to sell off all of its assets in order to pay off its liabilities. A ratio of 0.5 means that the company has twice as many assets as liabilities. This means creditors own half of the company's assets and the shareholders own the

Debt to Equity or Debt to Net Worth Ratio
Total Liabilities / Total Equity

Debt to Equity Ratio identifies the percentage of company financing that comes from creditors and investors. A company is viewed as risky when its debt to equity ratio is greater than one. This shows that creditors, rather than investors, have been funding operations.

The higher the Debt to Equity ratio, the greater the risk to a creditor. A lower ratio generally indicates greater long-term financing ability. If Net Worth is negative, the resulting ratio will be negative. A Debt to Equity ratio is considered favorable if it is equal to RMA standards, or at least 1:1.

	Ending Balance Sheet				Plan	Projected
2016	2017	2018	2019	Jan-00	2020	2021

Lower is Better	Higher is Worse
A lower debt to equity ratio implies a more financially stable business.	Indicates that more creditor financing (bank loans and leases) is used, rather than investor financing (shareholders).

A debt to equity ratio of 1 means that investors and creditors have an equal stake in the business assets. A ratio of 2-to-1 indicates a highly leveraged company, where monies owed are two times greater than owners' equity in the company.

Coverage Ratios

When shareholders own a majority of the assets, the company is said to be less leveraged. When creditors own a majority of the assets, the company is considered highly leveraged, and as a result, it has a riskier and less sustainable capital structure. Coverage Ratios are comparisons designed to measure a company's ability to pay its liabilities by calculating the company's ability to service its debt and other obligations.

On the surface, Coverage Ratios might sound a lot like Liquidity and Solvency Ratios, but there is a distinct difference. Coverage Ratios measure how easily companies can afford to meet the interest payments associated with their debt. The most common Coverage Ratios are the following:

Financial Leverage Ratio
Fixed Charge Coverage Ratio
Debt Service Coverage Ratio

Financial Leverage Ratio
Total Assets / Owners' Equity

The Financial Leverage Ratio reflects the relationship between debt and equity on the right-hand side of a company's Balance Sheet. It measures how much in assets a company holds, relative to its equity, by calculating how much debt the firm has accrued to acquire its assets.

The inverse of this ratio is "Debt to Equity," which shows that increasing leverage means increasing the proportion of debt to service, relative to equity.

A company must earn enough income to cover its interest expense and generate sufficient cash flow to meet the required interest and principal payments. Failing to do so can result in insolvency, financial distress, and, ultimately, bankruptcy.

	Ending Balance Sheet				Plan	Projected
2016	2017	2018	2019	Jan-00	2020	2021

Lower is Better	Higher is Worse
Owners have used more of their equity than debt when financing company assets.	Means that the company is using debt and other liabilities to finance its assets.

A financial Leverage of 1 or less means that the owners own all of the business assets. A ratio of 2-to-1 indicates that half of the assets were purchased through equity and the other half through financing.

Fixed Charge Coverage Ratio
EBIT + Fixed Charges Before Taxes / Fixed Charges Before Taxes + Interest Expense

The Fixed Charge Coverage Ratio measures a company's ability to pay all of its fixed charges or expenses with its existing income, before interest and income taxes, by comparing the company's income with its fixed costs. This ratio is an expanded version of the Times Interest Earned Ratio.

	Year-to-Date P&L Acutals				Plan	Projected
2016	2017	2018	2019	Jan-00	2020	2021

Higher is Better	Lower is Worse
Indicates a healthier and less risky business to invest in or loan money.	Confirms that the company can barely meet its monthly bills, and is not a good investment.

A ratio of 8 means that a company's income is 6 times greater that interest and lease payments. This is a healthy ratio that most lenders are looking for, and will view positively as an investment

Debt Service Coverage Ratio
Operating Income / Total Debt Service Costs

The Debt Service Coverage Ratio measures a company's ability to service its current debts by comparing its Net Operating Income with its total debt service obligations. Comparing a company's available cash with its current interest, principle, and sinking fund (see below) obligations help gauge a company's ability to meet its current debt obligations.

Unlike the Debt Ratio, the Debt Service Cover Ratio takes into consideration all expenses related to debt, including interest expense, pensions, and sinking fund obligation. The challenge with calculating this ratio is that the debt service amount is rarely provided in a set of financial statements.

A sinking fund is a reserve created to set aside cash or marketable securities investments

	Ending Balance Sheet				Plan	Projected
2016	2017	2018	2019	Jan-00	2020	2021

Higher is Better	Lower is Worse
Indicates more income is available to pay debt servicing that the business is likely to have more cash available to pay their debt obligations on time.	Less than one means the company doesn't generate enough operating profits to pay debt, and must use some of its savings to do so.

If a company has a ratio of 1, that means that the company's net operating profits equals its debt service obligations. In other words, the ratio is actually 1:1, because the company generates just enough revenues to pay for its debt servicing, with nothing to spare.

Throughput Ratios

In the business management theory of constraints, throughput is the rate at which a system achieves its goal. Throughput can best be described as the rate at which a system generates its products or services per unit of time. Throughput Ratios calculate the rate at which a business generates money. It measures the productivity of a machine, procedure, process, or system over a unit period, such as output per hour, cash turnover, or the number of orders shipped.

Throughput Ratios allow managers to understand better how efficiently they are manufacturing goods, or conducting services, by establishing both their baseline and the maximum rate, at which something can be processed. The most straightforward throughput measures to calculate from your P&L Statement are the following:

- Net Income Sales Productivity
- Gross Profit Sales Productivity
- Operating Income Sales Productivity
- Cash Throughput Volume
- Total Spend Productivity
- Direct Labor Investment Productivity
- Subcontractor Spend Productivity
- Materials Spend Productivity
- Equipment Expense Productivity
- Office Staff Investment Productivity
- SG&A Expense Productivity

The best managers use these formulas to quantify the gap between where they are and where they want to be or could be, across their business.

Operating Income Sales Productivity

Output (Operating Profit) / Input (Net Sales)

Operating Income is what's leftover from a dollar of sales after subtracting all of the costs of producing, acquiring, selling, and supporting your business. It represents what is available from each dollar of sales to pay the company's capital providers and its taxes, after all operating and overhead costs have been paid. It's one of the best measures of managerial performance.

Operating Income Sales Productivity or Operating Margin Ratio shows how well management puts the funds it has available for use through its operations.

Year-to-Date P&L Acutals					Plan	Projected
2016	2017	2018	2019	Jan-00	2020	2021

Higher Creates Opportunity
The more money that remains after paying operating costs, the more successful the operations and stable the company.

Lower Creates Challenges
Less money shows that operating activities are not sustainable when non-operating income is needed to cover operating expenses.

A ratio of 0.22 means that the company is generating 22 cents in operating profit for every dollar collected and held onto from sales. A 0.12 ratio means that $0.12 in operating profit is generated for every $1.00 sold and collected.

Cash Throughput Volume

Net Sales - COGS

Knowing how much incoming cash you can expect from sales is important. Knowing how much cash you'll have leftover after paying the direct costs for those sales vs. money that is simply passing through your bank account because there isn't enough margin in it is more important.
Cash Throughput Volume reflects how much money is left over after direct costs are subtracted from net sales. On a cash basis, this is the equivalent of "Gross Profit" on your P&L Statement. Simply put, having cash in the bank doesn't mean that it's yours to spend. Without a strong gross profit influenced cash inflow, it's impossible to build cash reserves in the bank. In short, Cash Throughput Volume reflects the proportion of every sales deposited in the bank that should be available to cover variable and fixed expenses and create cash reserves.

Year-to-Date P&L Actuals					Plan	Projected
2016	2017	2018	2019	Jan-00	2020	2021

Higher Creates Opportunity
Means you are likely to build cash reserves in the bank as long as SG&A expenses are less than the gross profit earned.

Lower Creates Challenges
Means that the company is probably using today's sales to pay yesterday's operating expenses.

Sales of $250,000 and COGS of $225,000 means only $25,000 from those sales is available to pay overhead expenses and leave an operating profit. If SG&A expenses are less than $25K, than you are likely to build cash reserves, if SG&A is more than $35K, you will burn through $10K of your cash reserves covering your operating costs tied to the $250K in sales.

Direct Labor Investment Productivity

Output (Operating Profit) / Input (Direct Labor Costs)

Direct labor productivity is a critical determinant of cost efficiency, and ultimately, profitability for most businesses. Direct Labor Investment Productivity is a single factor that measures how efficiently your direct labor investment converts wages, employment taxes, and assigned benefits into useful outputs (operating profit). It is calculated by dividing the ending output per period by the total costs incurred in that period. This throughput view is used to determine how much your direct labor contributes to the operating profit of your company.
Most of your employees have been hired to perform the work created by sales that produce profits. This measure tells you how efficiently you are managing this talent pool, overall, to produce profits during a given period. It isn't about anyone particular direct employee. The more productive your direct labor talent pool, the greater the profit return you'll earn from your investment in the employees who get the work done.

Year-to-Date P&L Acutals					Plan	Projected
2016	2017	2018	2019	Jan-00	2020	2021

Higher Creates Opportunity
A positive ratio moving up each year is usually an indicator of an upward profit trend.

Lower Creates Challenges
A ratio significantly below 1 indicates that your investment is not efficient in producing operating profit.

A ratio of 1 means that the company is generating 1 dollar of operating profit for every dollar invested in a direct laborer. A 0.6 ratio means that $0.60 in operating profit is generated for every $1.00 in direct labor compensation paid.

Gross Profit Sales Productivity

Output (Gross Profit) / Input (Net Sales)

Gross profit is the first level of profit from a net sale after the cost of goods used are deducted from the sale. The gross profit created is used to pay any remaining business expenses.
A falling Gross Profit Sales Productivity or Gross Margin Ratio shows that the cost of production is rising faster than the selling price, or, that inventory is shrinking due to fraudulent activity or product spoilage. Higher ratios can typically be achieved in one of two ways:

1. Through reducing costs by paying for materials or labor at lower costs
2. Through marking up your product's price

High Gross Profit Sales Productivity leads to more cash on hand and stability in times of economic downturn. A low ratio means cash is likely to be tight.

Year-to-Date P&L Acutals					Plan	Projected
2016	2017	2018	2019	Jan-00	2020	2021

Higher Creates Opportunity
Means more money for the company to make a profit after paying direct operating expenses.

Lower Creates Challenges
Indicates that the company is probably operating at a loss, with less money available to pay other operating expenses.

A ratio of 0.42 means that the company is generating 42 cents in gross profit for every dollar collected and retained from sales. A 0.26 ratio means that $0.26 in gross profit is generated for every $1.00 sold and collected.

Net Income Sales Productivity

Output (Net Income) / Input (Net Sales)

Net Income Sales Productivity is related to the Net Income Margin Ratio. It measures how effectively a company converts sales into net income. It's the best validation of a business's ability to set winning pricing policies, and its ability to control operating and nonoperating costs, relative to its net sales. It shows what the ratio of sales is after all expenses are paid.

Higher ratios are achieved by generating more revenues while lowering or keeping expenses constant, or, by maintaining revenues at a lower rate of expenses. A low-profit margin indicates high risk and the possibility that a decline in sales will erase profits and result in loss.

Year-to-Date P&L Acutals					Plan	Projected
2016	2017	2018	2019	Jan-00	2020	2021

Higher Creates Opportunity
Means that the company is running efficiently, creditors will be paid, and owners will see a return on their investment.

Lower Creates Challenges
Indicates that expenses are too high. Management will need to budget and cut expenses in order to avoid losses.

A ratio of 0.15 means that for every dollar of sales, 15 cents has been collected and held onto from sales. A 0.06 ratio means that $0.06 in net profit is generated after everyone has been paid for every $1.00 sold and collected.

Total Spend Productivity

Output (Operating Profit) / Input (COGS + SG&A Expense)

Productivity is a critical determining factor of cost efficiency and is often used to set performance standards. Total Spend Productivity is a measure of how efficiently your business strategy, structure, and processes convert inputs (all of your expenses) into useful outputs (profits). This number is calculated by dividing the ending output per period, by the total costs incurred in that period.

This throughput view is used to determine how profitable a company is concerning operations, and is a much more accurate picture of a company's success than gross sales. It's also the best proxy for how much cash is likely to be held onto after every operating bill has been paid.

Year-to-Date P&L Actuals					Plan	Projected
2016	2017	2018	2019	Jan-00	2020	2021

Higher Creates Opportunity
Means more money for the Owners to pocket or reinvest in the business after paying operating bills.

Lower Creates Challenges
Indicates less money for the Owners to work with after paying all operating bills.

A 1.2 productivity ratio means that for every dollar of sales that passes through the business, 20 cents will remain to cover interest and taxes, and have profit left over to pay the owner a bonus or reinvest into the business.

Subcontractor Spend Productivity

Output (Operating Profit) / Input (Subcontractor Expense)

Spending on subcontractors can have a significant impact on the profitability of most businesses—especially when the cost of paying the subcontractor is less than what you would pay your own employees to do the same type of work. Subcontractor Spend Productivity measures the efficiency of your subcontractor spend. It's calculated by dividing the operating profit as the ending output for a period, by the total costs incurred for that input, in that same period.
This throughput view is used to determine how productive your subcontractor spend has been in contributing to the operating profit of your company. Your outside service providers have been hired to help you generate revenues that produce profits. The more productive your subcontractor base, the greater the profit return you'll earn from your investment in outside help to get the work done.

Year-to-Date P&L Acutals					Plan	Projected
2016	2017	2018	2019	Jan-00	2020	2021

Higher Creates Opportunity
A positive ratio moving up each year indicates a well-placed investment in outside services.

Lower Creates Challenges
A ratio significantly below 1 indicates that your investment is not efficient in producing operating profit.

A ratio of 0.5 means that the company is generating 50 cents in operating profit for every dollar invested in subcontractors. A 0.0 ratio means that no operating profit contribution is generated for every $1.00 subcontractor spend.

Materials Spend Productivity
Output (Operating Profit) / Input (Materials Expense)

If your business primarily converts raw materials into finished goods, then smart material spending is likely to be the largest profit contributor to your business. If the size of this cost base in relation to other costs is large, it will have a more significant impact on profit, relative to other investments.

Materials Spend Productivity measures how important your material spend is to your business. It's calculated by dividing the operating profit as the ending output for a period, by the total costs incurred for that input in that same period. The purpose of this productivity measure is to help you determine how cost-efficient and productive your operations are in converting money spent on materials into operating profit.

	Year-to-Date P&L Acutals				Plan	Projected
2016	2017	2018	2019	Jan-00	2020	2021

Higher Creates Opportunity	Lower Creates Challenges
An increasing ratio is an indicator that this investment is becoming more important to your business's success.	A ratio significantly below 1 indicates materials are an insignificant contributor in producing operating profit.

A ratio of 1.2 means that the company is generating 1 dollar and 20 cents of operating profit for every dollar invested in materials. A 0.3 ratio means that $0.30 in operating profit is generated for every $1.00 spent on materials.

Equipment Expense Productivity
Output (Operating Profit) / Input (Equipment Expense)

Equipment Expense Productivity measures the importance of your spending on equipment to operating profits. This number is obtained by dividing the operating profit as the ending output for a period, by the total costs incurred for that input in that same period.

Businesses that have high equipment expenses are likely to see this expense have a significant impact on their business profitability. This throughput view is used to determine how impactful your equipment spend is in contributing to the operating profit of your company. The higher the ratio, the more critical it is to manage this expense so that you can hold onto more of each dollar sold.

	Year-to-Date P&L Acutals				Plan	Projected
2016	2017	2018	2019	Jan-00	2020	2021

Higher Creates Opportunity	Lower Creates Challenges
An increasing ratio is an indicator of that this investment is becoming more important to your business's success.	A ratio significantly below 1 indicates equipment expense is an insignificant contributor in producing operating profit.

A ratio of 1.8 means that the company is generating 1 dollar and 80 cents of operating profit for every dollar invested in equipment. A 3.1 ratio means that $3.10 in operating profit is generated for every $1.00 spent on equipment.

Office Staff Investment Productivity
Output (Operating Profit) / Input (Office Payroll Expense)

Changes in Office Staff Investment Productivity shows how efficiently you are managing this 'overhead' talent in producing profits during a given period. It's an overall gauge of where you're at, not a measure of any single office employee. Your direct labor productivity is impacted positively or negatively by your investment in-office staff who support the processes you've set up to get the work done. Office Staff Investment Productivity measures how efficiently your office staff can convert wages, employment taxes, and assigned benefits into operating profit contribution. This number is calculated by dividing the ending output per period, by the total compensation paid in that period. The more efficient your office staff is, the higher the likelihood that you are making money. They are foundational to your operation's ability to make or lose money based on their ability to keep score and collect payment for the work of your direct labor. Often, direct labor productivity tanks when the office isn't accurately paying them their wages.

	Year-to-Date P&L Acutals				Plan	Projected
2016	2017	2018	2019	Jan-00	2020	2021

Higher Creates Opportunity	Lower Creates Challenges
An increasing ratio is an indicator of that this investment is becoming more important to your business's success.	A ratio significantly below 1 indicates an insignificant contributor in producing operating profit.

A ratio of 1 means that the company is generating the equivalent of 1 dollar of operating profit for every dollar invested in Office Staff. A 2.3 ratio means that the equivalent of $2.30 in operating profit is generated for every $1.00 in office staff compensation paid.

SG&A Expense Productivity
Output (Operating Profit) / Input (SG&A Expense)

Any SG&A, also known as an overhead expense, can impact profits since no dollar spent on SG&A is directly attributable to a sell that contributed to gross profit earnings. To calculate SG&A Expense Productivity, divide operating profit as the ending output for a period by the total SG&A costs incurred for that input in that same period.

The smaller the ratio, the less impactful your overhead spend is on your operating profit. The higher the ratio, the more important it is to manage these overhead expenses if you are to make a profit. A negative ratio indicates that this area is a drain on your ability to produce a profit.

	Year-to-Date P&L Acutals				Plan	Projected
2016	2017	2018	2019	Jan-00	2020	2021

Higher Creates Opportunity	Lower Creates Challenges
An increasing ratio is an indicator of that this investment is becoming more important to your business's success.	A ratio significantly below 1 indicates an insignificant contributor in producing operating profit.

A ratio of -1 means that the company is generating a one-dollar operating loss for every dollar invested in overhead expense. A 2.0 ratio means that $2.00 in operating profit is generated for the equivalent of every $1.00 spent on SG&A.

Covering Your Cost Calculations

Making money starts with accurately knowing what your costs across your business. Another basic business truism is that money is "hard to earn and easy to lose." The best way to guard your money with care is by knowing the actual costs of your business so that you can price your products and service to make money.

The most basic business calculations to perform are the 'Covering Your Cost Calculations' that represent the starting point for achieving financial freedom. Use these formulas to increase your understanding of what it costs you to do business.

Financial freedom is not something that happens randomly for the fortunate few, it's something that you engineer by knowing the math behind your business costs. Below are the most common Cover Your Cost Calculations:

Cost to Do Business
Average Daily Costs to Do Business
Revenue per "ALL" Employees Average Net Profit per Manager
Overhead Absorption Rate
Breakeven Rate

When you can do the math for any area of your business, you can change the results for that area by changing the inputs used in its equation.

Cost to Do Business
Gross Sales - Net Income

Your Cost to Do Business is the amount that lies between your top-line Gross Sales and your bottom-line Net Income. You, and your business, win by continuously pushing yourself to more effectively manage the assets of your business, as you simultaneously control the expenses flowing through your sales, operations, finance, and administration functions.

Winning or losing in the game of business is measured by your ability to convert a dollar of sales into a profit. Knowing your costs across your business, at both the gross profit and operating income, is the key to shrinking the gap between Gross Sales and Net Income. Your financial statements and select finance ratios shed light on your field of play, so you'll know your next move with confidence to higher profits.

	Year-to-Date P&L Acutals				Plan	Projected
2016	2017	2018	2019	Jan-00	2020	2021

Lower Creates Opportunity	Higher Creates Challenges
The lower your total expenses paid out of each sales dollar, the higher your bottom-line results.	The higher your cost structure, the smaller your safety net to cover any "surprises" that always arise.

Gross Sales of $1,000,000 and net income of $50,000 is the same as $1.00 - $0.05 = $0.95 or your cost to do business on every dollar sold. Put another way you spent $950,000 chasing after the $50,000 you earned from the original million in gross sales. Every cent you don't spend is a penny that drops straight to your bottom-line.

Average Daily Cost to Do Business
COGS + SG&A / # of Days

Your business wins through building on daily success. Your profit or loss is the cumulative result of your daily actions throughout any given time period. You start controlling expenses when you know how much money is flowing through your sales, operations, finance, and administration functions on a daily basis. To more easily stay on top of your cost of doing business, you need to accurately determine your average cost per day to keep your doors open.

If at the end of the day, you have converted a higher share from a dollar of sales into a profit—then you can count that day as a win. If you spend more than you collected, you lost. You won't start making a profit again until you earn back the lost profit through higher sales and lower costs.

	Year-to-Date P&L Acutals				Plan	Projected
2016	2017	2018	2019	Jan-00	2020	2021

Lower Creates Opportunity	Higher Creates Challenges
The less you have in total expenses to pay out of each sales dollar, the higher your bottom-line number.	The higher your cost structure, the smaller your safety net to cover any "surprises" that always arise.

If your average cost per day is $2,400 and you make $3,000 then you're $600 ahead. If your next day cost structure doesn't change, and you only take in $1,700 then you're down $700 for the day and $100 for the two days, because you took in less than you spent.

Revenue for "ALL" Employees
Net Sales / # of Full-time Employees

The people you hire to generate and support the revenues that produce profits have a cost. The only way your employees benefit you is when you can collect more in sales than the amount it costs to keep them on the payroll. Put another way, the more productive your total talent base, the greater your profit return.

It's essential to look at revenue per employee—instead of profit per employee—because the revenue you generate is a direct result of your employees. If they aren't doing their jobs, then there is no revenue to collect, and therefore no profit, either.

	Year-to-Date P&L Acutals				Plan	Projected
2016	2017	2018	2019	Jan-00	2020	2021

Higher Creates Opportunity	Lower Creates Challenges
The more sales dollars you're able to retain, per employee, the more cash to pay expenses and leave you a profit.	The lower your sales dollars retained, per employee, the more likely you lose money unless you keep other expenses very low.

A company earning $100,000 in sales per employee is going to struggle against a company earning $1,000,000 in sales per employee. This is because the more employees you have on your payroll, the higher the risk of costly mistakes, so you need to push this number up continuously.

Average Net Profits per Manager
Net Profit / # of Full-time Managers

Your management team exists to help you manage the people you hire to generate that produce profits. Your managers are likely your most expensive employees have a cost. They only benefit you when they help your employees collect more in sales then the amount it costs to keep them on the payroll. Put another way, the more effective your management team, the greater your profit return.

It's essential to look at the change in your Average Net Profits per Manager since these are the employees that impact the amount of money you hold onto from each dollar sold and collected. If they aren't helping your employees be more productive each day in doing their jobs, then there is less revenue to collect, and therefore smaller profits than there should be.

	Year-to-Date P&L Acutals				Plan	Projected
2016	2017	2018	2019	Jan-00	2020	2021

Higher Creates Opportunity	Lower Creates Challenges
The higher the number, the more efficient your management team is in converting a sale into profit.	The lower the number, the more likely you are throwing money away on a management team that is not carrying their weight.

A company earning $100,000 in Net Profit through the work of ten managers is going to struggle against a company earning the same amount with seven managers. This is because the more managers you have on your payroll, the higher the risk of bureaucracy and employee frustration when you have more bosses than workers.

Owners' Compensation Ratio
Net Profit / Total Owners' Compensation

A business owner who is a big part of getting the work done in a business must pay themselves a fair wage, or you're subsidizing your customers by allowing them to buy from you without the value of 'you' built into the prices you charge. Don't do this. No business owner should ever allow themselves to make below minimum wage after they divide the monies they take out of the business by the hours they spend working in the business. The Owners' Compensation Ratio divides the Net Income by the total wages, benefits, bonus, and payroll taxes a business owner pays themselves for the work they perform in the business. The Owners' Compensation Ratio does not include equity distributions or owners' draws. These are Balance Sheet transactions reflective of the business owner, whereas the wages they take for the work performed should be treated as a cost of doing business.

	Year-to-Date P&L Acutals				Plan	Projected
2016	2017	2018	2019	Jan-00	2020	2021

Higher Creates Opportunity	Lower Creates Challenges
The higher the number, the more the owner recognizes through their compensation, the value they represent to their business.	The lower the number, the less the owner is paying themselves to work in the business, or they are not carrying their weight as they should.

A ratio of 0.05 means that for every dollar of sales, the owner is paying themselves 5 cents on each sale. A 0.0 ratio means that for every dollar in net profit generated after everyone has been paid, the owner is paying themselves $0.00 for every $1.00 sold and collected.

OVERHEAD ABSORPTION RATE
Total Fixed Costs / Total Variable Costs

To make a profit you have to cover both your direct (variable) and in-direct (fixed) costs in the prices you set for your goods and services. Overhead absorption is the amount of indirect costs not directly traceable to an activity or product. These are considered a cost of doing business, and must be paid through any sales dollars you collect.

Any money spent that isn't covered through your product and service pricing models is an immediate loss to your business. An overhead absorption rate is calculated, most simply, by dividing total fixed costs by total variable costs. This is the overhead rate that should be added to all direct costs and considered when calculating the price, you will charge for your products and services. Failure to include this figure in your pricing calculations and decisions robs you of profits.

	Year-to-Date P&L Acutals				Plan	Projected
2016	2017	2018	2019	Jan-00	2020	2021

Lower Creates Opportunity	Higher Creates Challenges
The less fixed costs you have to pay the less stress you carry each time these expenses come due.	The higher your fixed cost base, the higher your risk of not charging enough to cover your inefficiency and waste.

If your average cost per day is $12,400 and you take in $15,000 then you're $2,600 ahead. If your next day cost structure doesn't change, and you only take in $7,400 then you're down $5,000 for the day and $2,400 for the two days, because you took in less than you spent.

BREAKEVEN POINT
Fixed Costs/(1-(Variable Costs/Net Sales))

The breakeven point represents the point-in-time at which a business, product, or project becomes financially profitable. This occurs when revenue exactly equals the estimated total costs, such that loss ends, and profit begins to accumulate, on every dollar held onto during that accounting period.

The higher the asset base required to generate sales, the more important it is to know the breakeven point in your business cycle. For businesses with a low overhead and few assets to support, this number is fairly meaningless.

	Year-to-Date P&L Acutals				Plan	Projected
2016	2017	2018	2019	Jan-00	2020	2021

Lower Creates Opportunity	Higher Creates Challenges
A lower breakeven point indicates a healthier and less risky business investment.	A higher breakeven point confirms that the business has a high cost structure, with many moving parts to pay for before they earn a profit.

A company with a breakeven point of $500,000 will begin to earn a dollar of profit when net sales reach $501,000. As long as their cost structure doesn't change as sales increase every dollar sold and collected above $500,000 represents business profit.

CONCLUDING THOUGHT

Nothing matters if you don't make a profit with cash in the bank.

SmallBizTrends.com states that 40 percent of small businesses make a profit, 30 percent come out even, and the remaining 30 percent lose money. This is why half of all businesses fail in less than five years.

The bottom line is if you don't want to continuously be fixing the "C or P" in *B-CPR*, then you must fix the "R," or you will continue to suffer from financial mismanagement.

If you don't know who the money in your business is coming from (customers) or where the money is going (expenses), then you are on the road toward failure. If you don't want to make the necessary changes from the path you are on, then your best option is to take immediate action today to start the process for ending your business without further delay.

INDEX

CPSIA information can be obtained
at www.ICGtesting.com
Printed in the USA
BVHW092244301120
594477BV00008B/1127